Wearing Smooth the Path

25 YEARS AT ABBY'S HOUSE

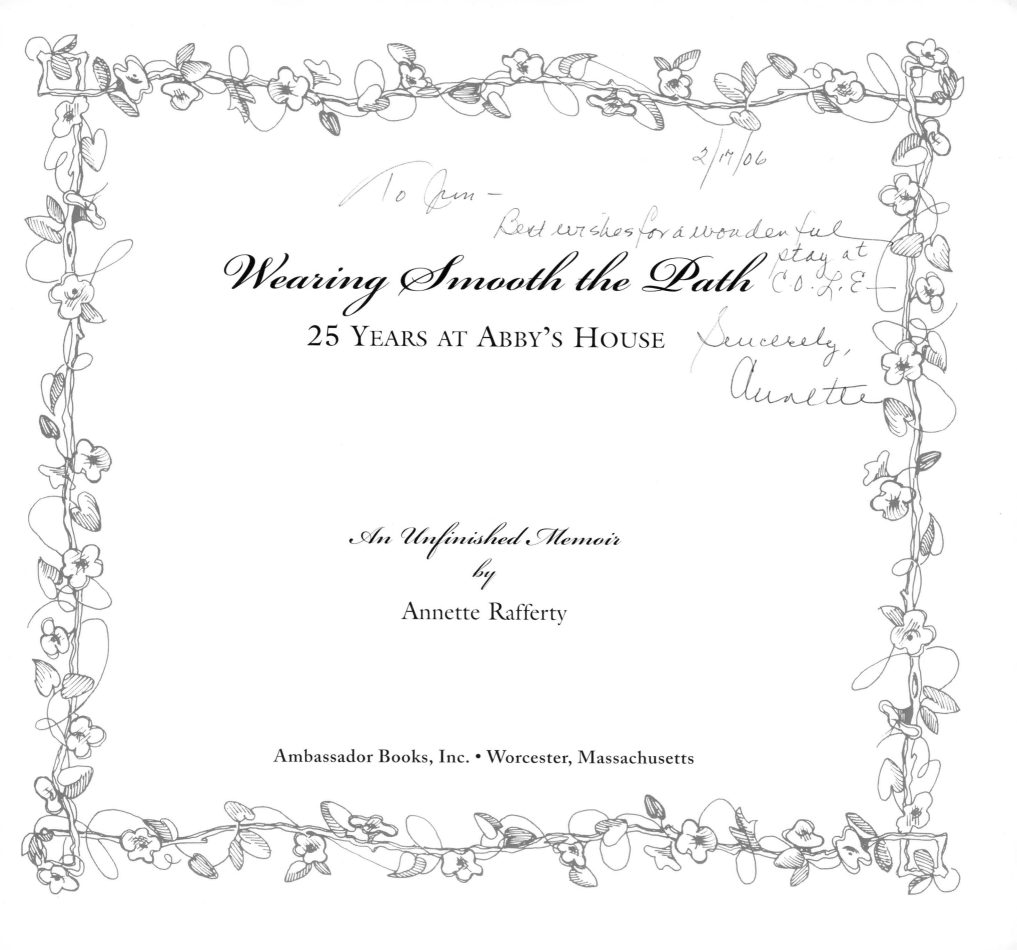

Wearing Smooth the Path

25 YEARS AT ABBY'S HOUSE

An Unfinished Memoir
by

Annette Rafferty

2/17/06

To Jim —

Best wishes for a wonderful stay at C.O.L.E —

Sincerely,
Annette

Ambassador Books, Inc. • Worcester, Massachusetts

We thank the *Telegram and Gazette* for permission to reprint the numerous photographs and articles appearing in this scrapbook. The following were invaluable resources on the life of Abby Kelley Foster: Margaret Bacon, *I Speak for My Slave Sister: The Life of Abby Kelley Foster*, Thomas Crowell Co., 1974; and Dorothy Sterling, *Ahead of Her Time*, W.W. Norton & Co. 1991. We gratefully acknowledge the following sources of inspiring words which appeared in Abby's newsletters and celebrations over the past twenty-five years: Joan Baez song, *My House*; W.E.B. DuBois, *Prayer for a New Year*; Norma Farber, *The Three Queens Were There*; J. Ruth Gendler, *Courage*; Denise Levertov, *Bright Morning Stars*; Rita MacNeil song, *Everybody*; Jan Phillips, *Campaneras Take Heart*; Marge Piercy, *To Be of Use*; Adrienne Rich, *My Heart is Moved*.

ISBN: 1-929039-06-9
Library of Congress Control Card Number: 2001087949

Published in the United States by Ambassador Books, Inc.
71 Elm Street, Worcester, Massachusetts 01609
(800) 577-0909

Cover and book design by Dagnello Design, Worcester, Massachusetts.

Printed in Canada.

Dedication to the Women of Abby's

To you who stay with us:

You are special people.
Under the worst of circumstances
You come to stay with us.
Coping with the impossible;
Trying to start again
And so often, you prevail.

To you who volunteer:

You are special people.
You sacrifice your time;
You lend your ears;
You care.
You are there for those who need you;
Helping them survive.

To you who are the core staff:

You are special people.
You dedicate your time to see all needs are met.
You fix what breaks, you improvise.
You find solutions.
When I can't handle a situation;
You are always there to guide me.

To All of you—The Women of Abby's:

You are special people doing special things.
I embrace you with my heart.

Denise Simon, Age 32, Volunteer

Acknowledgments

There are some special individuals who deserve my lasting gratitude for making these unfinished memoirs possible.

Let me begin with Nancy Kane, who was my faithful guide and competent consultant. She organized my material and did all my computer work. Nancy's father, Michael and my father, Andrew were great friends when our families lived in Oxford. Having Nancy as my 'angel agent,' available at all times, was one of the brightest spots of this three year adventure. Thank you, Nancy, for your invaluable help and for listening to me reminisce about those "good old days."

Thank you as well to Tess Sneesby, Abby's Executive Director, who encouraged me on a weekly basis to keep on keeping on and to Elaine Lamoureux, who made excellent suggestions and recommendations that improved the text. Also, I am grateful to Abby's staff, volunteers and Day Center guests for their warm support and interest. Sincere thanks to my editor, Margaret LeRoux, whose corrections and literary insights contributed greatly to 'wearing smooth the path' of these memoirs, and to Charlotte Fitzgerald, proofreader extraordinaire.

I owe a debt of gratitude to Gerry and Jennifer Goggins of Ambassador Books for their encouragement, support and expert advice, resulting in the publication of these memoirs.

Linda Dagnello, my graphic artist, designed the cover, produced the scrapbook effect I so wanted for this book and scanned more memorabilia and photos than she ever knew existed at Abby's. Thank you for this beautiful book.

Thanks are due to Ellen Grimm, Abby's grantwriter, to Greater Worcester Community Foundation and the Cultural Commission for mini-grants which helped finance this project.

Finally, to all of you who have contributed to Abby's in any way, accept my gratitude. Many of you sold house pins, made crafts, cooked and delivered meals, donated beautiful clothing, kept our shelves stocked with cleaning supplies, supported us with generous financial donations and provided additional safe housing for our guests at risk. These 25 years belong to you, too. I have tried to include as many of you as possible, but to personally acknowledge each of you by name was not humanly possible. I hope you will accept this acknowledgment as my sincere expression of thanks.

Contents

Preface   ix

Abby's from the Inside   xi

Chapters

1   From St. Elmo Road to Crown Street   1

2   Giving Birth to Ourselves   8

3   Here for the Long Haul   17

4   Building Community Years   29

5   Smoothing the Paths by Which We Came   33

6   Sisterhood Is Powerful   39

7   Molly, Meridel and More Milestones   45

8   A Brand New Day   55

9   Hello and Goodbye   59

10   True Women of Will   63

11   Progress, Pain and Persistence   69

12   Is Not Now the Accepted Time?   73

13   A House Standing on the Edge of Glory   77

14   Settling and Searching   85

15   Jumping into Work Headfirst   89

16   Walking In and Stumbling: Dirt and Humbug   97

17   The Queens Came Late   103

18   A Premiere Performance: the 20th Anniversary   107

19   Reconstituting the World: 77 Chatham Street   111

20   Our Lives Are Our Speeches   115

21   Guardians, Bright Minds and Good Hearts   119

22   Reminders of Our Mission   125

23   Fallow Ground for Future Deeds   129

24   Departures, Arrivals and Sidetrips   134

25   Compañeras, Take Heart   141

Epilogue   149

Voices of Volunteers and Supporters   151

Steering Committee and Board of Directors   154

List of Volunteers   155

"I hope that you do not feel that I speak to you in anger. I did not rise to make a speech—my life has been my speech. For fourteen years I have advocated this cause by my daily life. Bloody feet, sisters, have worn smooth the path by which you have come hither."

Abby Kelley Foster
October 15, 1851
Second National Woman's
Rights Convention
Worcester, Massachusetts

Preface

Several years ago, the idea of writing the history of Abby's House came up at one of our staff meetings. We talked at length of the importance of recording the events that led to the founding of the first emergency shelter for women and their children in Central Massachusetts. Without a written history, no one would know of the efforts, determination and conviction of the handful of women who established the shelter for women. They named that shelter the Abby Kelley Foster House after Worcester's most famous abolitionist and women's rights advocate.

This memoir is many things. It is a tribute to the community at large for participating in the growth of a small shelter into a present day multi-service organization. It is a testament of courage dedicated to the hundreds of women who have found Abby's House in their hour of need. It is a celebration of the contribution of more than five hundred volunteers who committed themselves to our mission of empowerment. It is a tribute to over ten thousand supporters and donors who believed enough in our vision to generously help us become and remain a bright spot in the city of Worcester. It is, in essence, a work of gratitude to every woman, man and child, to every church, business, school and civic group that has been a part of Abby's community. You have made so much possible for so many.

Finally, it is a work of love, inspired by the women who have been guiding lights over the past quarter of a century. What words can adequately pay homage to the staff and board of directors of Abby's House? All of them are women of will, who work with hope in their hearts on the front lines of homelessness and poverty accompanied by abuse, neglect, lack of self-worth and unimaginable needs. This chronicle of the trust and goodness of people involved at Abby's might appear false to someone not familiar with our organization. But twenty-five years later, what you see here is a glass always half-full. What else could keep us going and growing?

Personally, I found this assigned task a mixed blessing. The scrapbooks in which we kept the earlier history were an enormous help. I found so much was retained in those red volumes, however, that it was difficult choosing photos that would highlight the events as I remembered them. It was a gigantic undertaking sorting out what would make interesting reading. To me, of course, everything was interesting, because I was there. When this realization struck—that I was there, I made the decision to make this history very personal—one that would tell the reader how I got to Abby's House after years of formal education and teaching on a secondary level, and how Abby Kelley Foster influenced me and continues to inspire the mission of this organization. So, what we have here is really a life story, or one life within many. This is where the mixed blessing enters. The historian may have difficulty because I weave in and out of facts and interior spiritual meanderings of the mind and soul. The non-historian might relish the personal expression of my voice and have no real interest in the facts. So be it. The work is done for at least the first twenty-five years.

Let me add that the stubborn stand taken by our shelter's namesake, Abby Kelley Foster, in giving her life over to ending slavery, has been a strong force in our determination to end homelessness for as many women and children as is possible in one lifetime. Our daily work is her living legacy and I write with hope that this memoir will carry that legacy, to the next generation and beyond.

ABBY'S

Abby's from the Inside

Abby's from the Inside

Supper's ready. Tonight it was brought to the door by a woman who had made too much lasagna and delivered the excess just in time for five hungry women and three children to enjoy it. Dessert was already on the kitchen counter—fruit and brownies made by Cub Scout Troop #463. The two staffers are women from Holy Cross College, both with three years of staffing experience and about to graduate. Michelle and Beth, by name, will be heading out west to spend a year in a home for troubled adolescents. They had originally thought of business and marketing as future possibilities, until they attended a meeting of Abby's Friends on their campus. It offered an opportunity to be trained in night staffing at a place called Abby's House. They signed on and the experience has changed their lives and reshaped their future ambitions.

Tonight they are having supper with the women, patiently listening to their stories. Maria, 21, is waiting to get into a halfway program for drug rehabilitation. This is Edwina's first night. She came from M.C.I. (Massachusetts Correctional in Framingham) and, like Maria, is hoping to go into an addiction program. Barbara and Nadia and their children, Sandy, Hector and Junior, were burned out of a tenement on Charlton Street. They are having trouble finding decent, affordable housing. Everyone is in good spirits except Deidre, who sits quietly, removed from the group, no doubt protecting herself and her past. Hers is a long history of childhood trauma and eventual alcohol dependency. No one knows that she completed three years at Louisiana State University as a psychology major before the drinking and unresolved issues of incest and abuse pretty much destroyed her dreams and changed her life forever. Beth, noticing this, sits next to her at the table in an attempt to let her know Abby's is a place where, if she chooses, she can be herself. No one is a judge here.

When supper chatter and the clatter of dishes is over, Maria and Edwina pitch in, helping to clean up the dining room and kitchen. The two mothers, Barbara and Nadia, read to Sandra, Hector and Junior in the children's room. Sandy, the youngest and the only girl, discovers Emily, our doll-in-residence, a permanent fixture in that special room. She's busy talking to Emily, while the other two are showing signs of fatigue.

Meanwhile, Deidre has removed herself from any activity and is watching "Chronicle" on Channel 5. The ringing of the hot-line phone interrupts the flow of the evening. Michelle answers. It's the Worcester police. They have a woman who was beaten, and they're wondering if Abby's has an available bed. Of course she'd be examined at a local hospital first and then transported to Abby's if hospitalization was ruled out. Then Michelle spoke directly to the woman, who agreed to come. The conversation ended and the waiting for another guest began. The staffers tell the others that another woman is expected but won't arrive until well after lights are out at 11.

By 9:30 everyone has gone upstairs for showers and sleep. Sandy, the 4-year-old, asks Beth if Emily, doll-in-residence, can spend the night with her upstairs. Why not? Emily needs a good night's sleep, too. The boys, both of school age, are grumbling about retiring so early. Suddenly, except for the drone of T.V., the house is silent. Deidre is still in the living room. It was easy to forget her since she had nothing to say until—until then. "I'd like to wait with you for the new guest. Is it all right? She'll probably feel scared. I know that feeling." Ordinarily, the staffers would have discouraged the arrangement, since hospitals can take forever and the possibility of arriving at Abby's front door at 2 a.m. would deprive everyone of sleep. But Beth and Michelle, decided instantly to bend the rule. Deidre had spoken. Maybe she needed to say more. They were right. Once the silence had been broken, it was impossible for Deidre to stop.

"I know how that woman feels. Everything gets locked up inside your head and who's going to believe a kid anyway. My family was important in our town, so I buried it all, did my best to move on, and it worked for a long, long time. Then came the crash. I ended up in a state hospital. My life turned into a nightmare. Even with a disability check, I didn't have enough money for a decent place. Rents kept going up and finally I got evicted. I was and still am, totally overwhelmed and afraid of everyone and everything. This place wasn't where I wanted to be, but I had no choices left. But it's nice here—it reminds me of a house I lived in down South—homey and warm. And I don't have to pay for shelter or food. Gives me a chance to save. Elaine is always saying, 'Save your money,' and she's right. Maybe just going upstairs with this new woman, she'll know I'm staying here, too, and maybe she'll feel calmer."

And that is exactly how it happened. The staffers had made a good decision. When Sally arrived at 1 a.m., it was Deidre who welcomed her without saying a single word. She put her arm on her shoulder and, as Beth and Michelle made cocoa, Deidre and Sally quietly communicated in the dining room which for years has been the space of sharing where change can take place, where strangers become friends, and speak their own language and dance their own dances.

For twenty-five years, without missing an evening, including the Blizzard of 1978, women like Deidre, Barbara, Nadia, Edwina, Maria, Beth and Michelle, with or without children, gathered around the dining room table. Each one of the guests has her own unique story, with a litany of events suddenly out of control in their lives, that ultimately brought them to Abby's House. So it is with the women who are trained to staff at this emergency shelter. Each of them has come for some reason, usually a desire to help other women. We don't know each staffer's experience. We only know they are here with their sisters, willing to share, willing to say by their presence at Abby's that everyone has a right to physical and spiritual sustenance. Giver and receiver, receiver and giver. There can be no distinction. Each one stands on the common ground of struggle and hope.

How I got to Abby's is far, far less dramatic, but no less interesting. I, too, have a story that contains its share of humor, tears and joys. Did anyone ever imagine me here? Certainly not my family, not my college classmates nor the students I taught for so many years. Especially not I. So, how did I go from a secure profession into an area of work for which I thought myself ill-prepared, from a safe environment of a religious community into a search for a new sisterhood? Well, several funny things happened to me on the way to Abby's House on lower Crown Street, Worcester, Massachusetts.

CHAPTER 1
From St. Elmo Road to Crown Street

I was born in Worcester in 1930, spent my early years on St. Elmo Road and attended both Midland and May Street schools. Just before Pearl Harbor, we moved to Oxford, where I completed early childhood education at the Allen L. Joslin School. In 1948 I graduated from the old Oxford High School, and in September of that year, with feelings of loneliness and uncertainty, I entered the College of Our Lady of the Elms, a small Catholic college for women in western Massachusetts. It took several agonizing months before I adjusted to the routine of the Catholic atmosphere, having been dubbed a "pub" by some of the upperclass women who looked with suspicion on anyone who entered this sacred territory from a public education facility. Even though I wasn't accepted by some, their approval didn't matter so much when I discovered I had great roommates, one in particular, who shared my Democratic bias. Mary Crane and I bonded forever the night we kept the radio on (against the rules), eating onion and mayo sandwiches on pumpernickel while awaiting the results of the Dewey-Truman election. Of course, our personal favorite "give 'em hell Harry," was the unexpected winner, and we gloated in the victory. I kept thinking that my great-grandfather, Andrew Athy, would have been equally thrilled that a Democrat succeeded in upsetting the apple cart. After that victory, nothing interfered with my educational ambitions, and I grew to love the College and the faculty. At the beginning of my senior year, I was elected to the coveted position of Prefect of Our Lady's Sodality, the equivalent of a women's organization found on today's campus settings. There was no other organized group on campus held in higher esteem, and I was honored to have been elected into this leadership role, especially as a public school graduate! The final year at the Elms flew by, and I had firmly decided where the rest of my life would be spent. I would enter the Congregation of the Sisters of St. Joseph of Springfield to begin a lifetime commitment spent teaching high school students the two languages I loved, French and Spanish.

However, a two and a half year preparation period, called the Postulancy (six months) and the Novitiate (two years, one called the 'silent year,' meaning no company) was required before I would begin my active work. It was a rigorous physical and spiritual training and a great deal of patience and a lot of prayers were needed on a daily basis. We were reminded regularly that all this would pass and each of us would eventually be a young woman grown strong in wisdom, grace and humility. By March of 1955, when I was sent to my first teaching assignment, I was absolutely certain I had passed the humility part of the test. As for the wisdom and the grace components, I'm still working on those! Nevertheless, I was relieved that this testing period was over, and I arrived at St. Jerome's anxious to begin teaching the subjects I loved.

Well, not quite. It just didn't work out as I had envisioned. Subjects were handed out by "rank," that is, older Sisters, those who had spent the most years in the service of the Lord, got first choice! As the rookie, I really got the leftovers, which in my first year included U.S. History (we weren't allowed to read newspapers during the training period), English 3, using a parochial series that was not included in my public years of education, World History (see notes after U.S. History) and Biology. Just what I was prepared to teach to an average class of 57 teenagers who remained fascinated that someone as young and innocent as I had come to the inner city in the first place! If I thought the boot-camp training a bit harsh, the reality of teaching six different classes of nearly foreign material made it seem easy. In the convent, lights were out by 9:30, and a great silence prevailed— absolutely no communication was allowed under penalty of some kind of sin I've long since forgotten. Imagine me dissecting insects by night in the quiet of the kitchen pantry, trying to distinguish the various parts of the common earthworm. For

4 years old ... St. Elmo Road

June, 1948

Lifelong friend Mary Crane (r)

As Prefect at O.L.E.

Page 9

ENTERS CONVENT

Annette A. Rafferty, daughter of Mrs. Lillian Rafferty of 3 Clement street and the late Dr. Andrew A. Rafferty, who entered the Sisters of St. Joseph as a postulant this week at Mount Marie, Holyoke. She was graduated last June from Our Lady of the Elms College, where she was prefect of Our Lady's Sodality, co-editor of the school newspaper, and assistant editor of the yearbook.

September 14, 1952

Parish Buildings, South of Hampden Street

The old St. Jerome High, 1955

Biology class with Rosalie and Dorothy Renaud

years after I worried that the students who had expressed an interest in medical school had either flunked out or killed the first patient they had in the operating room based on the inadequate education I provided. To my great relief, I just recently learned from Maura Sweeney, a union organizer, and friend of Joseph Twarog, whose brother Francis was my biology student and about whom I worried most, had indeed become a very successful surgeon. To Maura's knowledge, none of his patients has died because of his incompetence! What a blessed relief.

Such was the story of my first assignment which lasted, by the way, ten and a half years. There were several rays of sunshine, however. I had the chance, finally, to teach Spanish and although I wasn't in my major field, the Reverend Mother sent me to get a master's degree in French Literature at Assumption College during the summer months. The best memories of these early years were the "kids" I taught. They were inspirational—hard workers and loyal to both the school and the faculty. Many a time, they saved me. I remember the visit of the Diocesan Supervisor whose real task was to highlight how little you really knew about teaching by asking the class to answer questions that would stump even Jeopardy champs. This class, the English students of 1957, stood their ground in the face of Sister Margaret Elizabeth, whose question, based on our reading of *The House of Seven Gables* was: "Please tell me what kind of candy Hepsibah sold in her store." They named everything from Mars Bars to penny candy, but failed to identify the correct response—rock candy! The students looked at me with questioning faces and, then remarkably, without prompting, burst into a delightful recitation of Emily Dickinson's poem:

> "I'm nobody
> ...are you nobody too?
> Then, there's a pair of us,
> don't tell....
> They'd banish us, you know.
> How dreary to be somebody
> How public like a frog
> To be stared at the day long by an
> admiring bog."

We were saved! Sister Margaret Elizabeth's face beamed. I kept my job, and the class went home relieved that their favorite teacher had escaped banishment.

In 1965, I was transferred to the most beautiful place on the face of the New England earth—Newport, Rhode Island on Bellevue Avenue, to St. Catherine's Academy, an all girls' school just down the street from the Doris Duke Estate and even closer to the Astors and Vanderbilts. For a few days, I thought I had died and gone to heaven. We walked to the ocean at night, went to Block Island on weekends if the weather permitted, and strolled down by the Colony House where George Washington made his mark. This assignment was well deserved after spending ten years in the heart of Holyoke's downtown area living in a convent that had a backyard leading to the former Providence Hospital and one sidewalk that led directly to the school. Here I was teaching in the master bedroom of Catherine Kernochan's home. She was Senator Pell's grandmother and her former home, with its gorgeous, highly polished parquet floors and a French door leading out to the beautifully manicured lawn, was breathtaking. I had the senior class marching on that beautiful lawn to the tune of Rudyard Kipling's famous poem, *Boots*. And, here I was finally teaching French and Spanish, with only one class of senior English. It just didn't get any better than this for a young teacher.

What I didn't anticipate was the tremendous change that was about to occur within me. I would move from being the docile, do-as-you're-told religious to a questioning, outspoken, creative woman, forever marked by the changes that came across the ocean from Rome where Vatican II and Pope John XXIII opened the windows of the Church. The transformation happened so quickly we can hardly remember a single incident that brought us all to life, except for the book, carefully covered so as to conceal its contents, that circulated in the chapel during that sacred hour called afternoon meditation. Actually, Sr. Claire Dugan was the facilitator of this famous internal rebellion. The book was John Gardner's *Self-Renewal: The Individual and the Innovative Society*—hardly an author or a text that could replace the *Lives of the Saints*. We devoured its contents, discussed what could happen coupling Gardner's ideas with the exciting writing found in *Perfectae Caritatis* (that section of Vatican II docu-

St. Catherine's Academy, 1965-68

*My friend
Claire Dugan, S.S.J.*

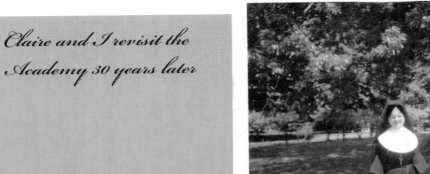

*Claire and I revisit the
Academy 30 years later*

Newport Revolutionaries

Claire as Sr. William Margaret, 1965

ments that would affect the religious women and men), and attended stimulating lectures at Salve Regina given by the "new" theologians. We even took the black serge offered to us by the Sisters of Mercy, hastened to the local fabric store, bought patterns and sewed into the early morning hours to get our experimental garb (modern dress) ready for exhibit!

Forgetting that I had struggled making a habit with ten yards of serge (that IS exactly the yardage involved in making a SSJ habit), I foolishly had selected a Christian Dior suit pattern. What was I thinking! But miraculously, the suit came together and I was a proud seamstress indeed. The Reverend Mother Mary Borgia established a "reviewing committee" to pass judgment on the new garbs. Three of us from Newport received a summons to appear and that we did, our hearts pounding, not with excitement, but with trepidation. All I recall of that fashion preview was receiving a reluctant passing grade. We were advised that not until a date specified by the Committee could we wear these experiments. I remember our local superior, Sr. Teresa Regina, questioning the Reverend Mother over the phone about the advisability of wearing our new robes in the convent. It would be acceptable as long as we didn't appear outside. Then, came Teresa Regina's famous question: "And, Mother, in the event of a fire inside the house?" An ear-shattering hang-up was the answer given.

It was then 1967. The Vietnam War and civil rights marches were the hot television news items, and within the convent walls on Bellevue Avenue, we were gearing up for our own war. We had no idea how fragmented we would become over interpretation of Vatican II documents, how many friends would become temporarily or even permanently alienated from one another, how many would eventually leave what had become an outmoded expression of religious life. We were ill-prepared to face the harsh realities of change or to learn what it was like to win a battle but lose the war. As I reflect now on my own experience, what became for me the harshest of the veiled realities was facing our collective inability to slip from under hierarchical control. We claimed our own identity as the church's conscience, not its cheerleader, and made external adaptations, but at heart we had remained unchanged in much of our thinking. The struggle led to life or death decisions. It was apparent that by 1968 the women of the community were on the move, for better or for worse. We were no longer the "little women" of the Church but were becoming vocal advocates for our future direction. I think it was in Newport that I finally grew up.

The date for those of us who had made experimental habits to appear in them had been set. It was June 24, 1968, at the summer retreat held at the Elms College. More excitement than fear filled the air. The older religious women, still in the traditional garb, had lined up outside the campus dining room early in the morning. I will never forget the encouragement those of us who were young and eager received from these women, who had lived for years in their habits and would no doubt be buried in them. Their hearts were opened wide and as I passed through their reviewing committee and heard only kindly remarks, I knew that the cordial charity all Sisters of St. Joseph promise at their vow-taking had triumphed. From that historic day forward, experimental dress slowly, but surely, replaced our centuries-old habit.

In the fall of 1968, I was transferred to the prestigious Cathedral High School in Springfield where I had only Spanish to teach to five different classes. That gave me the necessary time to continue my own brand of implementing the documents of Vatican II. My first venture into this new world was to write a proposal with three other brave Sisters—Cathy Leary, Jeanne O'Shea and Bev Rochford. We were determined to live outside the convent walls in an apartment in nearby Holy Name Parish.

We labored into the late evening, documenting our proposal with the necessary quotes from Vatican II and, with added confidence, even wove into the proposal our own Congregation's history that the first Sisters had lived among the people they served, not apart from them. This would be the "clincher." We were absolutely certain the hearts of Reverend Mother Mary Borgia and her council would melt, and we'd be moving in by the weekend! What we hadn't factored into our move was that we needed to request permission of Christopher J. Weldon, the Bishop of the Diocese. Since *Perfectae Caritatis* had launched religious women into the orbit of self-determination, it never occurred to us that the leadership would turn to the Bishop with our proposal to "experiment." Another battle lost! The Bishop put up a fight, calling in forces that we couldn't counter. Every

The Executive Board

1971-1975

CATHEDRAL HIGH SCHOOL

SPRINGFIELD, MASSACHUSETTS

April 2, 1969

Dear Sister,

We ask that decision on our experiment in Community living, submitted March 19, 1969 to the Experimental Board, endorsed by the Chapter, be withheld until such time that we have the support of our sisters, as it seems unlikely that approval from the local ordinary towards this experiment will be forthcoming, although he has not forbidden the doing thereof.

It is our sincere hope that our sisters will speedily realize that such an experiment is valid, necessary and desirable if renewal of the corporate group is to be achieved. It is also our earnest prayer that the Holy Spirit will help us all to see that continued disapproval of this experiment is de facto a continued refusal to re-evaluate our way of living, which always needs revitalization. We regret having to ask for this withholding of decision, but as service to the Community is our aim, we have decided that the goal would not be met if we launched out without support. It is on the basis of failure to see this goal being met that our decision has been reached.

In closing we would like to quote Thoreau: "If a man does not keep pace with his companions, perhaps he hears a different drummer. Let him step to the music which he hears, however measured or far away."

This explains our reason for not withdrawing this experiment. Please file it, until we can step to the music we hear.

Respectfully,

Sister Annette Rafferty

Annette in a quiet moment

Cele, Dee, Pat, Marion at 6 Birch St.

Canon lawyer from coast to coast was telephoned from the chancery, and, although the learned lawyers determined we were "legally" within our rights to "experiment," Bishop Weldon made his case to the entire Community, that it was the Spirit of the Law by which Sisters should live. The matter was ended. The case was closed temporarily, and the four of us who gave in to Community pressure to abide by the episcopal decision made copies of our proposal, and tucked them away in our trunks.

The following September, I was transferred out of the Springfield Diocese, to St. Peter's Convent in Worcester as the Sister-in-Charge. I imagine the Community thought I should be honored, but I had a much different perspective. The move was just the opposite of the small apartment group I had proposed—I was now a hotel manager. The convent had forty-eight sisters living in it, and I was in charge. Surprise! This was no reward. I must confess, the transfer brought me to another group of wonderful women, and I fell in love with the students I had at the high school. Those two factors were a source of continual redemption for me. And, from among those dedicated women were four who eventually received "permission" to move out of the convent into a small apartment near the school. Several years later they asked me to join them, and in my ecstasy, I sent notices of "I've moved into my apartment" to everyone I knew, including the Bishop of Springfield, providing him with exact directions on how to arrive at 6 Birch Street. Of course he never came, but when we met several months later at a community meeting in Holyoke, he actually sought me out and shook hands. No words were spoken, but I interpreted his cordial act as a subtle admission of my personal victory. And it wasn't accomplished in his backyard!

Those next two years flew by, and in the spring of 1971, for reasons known only to the Higher Powers, I was elected a member of the new governing body of the community. We were to be known as the Executive Board, with a president, vice president, and five area directors (local contacts). After long hours of discussion and reflection, I was assigned to Worcester, Worcester County and Rhode Island. This was no easy task in Worcester, since I came to the job with a "reputation" of advocating for the Sisters that had often required a confrontation with Diocesan authorities. To be truthful, I found Providence a more exciting, innovative place because no one in high places knew me, and the Sisters who worked in Rhode Island were, for the most part, doing direct work with the poor. It was probably the inspiration from this work and two unexpected invitations I received here in Worcester, that marked another major "conversion" in my life, culminating in my departure from the Sisters of St. Joseph thirteen years later.

CHAPTER 2 *Giving Birth to Ourselves*

Wearing smooth the path to Abby's House began with two invitations, one by phone, the other in writing. The first invitation came from Father Frank Scollen, Director of the Urban Ministry Commission, under the auspices of the Diocese of Worcester. Pastors, ministers and rabbis had been overwhelmed with requests to house the then "new homeless" of Worcester—women and often women with children, who, for one reason or another, were on the streets. Would I be interested in heading up a Task Force that would determine the extent of the need with the possibility of a concrete response? Of course I was, so I quickly responded in the affirmative. As a member of a women's religious congregation, I was deeply interested in finding ways to narrow the gap that existed in women's lives and in bringing about a more authentic sisterhood. Shortly after I sent my response to Frank, a second invitation came from Cameron McDonald who was beginning to form a committee of women within the Ecumenical Council to address the pressing concerns of women's future role in religion and society. I said "yes" again, since both invitations seemed challenging and exciting projects. It also occurred to me that both committees could be helpful in addressing the initial question: "What do we do with women who are homeless in Worcester?"

By the end of 1973, I was immersed in each committee's work, attending endless meetings, working at night to gather statistics and stories from homeless women themselves, connecting with neighborhood center workers for important "clues"

and in making conscious efforts to involve as many women as possible. But, by the middle of 1974, I had determined that women would have to be the initiators of any action. We just had to be the leaders, the designers and the doers! Working with the two groups had taught me a valuable lesson: women are creative. They see possibilities, not problems. The majority of men who served on the Urban Ministry Commision were interested in controlling the flow of the meetings as well as the suggestions made by the women. But to their credit, the members reached an agreement to establish a fund for homeless women, to be called the Abby Kelley Foster Fund, after Worcester's own Abby Kelley Foster who had been featured in an issue of the *Worcester Recorder*. (The City was preparing for the 1976 Bicentennial by publishing articles about important Worcester people. Since Abby herself had experienced homelessness, we thought it fitting that a women's shelter bear her name.) Our mailing address for the fund was the Ecumenical Office at 63 Wachusett Street, care of "Women, Religion and Society." In spite of growing concerns that the Urban Commission meetings were becoming endurance rather than energizing sessions, I was ecstatic that the two committees were working together in an informal way on the AKF Fund. The city of Worcester joined in by donating the first $1,000 to the fund—all due to the efforts of our women councillors: Barbara Sinnott, Barbara Kohin and Mary Scano. They had convinced city manager Francis McGrath that this $1,000, an anonymous gift to the city, would be well placed if donated to the fledgling fund for homeless women and children. The vote of the council was unanimous.

Meanwhile, up on Mount St. James, the young women of the Holy Cross Women's Organization, headed by Eve Gilmore, began mobilizing to collect monies to add to the AKF coffers. The momentum had begun. Interest in the issue of homelessness as it affected women and their children was drawing more and more women into the circle of concern. An announcement by Cameron McDonald that a conference would be held in the spring of 1974 at the YWCA came at just the right time. The conference, called Women's Rites, marked the first public presentation of the Abby Kelley Foster Fund that we hoped would result in a shelter for women. Our workshop was packed with interested women and men friends. To this day, I believe, without a shadow of a doubt, that this presentation got the issue of a women's shelter out of the boardroom and into the public arena, into a community that responded quickly with ideas, funds, invitations to speak, support of all sorts. Although it wasn't to open until 1976, Abby's House had been born, delivered into the Worcester community by a most fantastic group of women, whom I consider the "magnificent mid-wives of the '70s:"

Maureen Kroyak	Pat Cole
Mary Labunski	Joanne Bott
Leona Donahue	Carol Proietti
Cameron McDonald	Daria Meshnuck
Marge Dick	Doris Marcelonis
Kathleen Gooding	

These terrific women were followed by yet another group of pioneers, those who worked to get the shelter officially opened. During the rest of 1974, we gathered in the kitchen at my 6 Birch Street residence, planning and dreaming continued to buoy our spirits. Additionally, I received a great deal of support from the women with whom I lived—Dee Gaudette, Pat Archey, Carol Wren, Anne Marie Wildenhain, and Anna Marie Kane, who became a key person in developing the Holy Cross women component of Abby's House. Anna Marie used her role as the first woman Chaplain at Holy Cross to encourage women students to join in the struggle. The Congregation of the Sisters of St. Joseph of Springfield, of which I was then a member, was unbelievably supportive and gave me tremendous leeway to develop the dream with both emotional and financial support. My leaving the Congregation in 1986 had nothing to do with disinterest on their part. As I mentioned before, it had everything to do with a gradual shift in what was my primary community, differences in theological ideas and my need for freedom to shape a new kind of sisterhood.

June 1975 was here and it meant the final meeting of the Urban Ministry Commission for that year. The meeting, as I remember it, was held in the Commission's office at Plumley Village. It was a stuffy room with little ventilation. Who was present? I truly can't remember with accuracy. Of course,

Frank, Leona, Mary Matthew, Father Tinsley and I were definitely present. I do recall that it was a daytime meeting and an unusually small number of members were present, which made me very nervous. I had anticipated a "vote" on continuing work for the shelter. We needed a quorum. Or had a decision already been reached? No. We would decide here and now and I was ready for whatever the outcome. More than research and statistic gathering had occurred in these past two years. My heart had become invested in following through on my findings. What had begun as an interesting task had succeeded in changing my life. It wasn't a conversion as dramatic as Paul's fall from a horse, but it was an interior investment of my heart and mind in the outcome that motivated me. I know none of the men with whom I served on the Commission understood that. The opening of a shelter for women couldn't wait and neither could I. Often, during those meetings, the late Bishop Timothy J. Harrington (whom I later referred to as Brother Timothy), a man devoted to the poor, reminded me that teaching was my true calling and that I lacked a social work background. Both observations were accurate, but that didn't mean I wasn't qualified. I had good organizational skills acquired during my 21 years of teaching, and I knew instinctively how to connect with those people who had the abilities I lacked. This shelter would be a collective effort, not a one-woman show. Visualize Rosie the Riveter saying, "We can do it." That's how I envisioned myself and all the women who were involved. This does not mean I was without any moments of serious self-doubts. They came when I considered the seriousness of this effort and the reminders given to me in good faith and with good reason by Father Ed Tinsley. He possessed remarkable skills identifying much needed services in the city, noting that monies for shelters were not presently available and that we (I and those women interested) would require more on-the-job training. I agreed, and in the realm of practical considerations to follow his advice to wait for funds and training would have made sense. But I was no longer living in the realm of practical considerations. I had passed over, so to speak, to another space in time and was no longer willing to follow conventional wisdom. Can you understand that it had become impossible to ignore the need and I had to go forward, whatever the results?

Abby Foster: Worcester abolitionist, women's rights advocate

Cameron

United States Be

Abby Kelley Foster Fund
c/o Women, Religion and Society
Worcester County Ecumenical Council
63 Wachusett Street
Worcester, Mass. 01609

H. Women for Human Services
    What we can do, are doing for human services
    -Annette Rafferty, SSJ
    -Mary Bonina, Your Place,
    -Members of the Green Island Project

Abby Kelley Foster Fund for a Shelter for Homeless Women

1975

Rita Corbin

The Abby Kelley Foster Fund is maintained by women acting as individuals from many groups with a common concern: WHAT TO DO FOR HOMELESS WOMEN IN WORCESTER!

NEARLY TWO YEARS AGO, in response to the need for providing temporary shelter for homeless women in our city, a fund, namely the Abby Kelley Foster Fund, was begun and housed in the YWCA. The amount of money in the fund remained below $2,000.00, but as it was used, individual women and women's groups continued to replenish it. However, the limited facilities of the Y became a growing concern for us. Rooms weren't always available and referrals to the AKF Fund were often in no condition to share a room with someone already registered at the Y. Many women were helped by the Fund, but it became increasingly more difficult for the Y to admit Abby Kelley Foster referrals.

A GROUP IS FORMING NOW to create and maintain an emergency shelter for homeless women in Worcester. Will you be one with us?

HOW YOU CAN HELP:

(1) Do you know of any space that may adequately be used as a small shelter for women.....

(2) Do you have energy to join the group working to create the shelter.....

(3) Can you pledge a small monthly donation
    ____$1 ____$2 ____$3 a month ____$
    to help maintain the shelter.

By Amy Gaiennie

Abby Kelley Foster was one of the Worcester women attending the first National Women's Convention held in 1850 at the site of what is now the Commerce Building on Main St.

While Mrs. Foster was involved in the women's movement, the largest part of her work was as an abolitionist. Travelling throughout New England with little money, she spoke wherever sympathetic people could arrange a place for her to [speak].

Stanton said of her:

"Mrs. Foster was the most untiring and most persecuted of all the women throughout the anti-slavery struggle. She travelled up and down alike in winter's cold and in summer's heat, with scorn, ridicule and violence and mobs accompanying her, suffering all kinds of persecution, still speaking wherever she gained an audience, in open air, in the school house, barn, depot, church, or public hall; on week day or Sunday, as she found opportunity.

For listening to her on Sunday, many men and women were expelled from their churches. Thus, through continual persecution was woman's self-assertion and self-respect sufficiently developed to prompt her at last to demand justice, liberty and equality for herself."

Worcester Raised

Mrs. Foster was born in Pelham, Massachusetts on January 17, 1811. Her parents moved to Worcester in the spring of 1811. The family first resided on a farm at Washington Square. In 1835, Wing Kelley, Mrs. Foster's father, sold the farm and moved to Millbury.

[She] completed her education at Friend's School in [Provi]dence, and then [attended] school in Tatnuck [and Rox]bury and Lynn.

[She] was one of the first [wome]n to speak in public [again]st slavery, and in [1837] joined the anti-[slaver]y cause. She met [Stephe]n Foster, also an [aboliti]onist, and married [him i]n New Brighton, [Penns]ylvania in 1845. The [pair m]oved to Worcester [in 184]7, where they lived [on a fa]rm on Mower St in [Tatnu]ck. Here they [hid f]ugitive slaves [too], and their Mower [St f]arm became a [stati]on station in the underground railway. She

Barton at 100 Chatham St., Worcester on January 14, 1887.

The Worcester Historical Society has a letter, written by Mrs. Foster which describes how she decided to become a public speaker against slavery, and some of the experiences she had when she first took to the road to speak whenever the opportunity was provided. The letter was written about 45 years after she "first essayed to speak in public for the slave."

Mrs. Foster began her work by circulating petitions, to the state

"Pity The Slave"

Finally, after reading a passage in the Bible which seemed to speak directly to her, Mrs. Foster made the decision to travel, and speak against slavery:

"My way is clear...How true it is, as all history records, that all great reforms have been carried forward by despised and weak means. The talents, the learning, the wealth, the church and state are pledged to the support of slavery. I will go out among the honest-hearted common people, into the highways and by-ways and cry 'Pity the poor slave,' if I can do nothing more."

Mrs. Foster knew that there was danger for her as an abolitionist and public-speaking women:

"My mother still hoped I might be spared from taking up so heavy a cross. But I told her I had counseled the east, and that I must take my life in my hand as an abolitionist, and, as a woman public speaker, must suffer more than loss of life."

[publications,] [rai]se funds for abolition societies and throu[gh] "private conversation" explaining the [princi]p[le] of the anti-slave[ry] movement whenever s[he] found the opportunity. S[he] began to find that h[er] work as an abolition[ist] began to interfere w[ith] her duties as a sch[ool] teacher. She writes:

"At length my wh[ole] soul was so filled with [the] subject that it would [not] leave me in school hou[rs] and I saw I was not giv[ing] to this duty what was [its] due."

She decided to resi[gn] and after two more ter[ms] as teacher, was releas[ed.] At that time, the decis[ion] to become an acti[ve] public speaker two me[ant] [year]s as teacher, w[as] [discus]sed. At that time, [decis]ion to become [th]e public speaker w[as no]t [e]asy. The uncertai[nty, the] turmoil, [the] [quest]ioning of her o[wn abilit]ies was apparent [in her description] of [her] decision to "take [the] [work abro]ad."

[She] talked with h[er] [moth]er about the slave [quest]ion, she write[s, "talki]ng, but for the fa[ct that I] had so little co[mmand] of language, a[nd had] never any traini[ng in] public speaking, [but I] think I had a divi[ne call] to go forth a[nd] [spok]e...

[At o]ne point, when t[he abol]itionist societies we[re desp]erate for money, s[he sent] several of the me[n to do] [pers]asive articles in h[er ward]robe, "feeling tha[t I would] not withhold even [a feath]er's weight of he[lp that] might hasten t[he down]fall of the terri[ble syste]m, which, [in] [degrad]ing and cursing t[he slave,] had deprived t[his whole] country of t[he liber]ty of speech and t[he] [right to] the right [peace]able assembl[y and] [pe]tition."

H. Women for Human Services
    What we can do, are doing for human services
    -Annette Rafferty, SSJ
    -Mary Bonina, Your Place,
    -Members of the Green Island Project

The heat in the room suddenly cooled off. It was my turn to give the report on the shelter. I was shaking inside. That dreaded fear of rejection came over me. I felt like a little girl waiting to get a test paper back, hoping for an A, but anticipating an F. Finally, the waiting was over. The Commission's decision was not to establish the shelter at that time. I remember only my response: "Please accept my resignation, effective now." No reasons I can recall were given for this decision. Perhaps it really was a question of lack of money to do it and lack of experience to run it. Or it may have been a simple case of two different points of view: men are the planners and designers of such projects and women are hired into whatever positions the planners determine are necessary. To imagine women as both planners and doers was risky and radical! Father Frank urged me to reconsider my resignation. That was no longer an option for me. I had to act. Call it whatever you like—a decision made in anger, a foolhardy course of action, a response of an uppity woman. The truth is this: the decision came from a stubbornness of soul so powerful it frightened me, but it managed to push me forward with a strong sense of purpose. We women would create the model. We would get the money, find a place and staff it all in good time.

During the summer months that followed, Father Frank and I had many conversations about my resignation, which he thought at the time was not in the best interest of achieving the goal. Because of our mutual respect and long-time friendship, he did support the idea of sending out a letter to individuals and groups that expressed interest in helping with a women's shelter, inviting them to attend a December 4, 1975 meeting to be held at St. John's rectory on Temple Street. The letter, sent on Urban Ministry stationery, was drafted by the women members of the Commission and mailed to every neighborhood center, city-wide agency and to individuals who had joined the circle of interest. The purpose of the meeting was to determine whether those who came wanted to go forward. Everyone there would know by the end of the meeting how daring a move going forward was and how much energy was needed to achieve the dream. And, if the decision of the group was to proceed, it would be at its own risk and without the sponsorship of the Urban Ministry. It would be an independent venture, involving

women with lots of courage and determination and with an attitude that all things are possible. For now, we had to wait and see if the letter would draw in more help and support.

December 4, 1975 finally came. The long-awaited meeting began about 7:30 and the results exceeded all our expectations. After a number of reports about visits to other shelters in Boston and Providence, questions and suggestions began to emerge from the group. Excerpts from a letter written by Elaine Lamoureux best describe the proceedings:

"I do wish to share the outcome of the meeting called by Annette Rafferty concerning the problem of homeless women in the Worcester area. It was attended by well over 30 concerned people, present because of personal and-or group concern. Among the many organizations represented were: The American Friends Service Committee, Books Behind Bars, Catholic Worker Movement, City Council, the Correctional Exchange Group, FISH, NARW (National Assembly of Religious Women) Outreach, Senate of Religious, Urban Ministry Commission and parish groups. Several Religious communities were also present: the Sisters of St. Joseph, Sisters of Mercy, Sisters of the Presentation, Sisters of St. Anne and the Venerini Sisters.

Two years ago in response to the need for providing temporary shelter for homeless women in Worcester, a fund was begun, and homeless women were housed at the YWCA. At the present time, the limited facilities at the "Y"—along with the fact that many of the women referred are in no condition to share a room—have caused the YWCA to discontinue housing for our referrals. This dilemma prompted those involved to call on the Worcester community to find some solution to the problem. Because people are the best resource, it was hoped that a group would emerge and take action.

How should the problem be handled? Should we take a 'proposal' route or should we find an abandoned building and just begin? How should we define the problem

Doris Marcelonis

Marge Dick

Daria Meshenuck

6 Birch Street crowd

Barbara Kohin and Mary Scano

Barbara Sinnott

of homeless women in Worcester? Should we start with a place where women are just fed or where women are fed and housed? Are we being too naive and simplistic? What does it really mean to be in residential care? There was much dialogue among those present with experience and expertise in already existing models and people with a vision of creating a new model. As a result of this encounter, it was proposed that sub-groups be formed for people interested in formulating proposals in order to obtain funds, in creating a new plan or model, or finally, in promoting interest through public relations.

I personally found the meeting most rewarding. Every person present had a common concern—homeless women. Each felt accountable to and for them. Many are willing and ready to take a stand NOW, by giving their time and energy to help either in an active or in a supportive way. It was a beautiful experience for me to be a part of a group which is willing to give all in order to be of service to women who need to feel that they are 'somebody' and that they are loved. If anyone is interested, I would be delighted to share more in detail the input from the meeting as well as the information gathered from Rosie's Place and the Shelter...."

Sincerely,
Elaine Lamoureux

And thus was born the Women's Collective that continued to meet every two weeks at Hogan Center, Room 307, Holy Cross College. The plan that prevailed unanimously was to create a new model—a shelter for women done by women. By the end of February 1976, 2,000 flyers explaining the project and asking for assistance were distributed. Also, the process of incorporation as a non-profit corporation: The Abby Kelley Foster House, Inc., began! We had less than $1,000 in the fund, the plan was in its infancy, and we had no idea where the shelter would be located. The determination of the group was strong, and nothing would stop this movement now. Among the shelter pioneer-planners were: Muriel Audette, SSA; Mary Bonina,

Rev. Joan Bott, Geri Dinardo, Leona Donahue, RSM; Eileen Dooley, Penny Gaumond, Kathleen Gooding, Anna Kane, SSJ; Polly Kierstead, Barbara Kohin, Maureen Kroyak, Elaine Lamoureux, SSA; Peggy Marengo, Mary Labunski, MSBT; Carolyn Packard, Carol Proietti, SSA; Annette Rafferty, SSJ; and many other persons who continued to support us with time, talent, finances and the necessary ingredient: human concern. We had truly become committed to "Abby Kelley Foster House, Inc., a temporary, emergency shelter for homeless and battered women to be maintained by women acting as individuals from many groups with a common concern."

A progress report mailed out in early March outlined, however briefly, the hard work that was being done, often with no concrete results:

"We are in process of investigating property on Franklin and Highland Street. Pastor Bergstrom from Trinity Lutheran Church informed us that property on the corner of Wachusett and Highland had (already) been leased to the Mt. Olivet Pentecostal group. He is interested in our work and will let others know we are looking for a house. Also, we put our limited funds into a bank under the name of the Abby Kelley Foster Fund. I think we are officially an organization."

The meetings in Room 307 at Holy Cross were intense and interesting. We were all opinionated, but had a gift of being able to listen to each other. Eventually, we would reach consensus. Some of the issues that dominated the meetings were also recorded in that first progress report. Points discussed were the following:

1) The "where" of the home is important, especially if we want to use the facility all day. The Divorced and Separated Helpmates are interested in working with us.

2) What kinds of places are we considering? Will it be a storefront, a house, a three-decker, an apartment?

3) Who are the women who will come? An overnighter, a prostitute, a fire victim, a runaway, out-of-town people,

Eileen Dooley

Meredyth, Leona Donahue and Mary Labunski

PLANNING COMMITTEE

Muriel Audette s.s.a.
Mary Bonina
Rev. Jo-an Bott
Gerri DiNardo
Leona Donahue r.s.m.
Eileen Dooley
Penny Gaumond
Kathleen Gooding
Anna Kane s.s.j.
Polly Kierstead
Barbara Kohin
Maureen Kroyak
Peggy Marengo
Mary Matthew m.s.b.t.
Carolyn Packard
Carol Proietti s.s.a.
Annette Rafferty s.s.j.
...and many other persons who
are supporting us with time,
talent...financial contribu-
tions and necessary human
concern...

ABBY KELLEY FOSTER HOME, INC.

<u>A temporary shelter</u>

<u>for homeless women</u>...

To be maintained by
women acting as
individuals from
many groups with
a common concern.

ABBY KELLEY FOSTER
Worcester Abolitionist
and Feminist

Brief History

March, 1974 - Fund begun; housed in YWCA
October, 1975 - Fund withdrawn from YWCA (Y could no longer handle our referrals)
December, 1975 - Community Meeting of 40 women - results in a Coalition to make shelter
              a reality.
January, 1976 - Coalition meets to discuss models - "Rosie's Place", Sancta Maria, two
              Boston shelters for women.
February, 1976 - Our flyers are distributed - incorporation of Abby Kelley Foster Home
              completed.
March, 1976 - Worcester properties visited - committees formed for staffing and operation
              of home.
April, 1976 - Early summer promises to be opening date in Piedmont Street neighborhood.
              Nearly $100.00 <u>a week</u> has come in since distribution of flyers.

PLEASE SEND AMOUNT TO: N.B.

The Abby Kelley Foster Fund $1.00 a month from 150 people pays
c/o Program Unit of Women, Religion and Society   rent; $1.00 a month from 300 people
Worcester Ecumenical Council   covers utilities and heat. Pass a
63 Wachusett Street   flyer on to a friend.
Worcester, MA 01609   (757-8385)

-----------------------------------Please cut here and mail to us----------------------------

Your Name_____

Street_____City & State_____

   ed   ____$1   ____$2   ____$3   ____$ A <u>small</u> monthly donation
                                                is deeply appreciated.
ive our Newsletter? ___Yes   ___No

                                          Thank You.

The Women's Camp Project + the Abby Kelley Foster Fund
Cordially Invites you to meet
MARGARET HOPE BACON
biographer of Abby Kelley Foster, "I Speak For My Slave Sister"
on the topic
Worcester's Abby Kelley Foster: Her Message For Us Today
7:30-8   Book Party   9-9:30pm.

Thursday Evening
May 6, 1976
8 pm.

Science Amphitheatre
Science Building
Worcester State College

Sponsored by Worcester Area Campus Ministry at Worcester State College

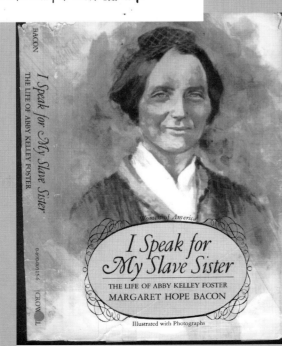

BACON

I Speak for My Slave Sister
THE LIFE OF ABBY KELLEY FOSTER

0-690-00315-6

CROWELL

I Speak for
My Slave Sister
THE LIFE OF ABBY KELLEY FOSTER
MARGARET HOPE BACON

Illustrated with Photographs

*Outside
21-23 Crown Street
April 4, 1976*

The red brick building spotted by Carolyn Packard

homeless women and children, women out of prison and mental hospitals, the chronically homeless?

After much discussion (and disagreement), we decided to deal with "any woman 18 years or older—homeless, battered, wandering, out of housing for whatever reason." Children with their mothers were to be included in this grouping. No one actively drinking or drugging would be eligible.

Eileen Dooley and I met in late February with lawyers filing our incorporation papers. Plans to file for tax-exemption were initiated. Bylaws were also in the works. Still, no place, but our determination had solidified. We proceeded as though we had all the money in the world and reached out to the community with confidence. Weren't we the greatest marketing firm in Worcester in 1976? I'd say yes. Numbers of people called and came and asked us to visit their women's groups to spread the word. Certainly, one of those women's groups I remember was the Tatnuck Church Cluster made up of the First Congregational Church, Christ the King and St. Luke's Episcopal. These women gave incredible support; and from those women came a commitment still alive and well at Abby's House. The women from the cluster I remember with fondness are: Margaret Baillie, Fran O'Connell, Eva Engel, Fran Wall, Ruth Gauch, Ethel Donaldson, Connie Hill, Bev Plucinski and Irene Allaire who joined them from St. Peter's parish. Both Fran O'Connell and Eva are still staffing the night shelter.

A March 19, 1976 progress report revealed that we were still without a place and money was coming in slowly and, of course, in small amounts. However, nothing deterred us. Our flyers were still being distributed, and our incorporation was completed. Now, all we needed was our tax-exempt status from the Office of the Secretary of State. Someone alerted us to property that was available on Claremont Street. We loved it, but after some attempts at negotiating price, the deal collapsed, and we remained "homeless." The sub-committee on public relations (which was also fundraising) had successfully planned another public presentation and had invited Margaret Bacon, author of *I Speak For My Slave Sister: The Life of Abby Kelley Foster*, to speak

in May at Worcester State College. It was to be called "Founding Mothers: Now And Then," and would be followed by a coffee and book-signing party. All our reports concluded with a familiar plea:

> "It seems very important and imperative that we begin to identify those women willing to commit themselves and some of their time to this house. Please come forward if you are interested or get in touch with someone who is...."

At the March 30th meeting, Abby Kelley Foster made her first of many public appearances. That is to say, a woman sent by the spirit of Abby Kelley Foster came to the meeting. She had not been present for any of the previous meetings although she was on the planning committee. As we were discussing the sad fact that we were still "homeless," Carolyn Packard spoke up and said: "Have you looked on lower Crown Street...there's a red brick building and one side seems empty." Mary Labunski and I wasted no time in following this latest housing "tip." On April 4, 1976, we found ourselves outside 21-23 Crown Street. This had to be it! The two of us decided to tell the landlord exactly what we would be doing. Honesty and directness would get the desired results! We approached the door. The landlord, Harry, was painting the front room on the 21 side of the duplex. I can still visualize him high on a ladder, looking down at us with a big, welcoming smile! He was delighted to rent not only one floor on the 23 side, but upstairs as well. The cost: First floor: $180...Second floor: $190...but he was willing to give us a rounded figure of $325, heat and electricity included. What a deal! Mary and I wrote up the report and presented it to the entire committee on April 14th with great enthusiasm.

Arrangements were made for people to see the house on Friday, April 16, at 12:30. Everyone loved the site, but questions still lingered: when do we plan to open the house; where can we find someone who will be there full time? We finally agreed that the date of opening depended on readying the house. I remember committing myself to three nights a week at the shelter and hoped that others on the committee would find a night to give. We were to make our final decision on

April 27, 1976, at noon. As usual I ended my written report of this meeting with an impassioned plea: "For the next meeting, please consider whether you are prepared to make a commitment of time to staff the house."

As I saw it, the time had come for that kind of commitment to the project. We were either going forward, or we would be forever stalled by questions and concerns that would only be addressed in the "doing." None of us had answers. They would eventually come. The challenge was imperative and the women in the group had to find their own individual answers. And they came. Unfortunately, some were unable to continue with the project. But the vast majority were willing to put their bodies there in a variety of ways. And so, on April 27, 1976, we signed the rental agreement with Haralambus Mironidis (fondly called Harry) and wrote our first rent check. Enthusiasm, a sense of great pride and accomplishment, the thrill of having come a long way, excitement, legitimate fear of the unknown, total conviction that the money and the volunteers and the donors would come, were all of the emotions that filled our hearts on that day. It was a new chapter in the extraordinary history of the Worcester landmark. Abby's House was a reality. Now, we needed to furnish her!

WANTED: for the Abby Kelley House (due to open 6/1/76)

DONATIONS OF:
FURNITURE (any kind)
POTS & PANS — DISHES — BED LINEN —
BLANKETS — PILLOWS — CURTAINS — ETC
— BEDSPREADS —
BEFORE YOU THROW IT AWAY
PLEASE THINK OF THIS WORTHY CAUSE.
FURTHER INFO: Eileen Dooley   Sr Anna
Ext. 2564   Ext. 2428 (3421)

CHAPTER 3 *Here for the Long Haul*

A colleague at American Friends Service Committee sent us a studio photograph of the lithograph of Abby. The original was forwarded to the American Antiquarian Society on Salisbury Street where the main body of Abby's papers are kept. Our lithograph hung in the shelter dining room until January 2000 when it was replaced by a Charlotte Wharton reproduction of Abby. Yes, the same Abby who now graces the walls of Worcester's Mechanics Hall. It was the gift of Mary Melville and framed for us by Dan Cavanaugh of C.C. Lowell on Park Avenue. I know Margaret Bacon's words which described the American Friends photograph still ring true as guests and staff alike look at the "new" Abby:

> "It makes me happy to think of Abby being present in the house named for her, listening to the stories of battered and abused women who now go there for comfort and for space. It is as though the woman I wrote about, the woman who died almost a hundred years ago, has returned. Abby Kelley lives."

Busy isn't an adequate enough word to describe the "furnishing" activities that were going on daily—and nightly. Through the efforts of Anna Marie Kane and Eileen Dooley, we found a dear friend in Dan Dewey (also of Holy Cross) who gave us access to the fancy furniture that departing students deposited in the dumpsters. We rescued bed frames and fairly decent mattresses, chairs and tables and some rather eclectic pieces of living room furniture. The house was shaping up, and within two weeks church groups had responded to our mailing by bringing towels, sheets, blankets and all sorts of necessary linens. Dishes and silverware also came in large numbers! A phone was connected, three articles about Abby's House appeared in local newspapers, the staffing calendar filled up quickly. The community of Worcester was responding with as much excitement and anticipation as we were experiencing. Abby's belonged to the people and they supported this effort. The only conveniences we were missing were a washing machine and dryer, but what we had instead were four amazing women who quickly took over the task of keeping the linens clean. How could we ever have gotten it done without Barbara Kohin, Marie Dugas, SSA, Fran O'Connell and the late Marilyn Dawson, who arrived quietly in the morning to pick up the laundry and then faithfully delivered clean sheets and towels by early evening? I can't imagine a more efficient delivery system. (A few years later a washer and dryer were donated.) We were fortunate to have our first "temporary" live-in staffer in place—Sue Geaney, a June 1976 graduate of Holy Cross College. Maureen Kroyak (our beloved friend who died of Hodgkins disease two years later) agreed to be the opening night staffer. We were definitely ready. On June 3 we had an open house for all our friends, supporters and neighbors. More than 150 people came to see, to encourage, to lend help and support. By day's end all had been strongly affirmed. Sue Geaney and Maureen Kroyak received our first guests on the evening of June 7, 1976, the historic opening of the only temporary, emergency shelter for women with or without children in Central Massachusetts. The porch light was on, and they came —women helping other women. By mid-June, church bulletins were carrying the following information about Abby's:

> "ABBY KELLEY FOSTER HOUSE at 23 Crown Street (756-5486) is a home for women, which provides temporary, emergency shelter for those coming out of prison, anyone out on the street or evicted. Stay is limited…Our emphasis is home, not rehabilitation…"

Ms.GAZETTE NEWS

FRAMING OUR FOREMOTHER

"The Prettiest Feminist"

The 19th-century feminists were too busy fighting battles to pose for pictures. What portraits remain are mainly made in middle age, and are a trifle grim.

Abby Kelley Foster, the first woman to be appointed an official in the American Anti-Slavery Society, was described by her contemporaries as the prettiest of the feminists. When I worked on a book on her life, I could only find an older Abby, pleasant-looking but battle-worn, for the book jacket (*I Speak for My Slave Sister: The Life of Abby Kelley Foster*, published by Thomas Y. Crowell). Some months later, I had a call from a friend in Worcester, Massachusetts, which is near Pelham, Abby's birthplace. A local feminist coalition had decided to establish a residence for women in transition, and call it the Abby Kelley Foster House. Would I come to a public meeting to tell the townspeople about Abby's life, and launch a drive for funds?

I said yes, and put down the phone with tears in my eyes. Abby would have been so pleased. After my talk, a welfare mother came up to me and grabbed my hand. "Abby Kelley lives!" she said.

The new Abby Kelley Foster House, which we visited later in the evening, was clean, but bare. A few weeks later, Beth Binford, a colleague of mine at the American Friends Service Committee, came into my office in a state of some excitement. At an auction in Chester County she had bought an old lithograph made in 1846, the subject of which was Abby Kelley Foster at the age of 36. The lithograph had been made by Robert Douglass, Jr., a black artist and [brother] of Sarah Mapps Douglass [a] teacher, feminist, and [abolitio]nist.

[It was] quite a find. Binford decided to offer it to the American

Antiquarian Society in Worcester, where the main body of Abby's papers are, and give the modest proceeds to the Abby Kelley Foster House. She also made a studio photograph of the lithograph, and sent it to the women who now staff the house.

It makes me happy to think of Abby being present in the house named for her, listening to the tales of the battered and abused women who now go there for comfort and for space. It is as though the woman I wrote about, the woman who died almost a hundred years ago, has returned. Abby Kelley lives!
—Margaret Bacon

Frank Kartheiser does some finishing touches

Mike Smolinski fixes up the outside

ABBY? 1978

WHO IS "Abby Kelley Foster"

a dramatic monologue

by whom? senior citizen Theodora Shearer

when? Friday, November 3 at 3:30 pm

where? Hogan 320

for whom? Abby's Friends & Benefactors & all interested folks

REFRESHMENTS will follow!

Polly Ellen Kierstead, September 1976

NEWSLETTER VOL.1 NO. 5
...a temporary for women...
Worcester, 01608..
2 a.m. each day.

ABBY KELLEY FOSTER HOME
emergency shelter
located at 23 Crown St.
open from 7 p.m. to
Phone: 756-5686
756-5466

ABBY KELLEY FOSTER, WORCESTER ABOLITIONIST AND FEMINIST

June, 1976

Dear Friends,

At long last, the Abby Kelley Foster Home is a reality!

We rented a duplex apartment in late April and spend the month of May getting ready and so many wonderful individuals and groups of people came to our assistance in a number of ways...furniture, bedding, bathroom supplies and kitchen items...along with lending hands to clean and arrange our home. In early May, we were happy to welcome to our city Margaret Hope Bacon, author of MY SLAVE SISTER, a biography of Abby, in whose memory our home is named. She lectured at Worcester State College about this remarkable woman and we shared the profits of her fund-raising appearance with the Women's Camp Project. Many churches have been more than generous with their financial support, too. But the steady, monthly dollars that come from you remain the 'backbone' of our continuity.

On June 3 we had open house for friends and neighbors. Many of you came to lend support. More than 150 new faces also came and we felt strong affirmation in our collective effort. We thank each and every one of you for your presence and, in so many cases, presents of all sorts!

Monday, June 7 we officially opened our doors and since then, we have been able to offer emergency housing to several women and children. One young woman came to us without work or housing. Fortunately, we have been able to help her through the Crisis Center. The Department of Social Services has referred a mother and three children to us...she, the mother, needs a permanent address for a few days in order to get AFDC. And so, we have begun. Our live-in person for June is Sue, a June graduate of Holy Cross. Around her, the rest of us have scheduled ourselves, so that at all times, there are two of us on duty. We meet again on June 22 to firm up staffing for July and August. Until we ourselves have a better idea of the direction the home will take, we are waiting before seeking a full-time resident staff person. In the meantime a great deal of interest has been indicated and some women are already asking about possibilities for the year. IF YOU KNOW OF ANY WOMAN WHO WOULD LIKE TO BE IN TOUCH WITH US, direct her to the June 22 meeting.

Carol Lareau, Jeanne O'Shea, S.S.J.

OA Worcester Sunday Telegram   May 8, 1977

Nun, Mental Health Leader Honored

Two Get Community Service Awards

Sister Annette Rafferty, the nun who helped found Abby's Home, a temporary shelter for homeless women and their children in Worcester, and Marjory Taylor of Southboro, an advocate and organizer of mental health services in the Southboro area, are Massachusetts winners of the annual Jefferson Award.

The award is presented for outstanding community service. It is cosponsored by The Boston Globe in cooperation with the American Institute for Public Service.

Sister Annette, 47, a member of the Sisters of St. Joseph of Springfield, was instrumental in the organization and operation in 1975 of the Women's Collective that is responsible for Abby's Home at 23 Crown St. After receiving the citation and bronze medal at a luncheon in the Globe building Thursday, Sister Annette said, "I was pleased that I would be able to accept the award in the name of the group. Because of our position, I feel the award was as much for the group as for me. I don't want to surface as a leader."

Sister Annette coordinated the planning, staffing and training programs for the volunteers who staff Abby's Home. She has proposed a voluntary pledge system to help fund the program.

Since the house opened in June, 1976, 447 nights of lodging have been provided for about 80 different women and about 30 children. Sister Annette said 20 of these women were "transients;" three were rape victims, and six were battered women.

Sister Annette was born in Worcester and was educated in Worcester and Oxford Schools. She is a graduate of Our Lady of The Elms College, Chicopee, received her master's degree from the Ecumenical Institute and taught in secondary schools in several towns.

Mrs. Taylor was born in Grosse Isle, Mich., and attended Hopkinton public schools. She is a member of the Governor's Advisory Committee on Mental Health and Retardation and is the chairman of the State Budget Committee.

The judges were Frieda Garcin, director of the consultation and education program of the Solomon-Carter-Fuller Community Mental Health Center in Boston; Malcolm Hobbs, editor and publisher of the Orleans Cape Codder; Kenneth Rossano, senior vice president of the Association for Mental Health. A clinic funded by the state Department of Mental Health opened in January, 1971.

Mrs. Taylor, 57, said she became interested in mental-health services about 10 years ago because there was none in the Southboro area.

She ran what has been called a "one-woman office" for the mental-health effort until 1968, when a group was organized as a chapter of the Massachusetts

First National Bank of Boston; Muriel Snowden, codirector of Freedom House in Boston; Richard C. Steele, president and publisher of the Worcester Telegram & Gazette Inc. and Robert Wood versity o

Sister Annette Rafferty

Foundation Encourages Grant Requests

By TERESA M. HANAFIN
Of The Gazette Staff

June, 1981

The Greater Worcester Community Foundation has money to give away. Lots of it.

But probably not enough for all the groups that are going to ask for some of that money.

For example, last year the foundation received requests for funds that totaled more than three times what it had to give away.

This year, according to executive director Kay M. Seivard, the foundation has about $150,000 to distribute, up from last year's total of $137,000. But $70,000 of that $150,000 already has been earmarked for certain charities by the people who donated the money. That leaves $80,000 to be distributed at the discretion of the foundation.

The foundation is an independent, non-profit organization established in September 1975 to help existing and new organizations in areas of health, education, civic, cultural and charitable needs.

It administers 14 funds, six of which were added last year.

The average amount of grants given out last year was $2,000, but organizations may submit proposals requesting $100 to $10,000. The foundation will allow up to 15 percent of the money they give to be used for administrative costs; the rest must be used for programming.

Those proposals must be submitted by July 31 to the foundation at 311 Main St. The groups must submit two copies of their proposal and eight copies of the foundation's summary sheet, which is available at the foundation office.

"I encourage groups that received money in other years, including last year, to come back and ask again if they need it," Ms. Seivard said in an interview. "Don't expect to get the same amount of money you got last year, but the chances are good you will get something."

An example of this as well as of the flexibility of the foundation is the $5,000 given last year to Abby House, a temporary emergency shelter for women. Abby House needed that amount to buy the house it has been renting and it also needed administrative money. But it didn't apply at first because it had received money the previous year.

Ms. Seivard encouraged them to apply and when she found out what they needed the money for, she said she was happy to recommend that they be funded. The foundation gave Abby House its money early so it could invest it and make the extra administrative money it needed. They bought the house.

"We took great pleasure in doing that," Ms. Seivard said. "They came to one of our board meetings to thank us and showed slides of their program. It was great."

Daybreak, a shelter and service for battered women and their children, received $7,000 last year; Big Brothers/Big Sisters of Worcester County and Piedmont Citizens for Action also received money, she said.

The foundation is eager to take on more funds to administer, Ms. Seivard said; a gift of any size may be made to the combined fund, which is for undesignated money given out by the foundation's distribution committee, headed by Helen Bowditch. A named fund may be started with $10,000 or with $2,500 and the intention to add on a regular basis until the fund reaches at least $10,000. The donor may designate the income to a field of interest or to specific charities or may allow the distribution committee to make the choice.

"We've received more than 40 requests for money already and the deadline isn't until July 31," Ms. Seivard said. "How many do you think we're going to get with all the budget cuts? Definitely more than 100."

The foundation requires that groups file six- and 12-month reports about their program and finances. This year, a new committee headed by Jean Hazzard will monitor and evaluate the funded programs.

"My advice to the groups out there is to apply," Ms. Seivard said. "Don't pad your request too much. The committee is very aware of that. Tell us what you need and why and we'll take it from there."

Kay M. Seivard

Kay Seivard (Marquet) GWCF comes to our aid

Dear friend, the late
Helen Pedone

Maria Pedone Whalen
follows her mom to Abby's

Anna Marie and
Paula Sasso
of Holy Cross, 1976

A 1998 reunion of Paula and Anna Marie

Our funds doubled, new volunteers signed up for training and information, and toys for the children came from Elm Park Community School. Chief Hanlon of the Worcester Police Department was aware of our existence, and policies regarding a working relationship with the police emerged, along with dates for training sessions with new recruits, arranged by Lieutenant John McKiernan. The front windows were repaired, the water was hot again, the downstairs readied for the arrival of the anticipated washer and dryer, and plans were made to send out a monthly newsletter!

Several young women came to Abby's as temporary, live-in staff in July and August of 1976: Paula Sasso and Meredyth Wessman of Holy Cross and Carol Lareau of the Sisters of St. Joseph. All the rest of us signed on the shelter calendar where there were openings. A letter from Carol contains some of her unforgettable memories of that first summer:

> "I remember being nervous, but by the end of my three weeks, I had become the 'expert,' and I learned something from it...that many things women undertake succeed because we learn from and help each other. One evening in particular stands out....the people living on the 21 side of the house had an argument that got out of hand. Loud words led to pushing. It resulted, finally, in a disconnected gas pipe...soon I began to smell gas at #23. So long after midnight, having reported the leak, Crown St. was crowded with police cars, fire trucks and the gas company workers repairing the damage! About the women? Of all the people who came, I specifically remember Lucky (Clarke). Her story, her life experiences and Lucky herself, touched me....I remember vaguely your cousin, Annette (Barbara Griffin). When you were around, she became your very distant cousin. When you were not there, she conned us with stories about her 'close' cousin, hoping (I suppose) to get 'special' treatment....I remember that it was not unusual for the doorbell to ring at 2 or 3 a.m. Battered women finally knew they had a safe place....I was struck by the number of volunteers and people behind the scenes....Women were able to recognize the breaking point in the other and were generous about watching and helping out with each other's children...so much gratitude for feeling safe and secure...many of the events and people changed my life after this three-week stay....my opinions about who was homeless and/or battered changed. Their ages, backgrounds, economic status destroyed my personal stereotypes....thanks for the "Abby" experience. Our conversations about such things as sexist language changed my opinion, attitudes and goals. It started me down a road I might otherwise not have chosen to walk."

By September 1976, we had our "permanent" live-in resident. Polly (Ellen) Kierstead came forward and donated her services five nights a week. It was a very busy year (1976) for all of us. We were everywhere—speaking about the need for this shelter and asking for a commitment to helping us help the women and their children. From March through April, we gave talks at Holy Cross, the First Baptist Church, Holy Name Church in Springfield, Colony Retirement Home (where we met the marvelously talented Phedora Shearer, who dressed up as Abby Kelley Foster and gave her own interpretation of her life to the residents), and finally, Anna Marie Kane and I presented Abby's House to the women of the UMass Medical Center staff! We had unbounded energy in those early days that even led us at our February staff meeting to begin to ask the following questions: "What could the daytime use of Abby's be? Should we be thinking about a permanent live-in person, and what are our goals for 1977–78?—will they lead us in the same direction or in new directions?" Years later, we answered those questions with decisions that have contributed to making Abby's House a multiservice organization. A day center began, a staff member lived in the shelter building, and we eventually moved beyond shelter to safe, affordable, permanent housing. But all lasting progress takes thoughtfulness and time. Since Abby's original steering committee had decided irrevocably that no programs we offered would be financed with state or federal funding, we needed the money to answer those early questions.

In May of 1977, the *Boston Globe*, in cooperation with the American Institute for Public Service, recognized my work done in Worcester by presenting me with the annual Jefferson Award.

Polly Kierstead and I traveled in to Boston to receive the award. After the luncheon and presentation, I had the opportunity to say what I have always felt:

> "I was pleased to accept the award in the name of the group. Because of our position, I feel the award was as much for Abby's staff as for me. I don't want to surface as the lone leader."

However, the Jefferson Award gave us an opportunity to celebrate Abby's first birthday on June 7th! Imagine, we were still here and growing slowly. I remember the following comments: "Can anyone believe that we have done this?" "Let's congratulate ourselves. We have done a wonderful thing—together!" "Abby Kelley Foster is the spirit leading us on. Don't ever forget that." "Does anyone believe that we will be here in 1980? Do you think the city, the state and the government will ignore the problem?" That last question haunted us. Ideally, we hoped our doors would close by the end of 1979 because an answer had been found. Realistically, we probably knew in our hearts that *we* would become *the* answer and that shelters would multiply. But what most of us silently pledged was to stay the course as long as there was a need. By the way, the election of 1980 put President Reagan into the White House, and within a matter of months, the deterioration of urban renewal began, alerting us that permanent, decent, affordable housing would not occur in his administration. Our pledge would be honored—Abby's House was here for the long haul!

It wasn't until I began to collect and to read all this historical data in our scrapbooks that I realized why in July of 1977, our steering committee met to establish some further structure in our fledgling organization. Abby had probably whispered in our ears during sleep that we had better prepare for that long haul—that we shouldn't expect any government to answer our questions for us. Weren't we, after all, a revolutionary (kind of) group of women with our own notion of how things should be done? Weren't we the daughters of mothers and fathers who had taught us to find our own answers? And hadn't we all read in our collection of historical data about our shelter's namesake the following editorial headline in the *Woman's Journal*: "Abby Kelley

Foster is Homeless"? Our course was set. We spent the entire day studying the structural area of Abby's, defining the "collective," developing job descriptions and the role of our staff, and reaffirming our basic philosophy:

> "...[Abby's] wants the person in crisis to gain control, to be empowered...each staffer becomes aware of what the person is capable of doing for herself for to do for a person what she is capable of doing is to disempower. Of necessity we must make judgments, but judgments are always open to revision. We provide support, back-up. We intervene when appropriate. We share information, resources and skills."

Later that philosophy would be incorporated into our mission statement.

We spent a couple of hours taking a second look at remuneration for services offered. How did that affect Abby's as a volunteer organization? Should Abby's offer stipends for tasks performed and if so, to whom and for what? We knew we needed guidelines for this effort. Just before lunch, we spent a considerable amount of time on accountability for money donated and how we could establish special relationships with other service agencies. Little did we know that within a year Abby's would be asked to make a very important decision that involved our shelter and a second emerging women's social service agency. For the remainder of the day we dealt with the future questions and logistical questions around meeting times and agenda development.

That same year, a number of important events took place. Abby's received a grant for operational expenses from the Campaign for Human Development, thanks to the excellent grant-writing skills of Leona Donahue, RSM. We received a support grant from the newly formed Greater Worcester Community Foundation, then under the directorship of Kay Seivard (now Kay Marquet). This was the beginning of a deeply-rooted relationship with the Foundation, thanks to a dear friend, Monsignor Edmund Haddad. Monsignor served on the first distribution committee, and that committee had to review hundreds of applications from Foundations that had been absorbed under the GWCF umbrella. I remember he told me the task

ABBY'S HOUSE
23 Crown Street
Worcester, MA 01608

I 74

Job description re: coordinator of a temporary, emergency shelter for women
(over 18) and their children.

The coordinator, though she works with and for the collective of women who
form Abby's, will assume specific responsibilities pertaining to the quality
of service offered in this shelter. She will be accountable to the core
committee and such accountability will be made in the form of an evaluation
at the end of the first three months of employment. Opportunity for mutual
accountability between coordinator and core committee will also be done at
this time. Further evaluation will be done on an annual basis to be determined
at a mutually agreeable time.

Qualifications:

1. ability to work with a group and to represent the shelter's services to
   the broader community.
2. a deep interest in human services.
3. an awareness of problems pertaining to women in crisis, in transition etc.
4. flexibility needed to deal with other people, agencies, etc.

Responsibilities: Even though present needs will be the prime factor in determ
the responsibilities of the coordinator, the core committee at this time sees
following responsibilities to be included. Both the coordinator and the cor
committee will mutually agree on the specific priority as to the execution o
these responsibilities.

I. Community Outreach
   a. collaboration with all agencies which deal directly with Abby's.
   b. public relations work
      1. arrangement of speaking engagements, training sessions and/or
         training of new volunteers.
   c. newsletter (communications)
      1. update of shelter activities, new directions
   d. investigation of new funding sources

II. General Management of Shelter
    a. liaison with landlord (for repairs, upkeep)
    b. update of shelter records (confidential file, etc.) This will
       conjunction with the Department of Mental Health Workers.
    c. response to mail:
       1. acknowledgements, thank yous, forwarding of checks, etc.
          finance person.
    d. response to others:
       1. phone/written to/from agencies
       2. supervisor of spin-offs, e.g., CES, M.H.A, volunteers
       3. public relations persons to groups
       4. close contact with finance person, legal helper.

Stipend: 1979-80 This stipend will be at least the set amount offe
employed at the rate of the Diocesan stipend. All other matters
negotiable.

Hours: 40 hour week. The distribution of this work time will be
to the priorities previously set under the section named respon

If interested, contact Abby's House, 23 Crown Street, Worcester,

	January	February	March	April	May	June	July	August	September	October	November	December
RENT	350.00	350.00	350.00	350.00	400.00	400.00	400.00	400.00	400.00	400.00	400.00	4650
TELEPHONE	20.12	18.84	21.80	22.48	19.22	23.89	19.20	27.83	33.84	26.05	21.74	267
ANSWERING SERVICE	15.00	15.00	15.00	20.00	20.00	20.00	20.00	20.00	20.00	20.00	18.84	22
EXTERMINATOR	8.50		8.00	8.50	8.50	9.00	9.00	9.00	9.00	9.00	20.00	96
STAFFING	60.00	45.00		22.50			150.00	30.00	22.50	7.50	9.00	382
PRINTING				60.49		12.00	20.93	97.37	18.48 2.89	30.00	15.00	227
POST OFFICE BOX		10.00							14.00	10.00	5.50	24
MISCELLANEOUS	2.50 BANK CHARGE		FLOWERS REIMB 15.00 20.00			DONATION 15.00			FLOWERS DECORATION 24.13			81
MEMBERSHIP	25.00											60
HOUSEHOLD	37.50		297.50	35.00								852
REPAIRS	16.00		115.11	20.00	40.03	37.94	31.13	22.30	262.53	148.00		86
STAMPS			25.00	13.00		20.56		45.00				82
FOOD	3.90				33.23	83.41	31.37	15.00	15.00	15.00		365
PETTY CASH	14.26 53.81	8.84 30.21	30.00					35.30	45.32			2?
								27.61				
EXPENSES	611.69	552.92	413.64	496.19	931.32	472.89	718.46	644.11	679.77	647.26	753.54	765?
INCOME	888.00	310.25	663.50	520.00	561.56	990.33	691.04	384.42	183.00	658.60	731.34	8512
	+276.31	-242.67	+249.86	+23.81	-369.66	+517.44	-27.42	-259.69	-496.77	+11.34	107.00 +2833	2014.65 +85?

seemed overwhelming, since most of the "distributors" were unfamiliar with the requesting agencies. Suddenly, Monsignor spotted our bold heading, ABBY'S HOUSE, and on impulse, he picked up the application, put it in the center of the table and said: "This organization I know—they do excellent work." Monsignor knew because he had asked me to educate the members in his parish, Blessed Sacrament, about the need. I did this during a series of talks I remember as "kitchen theology." This experience not only established our relationship with Greater Worcester Community Foundation, but also our friendship with Blessed Sacrament, which has contributed its Thanksgiving Food Drive to our Food Pantry for 25 years.

Other churches took their lead from this parish and Abby's House receives monthly food donations from many generous churches, including: the Christadelphian Chapel, St. Columba's Church, St. Christopher's Church, St. Charles Borromeo, Zion Lutheran Church, St. Luke's Episcopal, St. George's, St. Rose of Lima, Chaffin Congregational and semiannual donations from Park Congregational, First Baptist and Trinity Lutheran Church. Weekly donations also come from many other groups, churches, and individuals through Rachel's Table. A thousand thanks to Ed Haddad whose love for Abby's marked an important milestone in our history.

Our new lawyer, David Wojcik, whose services were obtained through Eileen Dooley, succeeded in procuring our tax exempt number and status.

Abby's House forged an important alliance with Comprehensive Emergency Services (CES) in order to better serve the needs of women and children. It was such a pleasure to work with CES and particularly to be inspired by the late Helen Pedone, who worked collaboratively with Abby's Steering Committee and whose daughter, Maria Pedone Whalen, has kept her mother's connection with Abby's as a volunteer.

Anna Marie Kane, chaplain at Holy Cross College, continued to challenge the young women students to reach out into the Worcester community and to volunteer at Abby's House. The following is a sample of her call of commitment which eventually led to the formation of "Abby's Friends," women students who have staffed the shelter for 25 years.

CONSISTENT COMMITMENT

"Go where you are least wanted because there you are most needed."

Even before the reality of Abby's House was incarnated in a red brick duplex at 23 Crown Street, the involvement of students, faculty and staff of Holy Cross in this important enterprise commenced. It was the struggling, newly formed Women's Organization who made the first financial contribution to Abby's approximately the same time as money was solicited from and donated by the Worcester City Council. It was this same organization that initiated not only the interest of female students to staff at Abby's but also challenged the entire campus to participate in a monthly pledge program to assist the efforts of Abby's and its guests.

So dynamic and so serious was this commitment that eventually the group separated itself and formed a new organization called "Abby's Friends." This change also affirmed the Student Government's support of those students attuned to the needs of Abby's.

Support for Abby's, however, does not stop with students. There is not a day that goes by that donations, either monetary or otherwise, are not made through the chaplain's office explicitly for Abby's. The consciousness of the need for such a place as Abby's has been awakened AND sustained by the Holy Cross Community.

This interest and involvement does not begin and end at Abby's for our students. Many of them have, in the course of the past six years, taken their shared experience of Holy Cross and Abby's to other cities and other shelters, extending their influence of Abby's beyond our imaginations and our geographical perimeters. Their involvement has extended as far as Indiana and Washington, D.C., to Springfield, to Rochester, and yes, even to Alaska!

I personally wish to thank those of the Holy Cross community, past and present, who challenge me to remember the implications of that age-old exhortation: "Feed the hungry...clothe the naked...shelter the homeless."

ANNA

In October of 1977, I received the following letter from Polly, who had been our faithful five-night staffer:

"I will have staffed for Abby's 13 months at the end of this month, and I feel it is time to leave. I am sending you this note so that the staff can have a month's notice. Abby's is doing well. The staffing has picked up, and house decisions have been made, and we have all come through an incredible journey together. I appreciated the opportunity to have been able to staff for this long. It has been an enriching experience…not easily forgotten. I find I am very tired and need to take time for myself. After October, I would like to put more energy into Books Behind Bars, plus spend time with the children."

Sincerely, Polly

Polly made an unselfish commitment to Abby's women and their children for which she'll always be remembered.

Margaret Baillie was our liaison to a group emerging at Clark University under the leadership of Beth Herr. It was a group committed to opening a house similar to Transition House in Cambridge that would offer six to eight weeks shelter time. (This was the beginning of what we know today as the YWCA/Daybreak Program.) By December of 1977, Daybreak had been selected as a significant name for their shelter. While Daybreak was searching for space, our agreement with their staff was to call the CRISIS CENTER (Daybreak's temporary administrative office) and ask for "Beth," only if we had a battered woman we could not accommodate. The Worcester Police had always brought battered women to Abby's House, as we accept a battered woman during the night. This policy has never been altered.

We drew up a new proposal for a continuity person, and began to talk about the need for a paid coordinator. In 1977 we had our first intern, Gail Zimmerman from Framingham State College! It was Gail who baptized Abby's House *A Bright Spot in the City*. Her final paper, *Summary of a Diary*, is a classic.

The year 1977 ended with our usual holiday gathering and pot-luck supper and the long-anticipated news from Mary Labunski that H.L. Rocheleau Insurance Agency had developed a liability insurance policy for us that was very affordable. We were grateful to Pauline Gifford for her effort in developing this initial policy that would protect the house, the guests and the staff. I viewed the policy as another indication that the Abby Kelley Foster House, Inc., and her mission had been taken seriously and that the business community had officially become a vital part of our support system.

Pat Dell-Ross (left) and Gail Zimmerman, our first intern

Summary of a Diary

Less than a week after attending a staff meeting at the Abby Kelley Foster House in Worcester, I had the following dream:

Someone is putting the pieces of a city together for me. It is Worcester. A hand is putting one piece on another, as one would in a flannel board presentation. All of the pieces are gray and black shapes of buildings. But then a red and a blue piece are added. I say, "At least there are a few bright spots in the city." Then I awaken.

As I recorded this dream the following morning, I recalled how dismal downtown Worcester had appeared to me when I went to the staff meeting. Though some new buildings have been added, including a beautiful glass building, it still looked run down and dismal in many respects. Some once flourishing businesses were closed, leaving empty hulks, and few people walked along Main Street. It was very different from the Worcester of seven or eight years ago that I had known. But then I put it out of my mind.

At the staff meeting I attended on September seventeenth, I got the impression that Abby's House supplies an important need for women, the need for a sanctuary at night for women of modest and low income. Until recently public service organizations have catered almost exclusively to men. Even the Salvation Army, were prepared to help only men who had an alcoholic problem. (At present they have detox centers for both sexes.) There are a variety of reasons why women need a place to spend a night or more, I learned at the meeting. However, the staff concurs that all the guests who come have been "battered" in some way, either physically, psychologically or socially. The prime purpose of the house is to offer a home atmosphere so women can relax and have a chance to come to grips with their problems.

After watching a moving slide presentation that depicted the types of women served by the house, I went away feeling that I would like being part of an organization that supplies such a worthwhile service.

Since that Saturday I have staffed overnight every Tuesday. It hasn't been the busiest night of the week, but nevertheless three to six guests have stayed each time. It's difficult to give individual descriptions of the many women who have come to Abby's and those with whom I have conversed on the telephone during the past six weeks that I have staffed there.

These women who have showed up at Abby's door have been women over sixty years old. The first one, Mary, came because she was afraid of all the noisy "goings-on" by people of a minority race in her new apartment building. The women, who were staffing with me that night, thought Mary was prejudiced. They questioned her so much she left. I think Mary had a legitimate fear; to be old and helpless is one hundred and eighty degrees away from being young and idealistic. That was my first night on staff. Therefore I kept my big mouth shut. Another old lady who come one night was so drunk it was impossible to understand what she said. She was all dressed up with furry slippers on her feet. We couldn't let her stay because it is the policy of the house not to accept guests who are drinking or are on drugs. So we gave her a pair of shoes and sent her on her way. She didn't mind; perhaps she came for shoes. The third one was a sad woman. She had taken up residence at a private boarding house just the previous week. The older woman who runs the house does not let any of the residents stay during the day. After a light breakfast, they have to leave until five o'clock when dinner is served. Lucile, as our guest is called, had paid two hundred dollars out of her two-hundred and eighty-five dollar state disability check for a month's board before the landlady put her out that night at midnight. It wasn't clear why they had a disagreement, but there was no evidence that Lucile was drinking or that she has any drinking problem. I slept in the same room with her that night. It was a mistake; she snored all night.

A number of young women have accepted Abby's hospitality since I've been on the staff. Two come together. They are alcoholics; they move from residence to residence; they often lose all their belongings; one has had her two children taken away from her; they change boyfriends frequently, and the men they "hook up" with usually treat them roughly. They are repeaters at the house. Another one, Marion, came because she had lost her key and couldn't get in her apartment. About twenty-two years old, Marion has been through a lot. She used to live in New York City. But one day she decided she couldn't stand living any more with her alcoholic husband who beat her, so she packed up her two small children and took the bus to Worcester. She knew Worcester a little from her childhood. For a while she was all right here. She got welfare aid and an adequate apartment and enjoyed a few months of peace. But then one day her husband found her. He has been with her for about a year now battering her quite often.

"You are a strong person to take your two children and make a move like that," I said to her while she told me the story.

"I thought I was," she answered, "but I'm not. I finally joined him drinking. I don't know why I did it. I guess it was because I couldn't bear it any more. Since then I've been bad off; I've had blackouts and everything. I don't even remember what happens." She told me a lot more that morning, while I drove her to the hospital where she attends group meetings for alcoholics. Her children are at present with her sister in New York. She's afraid she might lose them some day. Then there is Betty, a regular drop-in at Abby's House. Betty was sent to Lancaster reformatory when she was five years old. She was brought up there. She's young (early twenties), she's tough and she's pretty. She does not have a drinking or drug problem. However, Betty takes to men who beat her up. She claims it just happens, yet she repeatedly goes with cruel guys. She's had broken ribs and a broken wrist since I've known her. She is not very well in other ways, either; she's had a few serious health problems.

Another moving experience was my encounter with Carol. She is forty-three and it seems that she came to Worcester to try to find a future in the past. Her previous residence was in New Mexico, for the past five years. Divorced in her early twenties, she has since then traveled throughout the southwest and southeast. She has worked as a migrant farmhand, live-in maid, secretary, bookkeeper, factory worker, horse raiser, etc. She also speaks fluent Spanish. She was brought up in Worcester, so she came back to see if she would be happier here. As we sat in the living room, she relayed a lot of the experiences she had in Worcester while growing up. She talked a good deal about her mother, who has been deceased for sixteen years. Carol was lonely, very lonely. She said that she didn't know much. I think she knows more than most people ever will. I was in awe of her many abilities and interests and I told her so. She had a couple of other options, other than staying in Worcester. One was taking a job in South Dakota for a clergyman she had met in New Mexico. She took it, I found out a week later. I was pleased to hear that, because from what she told me, it was evident that she needed plenty of fresh air and [line missing - xeroxed out] … needed her.

As I reread my diary, I couldn't help noticing that a considerable amount of depression is expressed in my notes, especially in the first few weeks. Towards the middle the tone gets lighter, and as the weeks go on there is an appreciable change toward a more hopeful attitude. Staffing at Abby's House I have gone through the emotional progression that the diary reflects. At first, I felt absolutely overwhelmed by the seemingly dead end roads that most of the women travel. But as time went on I felt good about being able to help them survive. Each day that any one of them makes it without cracking up, or starving, or freezing is a day towards a better tomorrow. Now I know the true interpretation of my dream.

Maureen Kroyak,
dear friend

Kay, John and all the Kroyaks

Mass. Coalition of Battered Women Service Groups

C/o 46 PLEASANT STREET CAMBRIDGE MASSACHUSETTS 02139

Dateline: Worcester

Contact Person: Sr. Annette Rafferty, Abby's House, 756-5486

For Release on: Wednesday, June 7, 1978

The formation of a statewide coalition of agencies serving the needs of battered women was announced this afternoon at a press conference held at the YWCA.

Sister Annette Rafferty, S.S.J. of Abby's House and Beth Herr of Daybreak, two Worcester members of the coalition, said that the Massachusetts Coalition of Battered Women Service Groups was organized to meet the increasing demand for shelters, support groups, counseling and referral from victims of domestic violence.

The FBI estimates that every 18 seconds a woman is battered by her husband. Other estimates indicate that there are 28 million battered women in the United States.

In trying to meet these needs individually, each of the agencies in the Coalition found the same difficulties. Funding was tight; some welfare regulations were inadequate; and public awareness was lacking. The groups determined that a statewide coalition was essential to avoid duplication of services and to maximize and direct energies.

Sharon Smith Viles

14 **Worcester Telegram**   Thursday, June 8, 1978

Agencies Serving Battered Women Form Alliance

By JAN TOWNE
Of the Telegram Staff

A statewide coalition of agencies serving battered women was announced at a press conference yesterday at the YWCA by Sister Annette Rafferty, S.S.J., of Abby's House, and Beth Herr of Daybreak.

Similiar news conferences were held in Boston and Springfield.

While not intending to take on the welfare system, both women had some comments on its relation to battered and homeless women.

Ms. Herr said the Massachusetts Coalition of Battered Women Service Groups was organized to meet the increasing demand for shelters, support groups, counseling and referral for victims of domestic violence. She cited an FBI statistic that every 18 seconds a woman is being battered by her husband.

Daybreak, which opened recently, provides shelter only for victims of domestic violence and can be reached 24 hours a day through the hotline at the Crisis Center. Abby's House, which opened two years ago yesterday, provides shelter for homeless and transient women as well as those in possible abuse situations. To protect the women, addresses of shelters are not publicized. Other coalition members in Central Massachusetts are Women's Works, Inc., Athol, and Montachusett Task Force on Battered Women, Fitchburg.

There are several reasons why the groups decided to come together, Ms. Rafferty said. The agencies

Every 18 seconds a woman
is being battered
by her husband

ABBY'S HOUSE
Sister Annette Rafferty

will be able to share each other's services. And concerted community education will help raise public consciousness about domestic violence and homeless women. The group is considering a statewide newsletter which would include legislative items it may get involved in through some of its affiliates.

Ms. Rafferty said another reason is fund raising. Alone the agencies have little chance of getting funds, but as part of a coalition, they may have more clout, she said.

Ms. Herr said the coalition, which is a nonprofit organization, cannot lobby because of its charter and by law, but affiliate agencies can.

In reference to the welfare system, Ms. Rafferty said one of its "Catch 22's" is that it is very difficult for women without a permanent address to get assistance.

The six to eight weeks delay before a woman can receive assistance is also hard on her, Ms. Herr said. Through negotiations with the welfare department and proposals for changes in policy and procedure, the coalition may be able to help the victims of

DAYBREAK
Beth Herr

domestic violence. There is no strategy presently planned.

Ms. Herr said the agencies, in trying to meet the needs of battered women, found funding was tight (both Daybreak and Abby's House rely on contributions), some welfare regulations were inadequate and public awareness was lacking. The groups decided a statewide coalition was essential to avoid duplication of services and to maximize and to direct energies.

A meeting of more than 100 persons serving abused women was held last February, and the coalition was formed. Other states, including California, Connecticut and Pennsylvania, have coalitions.

"The coalition plans to strengthen existing services and to assist individuals and groups in organizing and providing new services for battered women and their children," Ms. Herr said. "It also hopes to train volunteers and to educate the police, the public and others who come in direct contact with battered women."

Ms. Rafferty said a precedent was set nationally for developing a coalition at the International Women's Year Conference in Houston last November. A resolution was passed outlining the need for strong legislation and adequate funding to aid battered women and their children. A national coalition and communications network have evolved from this.

State headquarters for the coalition is the Women's Center, 46 Pleasant St., Cambridge. A general membership meeting is scheduled June 17 at the Cambridge YWCA to affirm the constitution.

CHAPTER 4

Building Community

We welcomed the New Year of 1978 with an increase in our circles of involvement: we continued to be part of the collective forming of Daybreak and in late January we became members in the Montachusett Task Force on Battered Women, with full member rights and privileges (voting rights). Additionally, Abby's forged a strong relationship with the Rape Crisis Center, the Crisis Center, City Hospital De-tox, the Greater Worcester Women's Center that opened on Chicopee Street under the auspices of Worcester State College and Family Health and Social Services, on Main Street. Among the many great women we met because of this organizational growth were Marie McCarthy-Kaye, Susan Gately, Beth Herr, Fran Anthes and Carolyn Heusman. Publicity continued to bring us new volunteers and much needed donations. Our collective energy was high, and there was no sign of diminished commitment. Abby's House was gradually rooting itself in the community with increased visibility and those invitational pot-luck suppers, which brought not only new women, but also challenging ideas for our future work. We had our sad moments in April of that year as we bid farewell to two staunch members. Margaret Baillie left Worcester to settle at Wing's Neck, Cape Cod and Eileen Dooley moved to Buffalo, New York. It was our first experience of separation within the founding mothers' circle. That sadness intensified on June 7, 1978, our second birthday, at the death of our beloved Maureen Kroyak, who, for me, had been such a source of encouragement. Her spirit, along with Abby's spirit, is still guiding us through the continued dedication of her sisters, brothers and parents, John and Kay. On our birthday, we wept and honored this courageous woman. Fifteen years later, Abby's officially recognized this connection with Maureen when her Mom cut the ribbon at the dedication ceremonies of 19 Crown Street, site of our first supportive housing unit.

However, the day after Maureen's untimely death, a new birth occurred in Worcester: a statewide coalition of agencies serving battered women was announced at the YWCA by Beth Herr of Daybreak and me, representing Abby's House. The collaboration of the two agencies had been well worked out in advance, including our suggestion to Beth that Daybreak's shelter might want to occupy the #21 side of our shelter that presently had no tenants. It was a bold move, but one that gave Daybreak the opportunity to begin its mission while searching for a larger facility with an unknown address. Both apartments on the 21 side of the house were used as their offices, kitchen and dining room, while the upper floor housed the bedrooms. By May of 1978 a daycare facility for Daybreak's children was established in a small space occupied now by Abby's office kitchen area. For mutual protection, the cellar doors between the shelter side and Daybreak side remained secured. We also knew that we would be able to share each other's services and concerted community education would help raise public consciousness about domestic violence and homeless women. Since Abby's was "grand-mothered" into the Mass. Coalition charter in 1977 (the work of Pat Daly and me, Cindy Cohen and Gail Sullivan of Transition House in Cambridge), it seemed as though our fund-raising efforts would be made easier since we were members of a Coalition with "clout." Daybreak at that time, like Abby's House, relied only on contributions. It seemed such a good idea to be part of a state-wide coalition which would help us avoid duplication of services and maximize our energies. Abby's presence at these coalition meetings was continued by Sharon Smith Viles. In July of 1978, at a meeting of the Massachusetts Coalition held at the offices of Worcester Youth Guidance, Abby's House decided not to submit a proposal for monies that were available for shelters housing battered women and their children—a decision made for two reasons:

Abby's House Befriends the Homeless

By JAN TOWNE
Of the Telegram Staff

Abby Kelley Foster, a Worcester native, was a 19th century abolitionist and feminist who lectured around the country.

She often found herself without shelter while lecturing, but a large number of women now benefit from this woman's plight.

Abby's House, located in the city, provides temporary emergency shelter for women and their children. Often these women are in a stress situation and need to get out. Sometimes they are wanderers, abused or rape victims. By temporary, a three-evening stay is meant. By emergency is meant no other night agency could provide better care for the individual woman.

Abby's House has been open for 20 months, providing women with shelter for three nights at a time, although, with extenuating circumstances, this may be lengthened, said Sister Annette Rafferty, S.S.J., one of the organizers of the shelter.

In September, 1973, the Diocese of Worcester Urban Ministry Commission set up a task force on homeless women. Sister Annette was chairperson. The women on the task force began to study the needs of women in the city and the surrounding towns. They found that the greatest need was for a temporary, emergency shelter which could serve a broad group of women. They made a commitment to that need, said Sister Annette.

By Dec. 4, 1975, a group of about 40 women and several men were prepared to develop a model, search for sites and get into fund raising. The name had already been chosen.

In May, 1976, the property was rented, and Abby's House opened June 7, 1976. It has been open every

Sometimes they are wanderers, abused or rape victims. Some come and go quietly, sharing little of themselves.

night since then and staffed by volunteers who come from a wide variety of backgrounds and religious persuasions.

"We don't exclude anyone," said Sister Annette. "Anyone who comes across the doorstep is a victim. We are open to any woman, over 18, with or without children, who is in a stress situation and needs to get out. We work hard on referrals, and we work to get her moving again."

No One Excluded

Abby's House is prepared to handle 11 women and children nightly. A light supper and breakfast are provided. It is open from 7 p.m. to 9 a.m. because during the day the volunteers have other job commitments.

All kinds of women come to Abby's House from many places. "There are the transients who wander the country in a strange way," said Sister Annette. "They are like a lost generation. They share little (about themselves) with us and move on. We never see them again. They are human beings in need of shelter. There are the wandering mentally ill, we get them, too."

Because the women are sometimes fleeing a dangerous situation, the location of Abby's House is not

publicized. Most of the police departments know how to get a woman there and the house can be contacted by calling 756-5486.

Abby's House is run as a collective, said Margaret Baillie, a member of the coordinating committee. The staff, or collective, about 35 or 40 trained volunteers, staffs the house in pairs each night.

There are also other things to be done to keep the house running, and Mrs. Baillie's church group, for example, cleans it. The training session is informal. The type of volunteer covers a broad spectrum.

"Constantly new people are appearing, and that is what's beautiful," said Sister Annette.

When the task force was considering the needs of women, there were no statistics available on women in need of shelter. There are now.

Through November, 1977, the last month for which the statistics at Abby's House are available, a total of 150 different women and 72 children had been sheltered at Abby's House from one to 15 nights.

Of the 150 women, 65 were transient (stranded between cities, unable to get travelers' aid, seeking a better world here or unable to find shelter in the towns outside the city). Twenty-five were abused and 14 were accompanied by children. Four of the women were rape victims. Thirty were wandering mentally ill or alcoholic women, presently not drinking, their checks lost or stolen and their limited funds mismanaged. Sixteen came quietly, sharing little of themselves. "We are sure 150 were emotionally and/or psychologically battered," stated the report.

Mrs. Baillie feels certain, that although Abby's House hasn't been crowded and sometimes there is an empty bed, if another shelter opened, it would fill up.

Abby's House offers limited services, and this is by choice. It prides itself on the working relationships it has established with other agencies in the city, both municipal and state.

"Allowing this place to be open has presented new problems," said Sister Annette. "We are getting involved in other things. There are terrible gaps in human services. We are fortunate here to have people who are providers and advocates working to turn the system around."

"Sometimes we criticize ourselves for doing something the city ought to be doing," said Mrs. Baillie. Sometimes we wonder if by not doing it, it might stir the city into acting, she said.

Mailing Address

Funds for Abby's House come in fairly regularly. Flyers for Abby's House in both English and Spanish (La Casa de Abby) explain what the shelter is all about and gives Abby's House, Box 176, West Side Station, Worcester, 01602, as a mailing address for donations.

The collective relies on a mailing list of about 464 persons and organizations, and the Campaign for Human Development has provided a grant.

"It's really the little people's money," said Sister Annette. "We have stayed away from big money. We want it (Abby's House) to belong to everyone."

Abby's House began on a shoestring. It was a model on paper, but in its 20 months, it has proved a successful way to operate a shelter for women. What is the future of Abby's House?

"Our philosophy from the beginning was we wouldn't perpetuate ourselves," said Sister Annette. "If another group came along which could provide better or other services . . . we are committed to helping other groups."

Dorothy O'Brien

Claudia Russo

Pat Ushinski

Susie Sullivan

WORCESTER CITY HOSPITAL

EMERGENCY MENTAL HEALTH SERVICE

REFERRAL TO ABBY'S HOUSE:

A). Worcester City Hospital Emergency Mental Health Service (EMHS) shall screen appropriate female referrals to the Mental Health beds at Abby's.

B). Before a referral is made to Abby's, the Mental Health Worker at City Hospital shall call Abby's House and discuss with the staff the referral. Abby's House has the right to reject the proposed referral.

C). Upon agreement between EMHS and Abby's, the woman will be given a referral summary highlighting pertinent information and any plans for the woman next day. She will then be transported by cab to Abby's. Depending on the case and availability, a worker from City Hospital may accompany the woman to Abby's.

D). If a woman is to spend the following day at City Hospital, this plan will be so spelled out and it will be the responsibility of City Hospital to pick up the woman at Abby's before 11:00 A.M.

E). Abby's House may refer any of their guests regardless of referral source to the Emergency Mental Health Service for appropriate intervention, 24 hours a day or seek phone consultation 24 hours a day. (756-1551 Ext: 615)

f). The Abby's House Coordinator shall contact the EMHS with a follow-up on any referral made by City Hospital. Monthly coordination and review meetings shall be arranged between the respective services.

Fond memories of City Hospital

1) the amount we would get would be insignificant, and

2) we hoped that Daybreak would get our share since it was struggling financially.

Our minutes of that meeting reflect Abby's continual concern for other women:

> "As a gesture of support for Daybreak, struggling to make ends meet, we have offered continued use of the downstairs apartment for their overflow. Beth will present our offer to her Board."

It remains a mystery to those of us who have been here for these 25 years why in 1984 Abby's House no longer appeared as a member organization of the Mass. Coalition of Battered Women's Services. I certainly have speculated that when bigger funds were made available to battered women's shelters, Abby's was "dropped" from the rolls because we were not established exclusively for battered women, but accommodated any woman who was homeless. Was our gesture of support in 1978 misinterpreted? What happened to the grand-mothering of Abby's House into the charter that Pat Daly and I had worked on with Transition House? Did this severance of our organization from the Coalition occur because of money? Over the years, we have made many efforts through letters and phone calls to discover the cause, but no answers or responses were forthcoming. Nevertheless, Abby's continues to shelter battered women and their children and the Police Departments of Worcester and Worcester County still call us.

Meanwhile, John Ford of the Department of Mental Health made contact with our steering committee. He was interested in finding ways that Abby's House could help out with "some follow-up work for the wandering mentally ill." This contact resulted in one of the most critical structural changes that had taken place in Worcester and it happened because of our existence. That change occurred in the Department of Mental Health. During Abby's first three years, many of our guests were the wandering mentally ill; most of them needed much more than shelter. Repeated efforts to have the DMH become more

responsible for these women seemed futile. We held public meetings specifically to address the issue, but no obvious changes were evident. Our staff members made repeated visits to the Worcester State Hospital to plead for help to get some concrete evidence of concern for this fast growing population. Every evening, staffers were opening doors and responding to calls from the Police and/or the Salvation Army Shelter that women needed a place to stay. One had lost her address book and couldn't remember where she lived; another was locked out of her boarding house; another needed medication, but unfortunately for her, had no recent contact with her DMH worker.

In August of 1978, the Department contacted Abby's House and came to a staff meeting to discuss collaboration. DMH recognized the same needs that seemed obvious to us, but had been unable to find non-institutional structures with which to work. Finally, funds had been released and would be available to Abby's House to hire staff, thus enabling us to extend our services to women with mental health problems. We hired four part-time workers who would be available to our guests and what was miraculous about this funding was the lack of strings attached. We were under no obligation to accept referrals from DMH. Back-up services would be provided by a new mental health service, Emergency Mental Health, at City Hospital. We could make the decision whether Abby's House was appropriate for a particular woman. The three people responsible for this amazing extension of services were John Ford, Mike Gregory and Pat Ushinski. This blessed plan lasted for ten wonderful years and brought to Abby's the following staffers whom we would never have known without DMH: Mary Hennigan, Claudia Russo, Rena LeBlanc, Dorothy O'Brien, Susie Sullivan and Trudy Damiano.

As Abby's took each new step to broaden the base of service and involvement, problem areas continued to surface. We were faced with many questions:

1. How do we keep it all simple, or is that possible?

2. Is there a way to support new service groups and continue to energize our own initial group?

3. How do we find new people to commit themselves to the mission of Abby's House?

4. How do we find people concerned about women and their problems?

5. Is there an easy way to get funds?

6. Can volunteers and paid personnel work together in a model of collegiality and congeniality?

All of these concerns led us to another question: Don't we need to hire a coordinator to begin to find solutions to the bigger questions? It took a few meetings to work through the collective concerns, but in the end, we voted to hire our first coordinator. Funds had been solicited for the position from the Sisters of St. Joseph of Springfield who generously responded. Abby's House owes so much to the Sisters of St. Joseph who involved themselves from the beginning not only with funding, but with staffers who worked to root us into the Worcester community.

After several interviews, the collective voted to hire one of the "originals." In June of 1979, Elaine Lamoureux, who today is Abby's House Guest Advocate, became the first woman to formally head the organization. Elaine steered all of us to new heights in extended services, to the purchase of the 21-23 Crown Street property, to vast improvements within the shelter, to an amazing understanding of our women and their children and, finally, to a living example of what real empowerment can accomplish. Her inexhaustible energy fueled Abby's growth during the 1980s. It didn't take long before the collective realized what a gem it had in Elaine.

In October of 1979, we visited OPCD (Office of Planning and Community Development) to obtain Block Grant information. Initially, we were seeking funds to continue expanding our programs and to improve the inside of the shelter. By December, however, we were actually seeking funds to purchase Abby's House, which had already been designated by the Worcester Heritage Society as the *Carter Whitcomb House* and was listed on the historic register.

Elaine Lamoureux

CHAPTER 5

Smoothing the Paths by which We Came

The next two years were difficult ones for Abby's House. As we pushed forward toward purchase of the property, I remember endless Block Grant meetings in the City Council Chambers where we appealed our case for funding and endless meetings and correspondence with City Manager Jeff Mulford. Letters of support from the president of the Crown Hill Neighborhood Association, the Worcester Police Department, City Hospital Mental Health Unit and other agencies were forwarded to City Hall. We completed numbers of forms and were adamant that Abby's House deserved funding as we were providing an unprecedented service for Worcester. By January of 1980, nothing had been settled, but we did receive a very important statement from our landlord, Harry Mironidis, who had already expressed his interest in selling the property.

The entire 21-23 Crown Street property had been appraised at $33,000 by Patrick J. McMahon of Worcester County Institution for Savings, and Harry was asking $50,000. In March of 1980, we made an offer of $39,500, and outlined our reasons for the substantially lower bid. Our letter was composed by Theresa McBride, another "original" who had become an active member of the collective, now known as the board of directors. As expected, Harry rejected our humble bid and remained immovable. The board was reluctant to give him more than the original offer. Elaine and I canvassed the city for alternative sites that might become Abby's House should Harry freeze in his resistance. We looked at property on Pemberton, May and Chandler Streets. Nothing was satisfactory. Can you believe that by June 1980, Abby's House was about to become homeless? On an historic note, it was 138 years earlier in the month of June that Abby Kelley completed the disposition of her parents' property in Millbury and said her farewells to her "home, sweet home" forever. We would absolutely not let our "home, sweet home" be lost to us. The tug of war continued.

Elaine and I were so certain Harry would "cave in" that we left our community residences at Westminster and Dorchester Streets in June, agreeing to stay at St. Joseph's Home for Women on High Street until August 15. That would allow us proximity to our work and time to plan the women's center that we had in mind for the other side of the shelter. But by mid-August, negotiations were completely stalled and the members of Abby's House board were not convinced that we should negotiate further with Harry. That left Elaine and me without a place to stay, since we had left the home on High Street. Theresa McBride kindly and quickly offered to have this new center upstairs in her home on Oxford Place, but after several weeks of consideration, we mutually agreed that it wasn't appropriate for what we knew would be a very busy center, involving lots of people and even more traffic. What a dilemma. Where would we live while waiting for Harry to agree to our terms? There was obviously only one answer: Go to the shelter. And we did, occupying the back room, close to the bathroom. Had Abby Kelley created this situation? I have no doubt that she did. The first week in September, we moved in bag and baggage. Our stay was not without its inconveniences, but the funniest thing I remember to this day occurred one morning in the upstairs hall. One of the guests, who had come in to the shelter after we had retired, was dilly-dallying in the one upstairs bathroom. Elaine, who had been waiting patiently, finally banged on the door, asking the woman to come out. And she did. Elaine rushed in and the evicted guest looked into our room and shouted in a very loud voice: "Who does she think she is? The boss?" I had to look away and never let on that, indeed, she was the boss. The woman would find that out soon enough.

Finally, Harry succumbed to our persistence. The board of Abby's facilitated his eventual submission by deciding to buy the property and to enter into legal negotiations for a final sale.

The Commonwealth of Massachusetts
Department of Mental Health

GREATER WORCESTER MENTAL HEALTH
& RETARDATION AREA
Box 57, Worcester, Mass. 01613
TEL. 752-4681: EXTN. 356

Jan

Sr. Annette Rafferty
Abbey House
23 Crown Street
Worcester, MA 01608

Dear Sr. Annette:

The Greater Worcester Area, Department
supports the efforts of Abbey House
Development Grant.

The Department of Mental Health prov
House in the form of staff that work
The annual value of this staff cont
$18,000.

Your work is invaluable in the comm
to continuing our support and coope

Yo

dml   Jo
                             Ar

DEPARTMENT OF POLICE
CITY OF WORCESTER
MASSACHUSETTS 01608
617/798-7000

HALSTEAD TAYLOR
CHIEF OF POLICE

January 30,

Abby's House
23 Crown Street
Worcester, Massachusetts

It is with great pleasure that I write this l
of support for Abby's House. Since the opening of
House in June of 1976, our experiences have all be
positive.

Abby's House is an important resource to the
Police Department as it provides shelter and food
in emergency situations. This service is used by
ment quite frequently. Staff members from Abby's
have made their time available to the department T
Division providing instruction to police recruits
ling domestic violence and battered women.

It is with a great deal of assurance that I w
letter of support for Abby's House, an important r
for the Worcester Police Department.

Sincerely,

John J. McKiernan, Serge
Training Division
Worcester Police Departm

WORCESTER CITY HOSPITAL

PAUL F. MURPHY
SUPERINTENDENT

January 30, 1980

Sr. Elaine Lamereux
Abby House
23 Crown Street
Worcester, Ma

Dear Sr. Elaine:

It gives me great pleasure to be able to write this letter
endorsing your application for Community Block Grant Funding
from the City of Worcester.

We at City Hospital Mental Health Service are acutely aware
of the unique services that you provide to homeless women. Without your fine service, we would be forced to turn many women in
need of shelter on to the streets.

We look forward to continuing our fine working relation
and in the process building programs that meet the critical needs
of people in Mental Health Crises.

Sincerely,

Michael Gregory / KE S

Michael T. Gregory
Director of Mental Health

MTG:kes

26 QUEEN STREET, WORCESTER, MASSACHUSETTS 01610 · 617-756-1551

A Major Affiliated Teaching Hospital of The University of Massachusetts Medical School

---

January, 1980

To Whom It May Concern:

*I am willing to sell my property at
21-23 Crown Street, to the Sisters of
the Abby's House.*

*Sincerely,
H. Mironidis*

H. Mironidis

Abby's House
23 Crown Street
Worcester, Massachusetts
01608

March 18, 1980

Mr. Harry Mironidis
12 Townsend Street
Worcester, Massachusetts 01609

Dear Harry:

As you are well aware, we who represent Abby's House would like to purchase
the building at 21-23 Crown Street. We have been granted a Community Development
Block Grant by the Worcester City Council for $33,000 for the purchase of the
house. This grant has enabled us to offer you $34,600 for the property. We
understand that our offer falls substantially below your selling price of $50,000.
We have come to our offer from serious consideration of the various factors
outlined here.

An inspection of the house by Patrick J. McMahon of W.C.I.S. on November 2,
1979 appraised the property at $33,000. Mr. McMahon concluded that the "dwelling
requires interior and exterior redecoration, insulation, upgrade electrical,
delead, smoke detectors, upgrade plumbing and heating and modernize kitchens."
"The subject property is located in one of the City of Worcester's older residential
areas with many of the improvements exhibiting below average care." Based on this
inspection and analysis of other data, Mr. McMahon concluded that the market value
of the property was $33,000.

Rehabilitation Specialist, Robert L. Lunger of the Worcester Cooperative
Council Inc., also assessed the value of the property and noted that the hous
needs the following improvements:

1. Windows puttied.

2. Trim painting.

3. Insulation in the attic..

4. Insulation in the cellar.

5. Storm doors front and rear.

6. Ceilings on one side of duplex to be repaired, replaced, or
   suspended.

Mr. Lunger estimated the cost of these essential improvements at $12,000

In addition to the two appraisals, we received from a broker information
on all available residential properties in the immediate neighborhood. Sales
prices of the various buildings ranged from $28,000 to $39,500, including som

---

Mr. Harry Mironidis   -2-   March 18, 1980

single family and some multiple-unit structures. (These are simply the "asking
prices" for these buildings; as far as we know, no home in the neighborhood has
been sold in the past year for more than $35,000.)

From this survey, we concluded that despite improvements in the neighborhood,
house values remain relatively low.

As a result of those investigations, we have decided to make you an offer of
$39,500. The offer is based upon the following facts:

1. The appraised value of the property is $33,000.

2. Essential improvements on the building have been assessed
   at $12,000.

3. This offer, plus closing costs and essential improvements,
   comes to a total of approximately $52,500. As it is, this
   offer leaves us no reserve for the rehabilitation of the
   house and operating expenses.

We believe, therefore, that $39,500 is a just and equitable price for the
building.

If our offer is agreeable to you, we should like to take possession of the
building as soon as possible after July 1, 1980, when the Block Grant funds will
be made available to us.

In the intervening period, we intend to proceed with the following inspections:

1. Termite inspection.

2. Detailed structural appraisal, including electrical wiring and
   plumbing.

3. An investigation to discover whether any back taxes or other liens
   exist on the property.

In the meantime we hope that you will seriously consider our offer. We wou
be happy to confer with you further on this matter. In case it would be helpful
for you to consult him, the lawyer representing us in this matter is Paul Hempel
of Bowditch and Dewey, 311 Main Street, Worcester, MA.

On behalf of the board,

Theresa M. McBride

Theresa, a strong advocate

*Our Harry,
a very good man!*

Abby *had* to have been cheering us on. Only her spirit could have produced the unanimous vote of the Board of Directors. The move was a blessed relief and at the same time, marked another test of our patience, creativity and ingenuity. How do we get by these following obstacles:

- We upped our offer to $40,000, with $5,000 to be paid on a monthly basis at a no-interest rate and all transactions would take place with our respective attorneys.

- Abby's was already paying rent on the 21 side, left vacant after Daybreak moved to an undisclosed location. Our plans were to offer educational programs on the lower floor and transform the upper apartment into living space for staffers, thus complying with directives to have on-site management.

- OPCD rejected our request for funding to purchase the property, leaving us penniless.

- Beacon Corporation of Boston, a private corporation, about to begin renovation of the empty warehouses along Austin Street into low-income housing, had approached Harry with their own offer (much higher than ours) to purchase the house. They needed adequate parking space and would make a lot where Abby's House had been!

We got by under the drive of Elaine Lamoureux, who, as coordinator, couldn't imagine there was a hill in Worcester we couldn't climb and get to the top. Her upbeat spirit helped us to imagine we saw the light at the top and we did.

The plan to get to the top of the hill went something like this: we'd make no further bid to Harry, but we'd proceed to develop the women's educational center at 21 Crown Street, to be known as the Worcester Connection and to move ourselves upstairs, silently declaring a sort of squatters' sovereignty. We invited all the members of the Worcester City Council to an early morning breakfast served at the shelter by our guests. In this way they would see how valuable a service Abby's was providing the City and consequently recommend that OPCD funding be allocated to us. Abby's will always be grateful to the Council of 1980 for its funding approval vote. We're particularly grateful to those councillors who were able to attend our special shelter breakfast: Sara Robertson, John Anderson, Tim Cooney, Daniel Herlihy and the late Paul Leahy.

The next step in what I choose to call the Lamoureux Plan was to attend a Crown Hill Neighborhood Association meeting held in August, 1980 in the lovely home of Valentine Callahan. Beacon officials received invitations as well and responded that they would attend. (It was also at this meeting that Harry and Beacon Corp. learned 21-23 Crown Street was on the register of historic buildings and could not be sold for demolition!) Beacon company officials promptly withdrew their parking lot plans and Harry reluctantly agreed to sell. We felt we were very near success, but the negotiation on sale price delayed our celebration of purchase until January 14, 1981, exactly 94 years after the death of Abby Kelley Foster. Indeed, we were truly following in her footsteps. She had risen up at the Second National Woman's Rights Convention held in Worcester's City Hall to publicly declare:

> "I hope that you do not feel that I speak to you in anger. I did not rise to make a speech—my life has been my speech. For fourteen years I have advocated this cause by my daily life. Bloody feet, sisters, have worn smooth the path by which you have come hither."
>
> *Ahead of Her Time*

There were many people who helped us "smooth the path," in becoming property owners. The list is long and impressive. There are those who helped in the financing of Crown Street: Greater Worcester Community Foundation that voted us a sizeable emergency grant and the courageous women of 148 Elm Street, my beloved mother, Lillian, and her sisters, Mary Sheehan, Alice Sheehan and Ethel Cunningham, whose checks put us over the top. Then there were the legal experts who guided us through the muddy waters of closing and purchasing: David Wojcik, Paul Hempel, Diane Pierce Gonzalez and Chris Mehne of Bowditch & Dewey. Elaine especially will never for-

force the issue!!

Two Added to Block Grant List

Feb. 1980

A City Council committee yesterday approved allocations of $6.2 million in federal funds under the Community Development grant program, with amendments that would give money to Abby's House and the Worcester Heritage Preservation Society.

The full City Council will consider the recommendations of its Community Development Committee at Tuesday's council session.

The committee voted to allot $33,000 to Abby's House, a temporary shelter for battered women and their children, and $20,000 to the preservation society, allotted specifically for preservation and contractual obligations.

The extra allocations came from the program's $63,600 contingency fund, leaving about $10,000 for special funding of other programs.

There were requests for $33,000 from the Worcester Labor Co-op program, which offers to help low-income persons repair their homes; $30,000 for the Emergency Mental Health Respite Center, operated out of City Hospital, for its crisis intervention program; and $13,000 for additional funding for the Lead Paint Poisoning Prevention Program.

The Community Development Committee made no motions on these programs, saying that if there is money in the future, the proposals would be considered.

The committee voted to have the Office of Planning and Community Development help Abby's House in compiling information about the persons it serves to determine if it is eligible for funding. If not, the money would be returned to the contingency fund.

For a group to be eligible for block grant funding, the key criterion is that it must provide the bulk of its service to a neighborhood. Therefore, Abby's House must prove the service it performs is primarily for the Piedmont area if it is to be funded.

The preservation society was given $20,000 instead of the $27,000 it requested because there are already funds available for the administrative costs, the committee said.

The major appropriation sections of the program are for neighborhood stabilization, $911,000; neighborhood public works, $1.2 million; code enforcement, $231,000; parks improvements, $257,000; neighborhood facilities, $837,000; public services, $332,300; historic preservation, $55,000; Great Brook Valley Gardens improvements, $295,000; economic development, $232,000; and urban renewal (East Central and Downtown Public Works), $1.1 million.

We could have won the Oscar!

MINUTES OF THE FEBRUARY 13, 1980 STAFF MEETING

OPCD GRANT: On February 5, 1980 the City Council Voted to allot Thirty-three thousand dollars ($33,000) to ABBY'S

HURRAH!!

33,000

Two Added to Block Grant List

A City Council committee yesterday approved allocations of $6.2 million in federal funds under the Community Development grant program, with amendments that would give money to Abby's House and the Worcester Heritage Preservation Society.

The full City Council will consider the recommendations of its Community Development Committee at Tuesday's council session.

The committee voted to allot $33,000 to Abby's House, a temporary shelter for battered women and their children, and $20,000 to the preservation society, allotted specifically for preservation and contractual obligations.

The extra allocations came from the program's $63,600 contingency fund, leaving about $10,000 for special funding of other programs.

There were requests for $33,000 from the Worcester Labor Co-op program, which offers to help low-income persons repair their homes; $30,000 for the Emergency Mental Health Respite Center, operated out of City Hospital, for its crisis intervention program; and $13,000 for additional funding for the Lead Paint Poisoning Prevention Program.

The Community Development Committee made no motions on these programs, saying that if there is money in the future, the proposals would be considered.

The committee voted to have the Office of Planning and Community Development help Abby's House in compiling information about the persons it serves to determine if it is eligible for funding. If not, the money would be returned to the contingency fund.

For a group to be eligible for block grant funding, the key criterion is that it must provide the bulk of its service to a neighborhood. Therefore, Abby's House must prove the service it performs is primarily for the Piedmont area if it is to be funded.

The preservation society was given $20,000 instead of the $27,000 it requested because there are already funds available for the administrative costs, the committee said.

The major appropriation sections of the program are for neighborhood stabilization, $911,000; neighborhood public works, $1.2 million; code enforcement, $231,000; parks improvements, $257,000; neighborhood facilities, $837,000; public services, $332,300; historic preservation, $55,000; Great Brook Valley Gardens improvements, $295,000; economic development, $232,000; and urban renewal (East Central and Downtown Public Works), $1.1 million.

What a struggle!! But we DID it.

HOUSING COMMITTEE: Theresa McBride offered to look into other properties in the Piedmont area and then to meet with the small group of volunteers who will then meet with our landlord to compromise on a selling price for our building.

NEW OFFICERS: Congratulation to the newly elected officers of Abby's Friends: Lynn Murphy, Trissie Holland and Tracy Kennedy. Our sincere thanks to the outgoing officers who have been so much a part of Abby's: Renee Vita, Debbie Gendrop

NEW TREASURE: Pat Galy has accepted the position of treasurer for which we are most grateful. Our thanks to Fran Wall who has been such an assett to Abby's. We appreciate the tireless hours you have so generously given.

NEW MHA WORKER: We are very happy to have Ann Murphy join us. Ann works Mon thru Fri. from 6:30 to 10:30 p.m. so you will have an opportunity to meet her on your staffing night. Ann we are glad you decided to join us!

Abby's House awarded $33,000

by Richard Gagliano
News Editor

The Worcester city council has voted to aportion $33,000 to Abby's House, a women's organization to which 20 Holy Cross students belong.

Abby's house, located at 23 Crown St., provides emergency shelter on a temporary basis for tragedy-stricken women.

The house accommodates up to 20 people and is open between the hours of 6 p.m. and 9 a.m.,

according to Prof. Theresa McBride of the history department, faculty moderator of the group.

The organization plans to use their newly acquired funds to purchase the house out of which they now operate. It has been renting the house since it came into existence three and one half years ago.

The source of the money was a six million dollar grant from the Federal government, for which Worcester city council applied. In order to qualify for the funds, the federal government has stipulated that Abby's House must certify that at least 50 percent of its clientele lives in the Piedmont area in Worcester.

The grant is to be used as an "umbrella resource," according to McBride. Thus, some of the purposes it can serve include the restoration of old buildings, improvement of sewage systems, alcohol prevention programs, and housing projects.

Prof. John B. Anderson of the history department is a member of the city council subcommittee that prepared the budget for the appropriation of the grant money. McBride said "Prof. Anderson and Sarah Robertson, the chairwoman of the subcommittee, took keen interest in the promotion of Abby's request for funds, and were a great help."

McBride continued, "It should be made clear that this money will not be going toward the program. We continue to exist as a volunteer organization, and one which has to live off of the contributions of groups like Holy Cross students who pledge money and make up our staff."

Friday, February 8, 1980

Alice, Mary, Ethel and Lillian, my mother

October 16, 1979

Sister Annette Rafferty
Abby's House
23 Crown Street
Worcester, Massachusetts 01609

Dear Sister Annette,

On behalf of the Crown Hill Neighborhood Corporation, I am pleased to endorse your proposal to the Office of Planning and Community Development for the use of Community Block Grant Funds.

We feel that Abby's House is a significant service organization for the city of Worcester and would be pleased to see its services expanded. We have been impressed with the leadership of Abby's House and the supervision of its programing.

Since the Crown Hill Neighborhood Corporation is concerned with the revitalization of Worcester's inner city, we are strongly in favor of the purchase and rehabilitation of 23 Crown Street for the permanent home of Abby's House. As a group of residents concerned with improving the quality of our environment, we can only agree with your statement that it is important to improve 23 Crown Street, to turn it into a home for its inhabitants whether they be permanent or temporary.

In speaking with Board members our reservation was expressed. Should your services expand significantly over the next few years, we hope that the number of people will not overtax the resources of the neighborhood. Since your past performance has demonstrated your sympathy to this problem, we feel confident that your future judgements will be equally well conceived.

The Crown Hill Neighborhood Corporation wishes you success in your future work.

Sincerely yours,

Ellen R. Berezin
Ellen R. Berezin
President
Crown Hill Neighborhood Corporation

ERB/ls

Crown Hill Development Committee
5 Crown Street, Worcester, Massachusetts 01609

YWCA
... where the **W** makes the difference

2 Washington St.
Worcester, MA 01604
Telephone 791-3181

January 29, 1980

Worcester City Council
City Hall
Worcester, MA 01608

We at the YWCA understand that Abbey Kelly Foster is applying for a block grant to extend their services in the community. We are submitting this letter in support of this endeavor.

Abbey Kelly has a fine reputation in the community for their shelter service. There is a great need for providing free housing to women who otherwise would be unable to acquire shelter.

It has been our experience that Abbey Kelly's door is always open to needy women whether they be women in crisis, mentally ill, or transients without funds.

Sincerely,

Virginia P. Navickas
Virginia P. Navickas
Director of Services

Member of the Young Women's Christian Association of the United States

get the patience and persistence of Chris Mehne who finally completed the knotty negotiations with Harry and his legal team. Compelling letters of support came from other groups of supporters: Ed McCann of the Worcester Public Inebriate Program; Ellen Berezin, president of the Crown Hill Neighborhood Association; John Ford, area director of the Department of Mental Health; Mike Gregory, the first director of mental health at the never-to-be-forgotten Worcester City Hospital; and John J. McKiernan of the Worcester Police Department.

Meanwhile, we spent the rest of the spring and summer carrying out our mission in the shelter and developing the concept of the educational center, now based in the #21 side of the building. The Sisters of St. Joseph of Springfield were the women who made this center a reality. They decided to extend their Holyoke-based Center for Reflection/Action into Worcester. Besides carrying on their work of justice and peace, the Worcester Connection had an additional goal: to bring more women into the community of Abby's through programs that would produce positive, creative change in their personal lives. The center would be based on a philosophy of openness to all persons and respect for all cultures, and would offer an opportunity to pursue social issues, particularly the needs of women. I continued to have a vision of a place that offered consciousness-raising and increased awareness of the population we were serving in the shelter—a place where a new sisterhood could be fostered. To that end, I transferred my energies to educational expansion of Abby's House. An original member of Abby's steering committee, Carol Proietti of the Sisters of St. Anne, came forward to help shape that dream. Another chapter of Abby's House was about to be added to this city's bright spot.

A WOMAN'S PLACE

Where spiritual and social struggle converge is the Worcester Connection

By Bennie DiNardo

WORCESTER CONNECTION

FEMINIST EDUCATION
REFLECTION ACTION

21 Crown Street
Worcester, MA 01609
(617) 756-1038

A chance to explore the root causes of women's struggle by offering:

* Courses and workshops pertaining to issues that affect women
* Meeting space for groups of 20-25 by arrangement.
* Media rentals of slides & films Re: World hunger, Womens' issues, Third World, disarmament... A directory is available.
* Free rental library on feminist issues

Open Sept.-June
Tues., Wed., Thurs. 9-5 p.m.   Call or write for info.
Mon. 7 p.m.-9 p.m.

—We publish our own quarterly,
AT THE CROSSROADS

Educational Component of Abby's

The 21 side of Abby's House

POETRY:
at the WORCESTER CONNECTION

A place to live
is all that's needed.
The Aurora or The Albion.
Someone with grand thoughts
built, in another time,
hotels on Main Street
now city rooming houses like these
and the one called "The Palace".

On some streets
a porch railing leans
on a weakened frame
left standing in an empty lot.
Or stairs
remain cut out of a cement wall
that surrounds no house.

Worldly possessions.
A place to live.

At the housing office
the summer client walks in
carrying a suitcase
and an electric fan.

Smoke.
That's what
the blades of the electric fan
bring in tonight.
At the window I listen
to a cop radio blaring
" '78 Ford Fairlane. Castle Hill Park.
In flames."

MARY BONINA
Wednesday, 8:00 pm
Oct. 14, 1981
21 Crown St.

Worcester Connection
celebrates
Women!
March 10, 1981
tues. 7:30 p.m.

Presentation on:
Women's Work
and Industrialization:
19th century perspective.
by Dr. Theresa McBride,
history dep't., holy cross
college

Public invited.

We commemorate
Women's History Week
March 8 - 14, 1981! Come

Guerilla Commander Dora Maria Téllez, "Commander Two" of the assault on the National Palace (August 22, 1978), "Commander Patricia" of the taking of Leon at the end of the war, was 23 at the time of Nicaragua's victory. Today she is Vice President of the Council of State, Ideological Secretary of the FSLN in the capital city and a member of the vanguard's Secretariat.

Photo by Margaret Randall
from the book Nicaragua Libre!

Worcester Connection
Women's Project
presents:
Update on Nicaragua.....
an inside story... from a recent fact-finding tour
Sat. Jan. 23, 1982
Speaker: Jeanne Gallo s.n.d.
of Overview Latin America, and a former Brazilian missionary.
Time: 8 p.m
Place: El Centro
11 Sycamore St.
— Public Is Invited —
please post!

Some of the Connection women

Dear Annette,
You have been in my thoughts lately and I've finally decided to get in touch with you. I know you are very busy, so I am a bit hesitant to ask if we might get together — but could we?

I've been groping my way through a lot of loose ends, and in the process discovered a lot that is really unsettling and unclear.

For a lot of reasons (many unknown!) I would like to talk with you.

I hope this doesn't put too many demands on your time —

I'll give you my address + number, and hope to hear from you.

Tess

Tess comes to wear smooth the path, 1981

CHAPTER 6 *Sisterhood is Powerful*

With the untiring devotion of the shelter coordinator and the help of dear friends, we spruced up the 21 side, even laying carpets that Elaine and I dragged out of Worcester Center. A card company decided to re-carpet its store and called to see if we had any interest in their used carpet. In our enthusiasm, we said yes, having no idea what a tedious, exhausting task we were undertaking. Weeks later, the job was done and so were we. The carpet had been laid, shampooed, trimmed and sliced to fit the irregular floor design with the help of Charlie and Richard Monroe. And, I must add, the center looked spectacular. Our muscles ached for weeks, but the compliments we received on home decorating compensated for the pain.

Then the women came, not in droves, but steadily and with curiosity about what this Worcester Connection could do for them. By October of 1980, we had courses in place and had opened our doors to groups seeking to plan many anti-war activities, including the nuclear freeze campaign. A Central American solidarity group had emerged, as well as programs on rape prevention, women's nutrition, poverty and economics. A dedicated group of women, who named their meetings Sisterhood is Powerful, was at the heart of the Connection's development. I remember most of them: Marge Dick, Ann Kaminski, Mary Haberstroh, Lynn Gostyla, Pauline Kalagher, Pat Daly, Marion Bergin, Mary Pat True, Pauline Turner, and Brenda Kartheiser, who is still at Abby's as our H.O.A.P. (Homeless Outreach Advocacy Pogram) nurse in the Day Center.

In early August of 1981, I received a letter from a young woman whom I met several years before. She was the niece of Sr. Helen Turcotte, one of the SSJs with whom I had worked for eight years. At the time of our meeting, I had explained what Abby's was and what this new center might become and invited her to come and join us. The letter was a response; yes, Tess Sneesby would be glad to come.

I believe that Tess' arrival at Abby's House marked the beginning of our sense of a community, firmly rooted and committed to the lives of women and to the development of a feminist perspective, all shaped out of "hands-on" experience. Tess first applied her energies to the Connection, working closely with the local disarmament group on the nuclear freeze issue. In November of 1981, together with Katie Green and Barbara Morin, Tess and our Elms College intern Dot Joseph traveled to Washington, D.C. to participate in the famous Women's Pentagon Action. By Christmas, she wrote in the Connection's publication, *At the Crossroads*, the following:

> "I have spent the past few months living and working on Crown Street. Here at this place, individual women have come together, very simply, to be present to one another. Imagine nearly one hundred women creating, recognizing, sharing in this place! Some are present in that space called "shelter" doing the morning shift, staffing once a month or five evenings every week, or cleaning each Wednesday morning. Some are present in that space called "center" giving programs, doing clerical work, answering phones, attending programs. Some live here; some are part of a daily working collective. All of us are, by turns, empowered.
>
> Our presence to each other allows us to step aside from our everyday struggles and recollect ourselves. A guest at Abby's may be living in a crowded, noisy rooming house and needs to get away for a while. Or maybe she has an abusive partner and has to get out of that situation. Someone has been discharged from a psychiatric ward, not sure what the next step is; or a woman has run

Tess and Eva Engel

Marie Therese Martin

They 'Bee' Quilting

Pat Daly, left, of the Worcester Connection, explains the intricacies of a quilting pattern to Sisters Margaret Curran, center, and Pauline Kalagher. The women are participants in a "Quilting Bee," held the fourth Thursday of each month at the Worcester Connection, 21 Crown St. In addition to its quilting sessions, the center offers a variety of programs for women including a free lending library, formal and informal courses, workshops on religion and educational resources. Hours are 9 a.m. to 5 p.m. Tuesday through Thursday and 10 a.m. to 3 p.m. on the first Saturday of each month. Scholarship aid is available and child care is possible for Saturday events. The next scheduled event is a support-discussion program with members of the Women's Peace Group. It's planned for 7 to 9:30 p.m. Tuesday.

Carol Proietti, Pat Simon and Annette

Elisabeth Fiorenza at our 3rd Women's Weekend

Carolyn had us singing with our hearts

out of money and can't find housing. For the staffers, Abby's is sometimes a respite from the hassles at work or in the family. Then there are the women who stop in at the Connection during the day for coffee, to talk or to browse. Maybe she can leave her child here and go shopping by herself! And at night she may be involved in a course. Whether it is five nights or two hours, we give each other the space apart that we need."

Tess' clarity of purpose and depth of thought process have been guiding lights since her arrival. Over the next two years, she spent more time with the women at the shelter where her innate gifts of compassion and understanding combined with an amazing firmness with the guests eventually led her to become Abby's House co-director (shared with Elaine Lamoureux) and then to the position of executive director. I continued to rely on her insights as we developed both our program component and the Connection publications.

The first years at the Worcester Connection (1980–82) were full, exciting and challenging. Marie Therese Martin, CSJ from Boston, offered to give a course on *Mary*; Theresa McBride of Holy Cross gave an inspiring talk on *Women's Work and Industrialization*; Mary Duffy, Nancy Sheridan and I gave women's retreats; and Carol Cross and Pauline Kalagher taught courses on *Nutrition and Exercise*. Pat Daly's course on *Economics and Women* was a huge success. A flood of wonderful speakers flowed into the Connection those first years, as well. We entertained Tom Cornell, the late Anabelle Wolfson (both conscientious objectors to the draft), poet Mary Bonina, Joan Morris (author of *The Lady was a Bishop*), Sally and Phil Scharper of Orbis Press; Midge Miles, storyteller par-excellence; nutritionists Irene Timlege, Dr. Lucille Sadwith and Elise Schlaikjer; anti-war and non-violence champion, Joanne Sheehan; Pat Simon, Gold Star Mother for Amnesty; Penny Lernoux, expert in Latin American politics; Jeanne Gallo of American Friends Service Committee. The course given by Pauline Turner on Religious Mythology of Woman was sensational. Irene Mizula, on the Connection staff, offered craft courses.

The response to the Connection offerings was so encouraging that the staff decided to establish an annual "Women's Weekend" to be held each November. These weekends brought wonderful facilitators to Worcester, among them: Madonna Kolbenschlag, well known author of *Kiss Sleeping Beauty Good-Bye*; the late Marge Tuite, nationally recognized community organizer who concentrated on Women's Work and Economics; Elisabeth Schussler Fiorenza, author of *In Memory of Her*, now at Harvard Divinity; Pam Wright who, at the time, taught in Clark University's COPACE; and lastly, the feminist musician Carolyn McDade, who had us singing with our hearts.

At the first weekend, conducted by Madonna Kolbenschlag, we introduced our newest staff member, Marie Therese Martin. All of us were thrilled to welcome another woman into our collective and one who would eventually establish some powerful programs, such as "Rootwomen" and "Women's Project," both ongoing opportunities to explore feminist spirituality in individuals' lives and in the lives of other women. Marie continued to be the source of inspiration to the Connection until 1988 when financial concerns about the future of such a women's center led to its closing. Funding sources for the center had dried up. Most foundations were inclined to allot dollars to the shelter component of Abby's rather than to the women's educational branch. Furthermore, Abby's board had determined that the space could be better used for other expanded services. The women's center relocated to the Central Building downtown where it continued to thrive for several more years. In her own words, Marie described her recollection and fond memories of being part of Abby's educational component in, "We Had a Dream ... and It Lives On!"

Among the greatest contributions offered to the Worcester community during the nine year history of the Connection, was the publication of a feminist journal, *At the Crossroads*. In Abby's history room, located at 77 Chatham Street, I have all of the volumes. It would be impossible to include in this history each and every inspiring article. There are so many memories connected with this quarterly, beginning with our long and painful discussions about the title, which we finally agreed described where most women found themselves at the time. Each of us was struggling with redefinition and a strong, emerging consciousness about where we should spend the rest of our days. During this time, two of us, Elaine and I, left our religious communities to continue our work with women. The Connection had provided us with a new model of sisterhood, something I had always envisioned for myself. In 1986, I made the move from one community into another. Others remained in their chosen area, but were decidedly more aware of how to recognize and avoid the patriarchal traps. At any rate, *At the Crossroads* said it like it was in the '80s.

Ms. Morris, noted British scholar and lecturer will address the topic:

IN THE EARLY CHRISTIAN CHURCH, THERE WAS A TRADITION OF WOMEN CELEBRATING THE EUCHARIST

In her presentation, Joan will include slides of the catacombs of Priscilla in which was found the Eucharistic scene depicting women celebrants.

Her best known work, The Lady was a Bishop, was published in 1973. In this book she uncovered previously unnoticed evidence of women celebrants.

This lecture is open to the public.

For further information, call Worcester Connection 756-1038 Monday-Friday 9-5.

Worcester Connection Women's Project announces the special visit of Joan Morris, author of The Lady was a Bishop, to 21 Crown St. Saturday October 31 2-4

3RD ANNUAL WOMEN'S WEEKEND

AT THE WORCESTER CONNECTION
21 CROWN STREET
WORCESTER, MA 01609
(617)756-1038

1983
NOVEMBER 4th and 5th

In Memory of Her

-WHAT ARE WOMEN SAYING?
-WHY IS FEMINISM A PRIORITY?
-HOW DO WOMEN INFLUENCE THE DIRECTION OF SOCIAL CHANGE?

A PIONEERING WORK IN THE ROLE OF WOMEN IN THE ORIGINS OF CHRISTIANITY

with Elizabeth Schüssler Fiorenza

A FEMINIST RECONSTRUCTION OF CHRISTIAN ORIGINS

Elizabeth Schussler Fiorenza is a Professor of New Testament Studies and Theology at the University of Notre Dame. She has authored numerous books and articles on feminist theology and served on various task forces and commissions on the problems of women in church and theology. Her latest book IN MEMORY OF HER keeps alive the story of the unnamed woman who anoints Jesus in the Gospel of Mark - "Wherever the gospel is preached in the whole world, what she has done will be told in memory of her." Mark 14:9

FRIDAY, NOVEMBER 4, 1983
7:30 P.M. Registration
8:00 - 10:00 Session I

SATURDAY, NOVEMBER 5,1983
9:30 a.m. Registration - Coffee
10:00 a.m. - 4 p.m. Presentation and Sharing

DONATION: $15.00 for weekend
$10.00 student
SCHOLARSHIP AID AVAILABLE
$5.00 (non-returnable) registratic
fee due by
November 1, 1983

We Had a Dream ... and It Lives On!

The Worcester Connection: 1980-1989
by Marie Therese Martin, CSJ

We had a dream ... of strong vibrant women gathering, learning, living, loving, hoping, singing, dancing, teaching, healing, advocating for justice for all people, "be-ing," celebrating themselves as gift ... a "womanspace" connecting the spiritual, political, cultural, economic and social realities experienced by women locally and globally.

Founded in 1980, the Worcester Connection was born of the vision of Annette Rafferty and the Sisters of St. Joseph of Springfield as a reflection/action center. For ten years this "womanspace" was a vital force in the Worcester community, a place where women's voices were heard and women's experience was valued. Annette invited me to join the staff as director of the Women's Project in 1982, sharing the common vision of Sisters of St. Joseph always to move toward love of neighbor without distinction. Focusing our energy on the empowerment of women, this vision gave shape to our feminist perspective of a worldview which includes all people and all cultures. These were wonderful years, filled with rich memories of women, and a few men, who gathered and connected at 21-23 Crown Street to staff and reflect on women's experience. Retreats, courses, workshops, films, At the Crossroads, discussion groups brought together a litany of women espousing feminist values and organizing for change, nurturing the birth of many lifelong frierndships ... with strong connections to Abby's House. It was a space of weaving the stories of the guests at Abby's with other change-makers who recognized that planetary survival depends on the emergence of feminine principles of interconnectedness, responsibility and cooperation.

I remember: the blessing of music with Carolyn McDade, Marsie Silvestro, Kathleen Principe, Betsy Rose; the capturing storytelling and drama of Roberta Nobleman; the sculpture and performance of Suzanne Benton; the photography of Ann Marie Grady; the art of our cardmakers; the weaving of Barbara Liberty; the energizing commitment to change in church and society brought by Marge Tuite, Ada Maria Isasdi-Diaz and Joan Sabola, Joan Morris, Elisabeth Schussler Fiorenza, Theresa Kane, Madonna Kolbenschlag, Midge Miles, Angela Dorenkamp, Alice Laffey, Penny Gill, Kathy Hasagawa, Elizabeth Petroff, Pam Wright, and the "regulars" who brought life to both sides of the house, Annette, Tess, Elaine, Pauline Turner, Mary Haberstroh, Margaret Curran, Ann Kaminski, Paula Kelleher, Carol Proietti, Irene Mizula, Anna Marie Kane, Ann B. Day, Elise Schlaiker, Joan McGinn, Marie T. Sullivan, Sara Reynolds, Sue Ardizonne, Dee Graney, Joanne O'Brien, Mary Pat True, Pauline Kallagher, Kathy Sullivan, Carol Cornacchioli, Helen McCarron, Carol Burns, Marion Bergin, Marjorie Dick, Karen Dorhamer ...; our connections with NETWORK, Church Women United, Mary's Pence, National Association of Religious Women (NARW), Women's Ordination Conference, Religious Task Force on Central America, Womancenter at Plainville, Women's Alliance for Theology, Ethics and Ritual (WATER), New Ways Ministry ... May they, and all who passed through the doors on Crown Street and 332 Main Street, The Connection's second home, be blessed! Believe it, these are the women who continue to transform the world.

The struggle was never easy, but each day brought renewed energy as women discovered and celebrated themselves as gift, and raised consciousness, advocating for the rights of women in society and church. Hardly a day passes in my journey that I don't "connect" with someone who remembers the "connection days" and the spirit of life experienced in our space. We keep meeting and celebrating life together creating sacred spaces and experiencing the joy of gathering old friends and new for blessed events as we journey on. We do keep meeting, connecting, visioning and being a support for each other on the way. The dream lives on!

Open for business

The food pantry

The renovation of the garage

INVENTORY FORM CONTINUATION SHEET

MASSACHUSETTS HISTORICAL COMMISSION
Office of the Secretary, Boston

Community: Worcester

Form No: 130-P

Property Name Extension District

Indicate each item on inventory form which is being continued below.
7. Property list - cont.

\# 1st owner (occupation) date style other info.
Austin Street (cont.)
111 Edwin A. Morse (machinist) ca. 1851-1860 side-hall Victorian -
    Morse 1st known owner-1870
113 Josiah P. Houghton (water wheels) ca. 1851-1860 side-hall Victorian
    Houghton 1st known owner - 1870.
117-119 Edwin Ames (mason) ca. 1870 Second Empire

80-84 D.G. Rawson's Boot factory -wood section ca. 1870, brick section-
      ca. 1878-1886
86 Warren Leather Goods factory - ca. 1896-1911
98 Amos White (clothes dryers) ca. 1851 Greek Revival - White, 1st
    known owner-1878.
102 Miss Elizabeth Scott (none given) ca. 1870-side-hall Victorian-alter
110 David G. Tapley (pattern maker) ca. 1860 side-hall Victorian
114 Rufus Chase (painter) ca. 1851-Greek Revival/Victorian-Chase 1st
    known owner-1870
120 George Bradford (cigar maker) ca. 1855-Greek Revival-altered

Chatham Street (named Division Street prior to 1849)
77 Willard Jones (Willard Jones & Co. ca. 1869-Second Empire

54 John Kendall (hats, caps & furs) ca. 1845-Greek Revival-Kendall 1st
    known owner-1870
78 Charles White (boot manufacturer) ca. 1851-Italianate
80 Amasa Ballou (painter) ca. 1878-1886-Second Empire-Ballou not
    a resident of this house

Congress Street (opened 1846)
1   John Spaulding (carpenter) ca. 1851-1860-Greek Revival/Victorian-
    Spaulding 1st known owner-1870
5   John Spaulding (carpenter) ca. 1858- side-hall Victorian
7   Alex J. Warfield (boot crimper) ca. 1851-Greek Revival
11 W.H. Hathorn (salesman) ca. 1851-1860-side-hall Victorian - Hathorn
    first known owner-1870
13 Edwin J. Leland (photographer) ca. 1851-1860-Greek Revival cottage-
    Leland 1st known owner-1870
15 Simon T. Jacobs (carpenter) ca. 1855-Greek Revival

4   S. John (unknown) ca. 1851-1860-Greek Revival-S.John 1st known
    owner-1870
6   Cyrus K. Hubbard ("Fruit, confectionary & eating house") ca.1851
    Greek Revival-Hubbard 1st known owner-1870
8-10 Hiram Barnard (Barnard Bros.) & George Bliss (hats, caps Etc.)
     1890-1891-Queen Anne double house-Barker & Nourse, arch'ts
                                                          (cont.)

Staple to Inventory form at bottom

How we learned about the neighbors circa 1850

INTORY FORM CONTINUATION SHEET

ACHUSETTS HISTORICAL COMMISSION
ce of the Secretary, Boston

Community: Worcester

Form No: 130-P

Property Name: Oxford-Crown Extension District

cate each item on inventory form which is being continued below.

Property list - cont. page \# 3

1st owner (occupation) date style other info.
ress Street (cont.)
Nelson Cowen (none given) ca. 1851-1860-Greek Revival cottage-
  altered-Cowen 1st known owner-1870
Alfred Metcalf (machinist) ca. 1860-Greek Revival cottage-altered
Joshua Wheeler (machinist) ca. 1857-Victorian (curiosity)

n Street (partially opened prior to 1851)
Granville Langley (Bigelow & Langley) ca. 1870-Second Empire
3 Carter Whitcomb (manufacturer) ca. 1851-1860-Greek Revival/Ital-
  ianate double house (brick)

George Rice (?)-(Goddard, Rice & Co.) ca. 1851-Italianate
Elijah Brooks (clicker) ca. 1867-side-hall Victorian
Jonathan Luther (none given) ca. 1851-1860-side-hall Victorian cottag
  Luther 1st known owner-1866

rd Street (laid out before 1851)
Alonzo Whitcomb (manufacturer) ca. 1861-Italianate double house
Luther Stone (accountant) ca. 1852-Greek Revival
Alexander H. Dean (leather dealer) ca. 1851-1860-Greek Revival-
  Dean 1st known owner-1870

sant Street (eighteenth century road)
210 Amory Carter (carpenter) ca. 1850-Greek Revival double house-
    altered
    Danforth Brown (real estate) ca. 1848-Greek Revival
    Joseph Raymond (supt. telegraph repairs) ca. 1870-Second Empire
    George Bigelow (bank clerk) ca. 1870-side-hall Victorian

Staple to Inventory form at bottom

We are in the Carter-Whitcomb house

Irene Mizula

CHAPTER 7

Molly, Meridel and More Milestones

Meanwhile, on the shelter side of Abby's House, there were many exciting new developments. In 1982, the sad-looking garage with its three stalls was completely renovated to accommodate a food pantry that would serve the needs of shelter meals, former guests and the soon-to-be-neighbors at what became Whittier Terrace developed by the Beacon Corporation as low-income housing. In August, a notice from the Worcester Preservation Society informed us that we would be included in an historic marker program. This meant quite simply that 21-23 Crown Street (previously designated an historic building) would bear an official historic marker. Thanks to supporter Janet McCorison of the Preservation Society, the marker was donated. Within a few weeks a stunning looking marker was placed on the building, to the left of number 21, noting that this had once been the home of Mr. Carter Whitcomb, manufacturer circa 1850.

We were very aware that Abby's was located in the historic Oxford-Crown District, which still preserves a large portion of one of Worcester's earliest residential areas, one that mushroomed in the boom years of 1845–1860. Although some homes have been destroyed, the majority of buildings constructed here prior to 1870 remain, complemented by the area's abundance of granite walls, gate posts and stairways. It wasn't long before we learned that streets in this district were settled by artisans, small-scale business men and manufacturers. On Austin Street there was the Warren Leather Factory, a painter, cigar maker, machinist and a maker of water wheels. (This factory is today Whittier Terrace.) On Chatham Street lived a proprietor of a shop for the fanciest of hats, caps and furs, while on Oxford Street there lived an accountant and a leather dealer. Congress Street boasted a few carpenters, a photographer, a boot crimper and a Fruit, Confectionary and Eating House owner. Abby's House, built around 1850, is a double house made of brick, combining elements of Greek Revival and Italianate architecture. When it was sold to its second owner, Mr. Whitcomb, in the deed it was noted that he (Whitcomb) retained the right to all the produce from the fruit orchards surrounding the property for one year. What is today a Whittier Terrace parking lot was once a wonderful orchard of pear, apple and peach trees. I learned more about this from the late Ed St. George, a former comptroller of the Diocese of Worcester. His family had lived in the Carter Whitcomb house, and he told me that on his way to school, he took fruit for his lunch!

By the time we opened the Carter Whitcomb house as a shelter for homeless and battered women in 1976, the neighborhood boasted a series of well-kept and strictly-run boarding houses. A woman could easily find a room that was decent, clean and affordable within three days. But that was then and could never happen today. It is important to all of us that women coming to Abby's learn not only the history of the neighborhood, but also become aware of our rich "herstory," told through scrapbooks, files, oral histories and our newsletters that are now retained in the History Room at 77 Chatham Street.

Meanwhile, we were all conscious that an annual fundraising event needed to be woven into that "herstory." The best idea came from Irene Mizula, SSJ. Thanks to Irene, in September we held our very first tag sale in the old cellar under the 21 side of the house. We made about $300 and rejoiced that we had a few more dollars to continue our services. In reviewing the newsletters, I noted the following increase in sales: the third tag sale netted $1,428; the 1985 sale brought $1,500; and by 1989, we had reached an all-time high of $4,125. Each year this tag sale, still our major yearly fundraiser, has improved in size, in the quality of the items available and in the number of tables, and in the dedication of the organizers and the volunteers (at least 130 show up to participate and to run a table). Our 18th annual,

Our Tag Sale 1980-1997

Marilyn Hildick looks the paintings over

Ruth Dow (r) waits patiently to make a sale

Jaycee Eileen Mitchell helps out

Sally Brown selling dishes

Otis and Anne Wickwire make a furniture deal

"Whitey," Elaine, Maryellen and Don Lamoureux - old faithfuls

Hilda works her way out of the garage

Mary Ann McGrain and Ann Harrington - the toy specialists

The crowd gathers at 9 a.m.

Patti Conzo makes a half-price announcement

Brenda Kartheiser and Julie Komenos take a break

Veronica Griffin and Joyce Ronka selling their wares

held in 1998, yielded over $17,000. Buyers and business sponsors made the day a huge success. Undoubtedly, this is the social event of the year, "the inner city Brimfield Flea Market." It remains a monumental testimony to the level of support Abby's house has within Worcester and Worcester County communities.

Abby's House was nearly ten years old and all of us, those doing the sheltering and those doing the educating, decided to celebrate this anniversary in style. We set up committees and began planning. With the help of Lynn Kremer-Babcock of the Theater Department of the College of the Holy Cross, we received some interesting information about a one-woman performer, Molly Culligan, who would probably be willing to come from St. Paul, Minnesota, to do a performance called "Ripenings," based on the prose and poetry of Meridel LeSueur, a distinguished writer and activist who was blacklisted during the McCarthy years of the 1950s and had disappeared from the public eye. We eagerly read the comments sent to us by Lynn and began to get insights into the spirit of LeSueur and Culligan. I remember writing about them in the booklet we compiled for this 10th Anniversary:

> "Running through all of Meridel's work is the examination of what being a woman feels like. Molly continues to muse: 'Simple, but so little encouraged in the linear world. It was brave and she is brave and speaks for all of us. Because of the few like Meridel, we are learning to take up our pride in being creatures of the earth, not 20th century prisoners of our over-stretched minds.' Molly resonates with Meridel's love and respect for the land and her concern for its survival, which they both believe is possible only through community energy. They are both concerned that women grow to full self-worth in their home lives and in their working lives, while not denying their ability to perceive life subjectively. And so, in this adaptation of the work of Meridel LeSueur, Molly Culligan focuses on everyone's common humanity. It's about women's qualities; of lovingness, pliancy, perplexity, simplicity, wonderment, compassion, patience, formidable strength, modesty, mother-instinct."

It didn't take us very long to contact Lynn at the Cross and say: How can we get Molly Culligan? Contact made, the contract was signed. We needed the best kind of format in which to introduce this amazing woman. A dinner-theater was our choice and what a good one it proved to be. The response to our first mailing in January of 1985 was overwhelming. April 12th, the agreed upon date, couldn't come fast enough and when it had come and gone, we raised $10,000 (a thousand for each year), celebrated with much gusto, eaten a delicious meal, catered by Saga of Assumption College. We were treated to an outstanding, unforgettable performance by Ms. Culligan. As someone stated after the event:

> "I didn't know what to expect. I was puzzled, embarrassed, saddened, depressed and finally joyfully exhilarated! That it was a woman's play about a woman and her feelings, I don't doubt ... that it was any human being rising above circumstances because of the principle of love is hopefully universal. As an actress, Molly drew the emotions and married us, the audience, to the characters of the play."

There are so many people to thank for that celebration—the sponsors and those who gave special help in funding the printing, the performance and the transportation costs: Norton Company Foundation, and the late Rev. William O'Shea and Ethel S. Cunningham. Bouquets should also be given to the Committee Chairs: Claudia Lacerte, Carol Burns, Vickie Powers, Karen Kappes, Pauline Kalagher, Ruth Sanders, Claudia Russo, Everett Lacerte and Rita Chasen. Finally, thanks to all the women and men who helped out in any way with mailings, placing of posters and the buying and selling of tickets.

Another milestone within the shelter component was the opening of Abby's By Day on March 17, 1986. It began in the dining room, one day a week and reached out to the women who had moved on to their own places from Abby's, but continued to fight the demons of loneliness and isolation. It was here, in the warmth of Abby's, that those who came found support, understanding and friendships, many of which continue to this day. Julie Komenos came to Abby's, asking to help and

The performer:
Molly Culligan

415 Laurel Ave
St. Paul, MN.
55102
1-612-291-0195

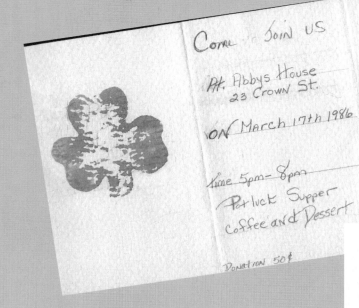

Come + Join us

At Abby's House
23 Crown St.

on March 17th 1986

Time 5pm – 8pm
Pot luck Supper
Coffee and Dessert

Donation 50¢

Another Abby's milestone

RIPENINGS

based on the prose + poetry of Meridel Le Sueur
directed by Lynn Kremer-Babcock
script adapted by Phyllis Paulette
performed by **MOLLY CULLIGAN**

She was superb!

*Julie Komenos began
the Day Center, 1986*

Opening day

Chef Ellen Shepherd fills the plates

Welcome to the Day Center

Holly and Edna prepare dinner

Joan and Kathy wait for it

Carolyn Sheldon and "Cher" entertain

Georgia and Mary enjoy the show

Open House
10:00 a.m. - 2:00 p.m.
March 17, 1987
1st Year Anniversary
Abby's - by - Day
23 Crown Street, Worcester, MA

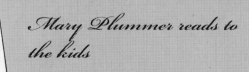

Mary Plummer reads to the kids

Linda Wakefield decorates the dining room

within a few weeks, she initiated the program along with a few courageous volunteers—Ellen Shepherd, Linda Wakefield and Paula Sullivan, a nurse who came from Pernet Family Health Service to discuss health issues with staff and guests. The seed was planted that blossomed into a five-day a week Day Center that still reaches out to those women who have left the shelter, to those staying at Abby's and to women with or without children who are struggling financially and socially in our neighborhood. Now, in its 14th year of operation, the Day Center continues to follow Abby's unwavering and underlying philosophy of hospitality and empowerment. And its mission has been faithfully carried forward in these years by many capable women coordinators, among them Julie Komenos, Annette Rafferty, Elaine Lamoureux, Karen Staropoli, Terri Griffin, Judie Cofsky, Ellen Laverdure and Jeanne Adler. All of these women help other women find a refuge of companionship. As Tess wrote in the first issue of the 1987 edition of our newsletter:

> "We are very excited about our newest program called Abby's By Day. Its purpose is to translate the same sense of hospitality, acceptance, belonging and empowerment that is found in the shelter at night. We want to reach out to former guests with social, emotional and practical support as they try to maintain a permanent home. Since March of 1986 approximately 12 women have been meeting each Tuesday. In the coming year, we hope to complete a renovation of our cellar to provide us with more space. We also hope to increase the number of participants and days open. This will depend on more volunteers responding. With a grant from the Greater Worcester Community Foundation, this program will 'see the light of day'."

And, indeed, we did "see the light of day" with the help of a very generous grant of $10,000 from GWCF to renovate the cellar into a bigger site for the Day Center. By the close of 1987, a new Center had been created in what had been the two cellars of 21-23 Crown Street. The amazing transformation of this once dark, foreboding space into a bright, welcoming area was accomplished by Brian Shorten and his assistant Art Flora. Their skills in making this Center the heart of Abby's By Day were just short of miraculous. So, within the space of two years, the concept of daytime hospitality had expanded from a small dining room area into two renovated cellars. It continued to grow, and not much later the number of women and children coming to the Center required another miracle. Could this possibly happen?

In January of 1988, I became the first full-time coordinator of the Day Center. Julie, who had begun the Center, had gone back to nursing, but she assured us that within a few years, she would come back to Abby's. We needed her incredible energy, magnetic personality, warm heart and her contagious laughter. Fortunately for Abby's she kept her promise. What a great experience for me! I knew most of the women who came. We had established bonds through my years of sheltering and educating at the Worcester Connection component. Working with these women would be comparable to enjoying old friends. By June, I submitted the following reflection to Tess:

> "In its second year of existence, but in the first years of a five-day week, Abby's By Day is already established as a space where every woman is welcome, safe and befriended by a dedicated staff and volunteers. Since the philosophy of Abby's is one built on mutuality, empowerment and respect for individual difference, the Day Center reflects that philosophy in the way guests and staff interact, in the way activities are planned and in the way policies are shaped. As the recently hired coordinator, I am thoroughly enjoying juggling these three components. Each day brings new challenges, lots of laughter as well as opportunities to grow. We are all being pulled beyond the limits we've set for ourselves. The words, 'I never thought I could handle communicating with ten women, preparing a meal and keeping an eye on the kids,' have gradually translated into, 'I felt strong and pretty powerful as I drove away today.' All of us are drawing on inner resources we never imagined were there and find we can and do offer a quality presence."

By the close of 1988, on November 29th to be exact, Abby's Thrift Store opened its doors on the first floor of the 21 side of

Aurea

Lucy

Rita and Connie

Mary and Helen

Carolyn looks on

Hermania, Carmen and Venecia

Juanita, Clint and Hilda join in

Now, it's time to eat!

Some of our volunteers

Jeanne opens for business

Marilyn and Mary, Monday staffers

Gloria Todd and Anne Schneider

*Dorrie Hutchins (l)
and Fran Keller (r)
getting the sales ready*

Abigails help with our Annual App

Pam Ruah

Nancy Hastings and Pat Thomas

the house, in that space once occupied by Worcester Connection. The purpose of the store was to serve shelter guests by providing clothing for women and children at no cost. The shop would also serve as a fundraiser for shelter operations by asking donations of clothing from the general public, friends and neighbors of Abby's. Our hope was to involve the women in the Day Center in running the store, giving them a chance to learn new skills and to socialize. Eventually, this dream fostered the birth of the "Abigails," a program developed and nurtured by volunteer and retired social worker, Jeanne Rosenblatt, who has in these later years become an integral part of Abby's community. Jeanne had this to say about the program:

"I had observed the need to empower women I was meeting at Abby's as well as the women who live in the neighboring low-income housing project (Whittier Terrace). So, knowing how much these women would benefit from learning new skills and accepting increased responsibility, I organized what became known as the Abigails. The women began working in the Thrift Store, in the Food Pantry, in the Day Center, in the office doing clerical work. Through these efforts, the women earned credits that would translate into clothing at the store and food in the Pantry. It has proven to be a great incentive for women who struggle daily with low income. This collaborative effort has helped Abby's greatly and has been greatly valued by the participants themselves."

The "Abigails" are still a vibrant part of the organization and I am reminded often of Abby Kelley Foster's words when Jeanne is registering another woman for her program:

"There are thousands of women in these United States working for a pittance who know they are fitted for something better and who tell me when I urge them to do business for themselves, 'I do not want the responsibility of business. It is too much. ...' "
Spoken on October 15, 1851, at the Second National Woman's Rights Convention.

Jeanne, who knows well the concept of empowerment, is Abby incarnate. None of her Abigails will pass up the opportunity to assume more responsibility. Thank you, spirit of Abby Kelley Foster, for directing Jeanne to us.

Today, the Thrift Store is open six days a week and is run by a capable and dedicated staff of volunteers. We pay special thanks to Claudia Hamlet-Lacerte for creating this place where families could find wonderful bargains. As with every other area of Abby's House, the Thrift Store continues the tradition of providing quality, care-filled service and hospitality to those who visit, shop, donate, purchase and help support the shelter needs.

Women and their children will always need a safety net!

Children of Abby's House

CHAPTER 8 *A Brand New Day*

During the summer of 1988, we published *Abby's Anthology*, a collection of writings from the guests and staff of Abby's. The editor of this anthology was Denise Simon, who spent considerable time as a shelter staffer and was eventually inspired to compile the thoughts, poems and musings of our guests. In the Preface of the booklet, Denise wrote:

"Last March, having never done anything charitable in my life, I decided to donate some time to helping the homeless. I contacted the Worcester Committee on Homelessness, asked where I could do this type of work and they directed me to Abby's.

When I started volunteering, I had no idea what it would be like. I guess I expected to find people that were down and out, bitter about life and uncaring. No one will ever know just how much fear I felt, stepping in to volunteer for my first night of work. What I found was a far cry from anything I ever expected.

The women I encountered at Abby's were there for various reasons. Some had been battered; some had jobs, but didn't make enough money to pay the rent; some were new to the area and just needed to stay somewhere while looking for an apartment. We had others who had been released from mental care and even a student or two passing through, looking for a place to stay.

Sure, there were a few that met my worst expectations, but by far, most of the women I met and have continued to meet have been people who, no matter how bad their situations, had decided to pick up the pieces and turn their lives around.

Early on, I noticed that many of our guests were writers. I brought this to the attention of the Board of Directors and asked if I could put together an anthology of their writings. What you see here is the result of that request.

As you read through the following pages, realize just how human our guests are. They are warm, caring, loving people. Then next time you encounter a homeless person, don't look at her as a 'problem,' look at her as a sister human being—and care!"

Some samples from this beautiful booklet are included in my own account of Abby's House history since they reflect the beauty of the women and children who make up our family.

It seems to me that revisiting the poetry of former guests is a very important way to reconsider our mission and to reaffirm our commitment to one another. During the many hours of extracting facts, reconstructing the timeline of our slow, but steady development as a multi-service organization, of laughing and crying at the mountain of photos and slides, I always returned to the anthology and to the newsletters written by Tess to recapture the true spirit of Abby's House. We were founded on and grounded in the belief that things can be different for women with the help and support of other women.

Perhaps the most powerful change that was occurring within all of us during the 1980s, the years of the unforgivable neglect of urban renewal and of punitive state and federal policies, was expressed in one of the final editions of "A Bright Spot in the City":

"In the midst of this changing season, we received an article whose contents seemed to challenge our energy.

Published by the Boston Foundation, it relates the thoughts and feelings that many shelter providers have about the present state of homelessness. Since each one of us involved with Abby's, whether staffer or supporter, is a shelter provider, we have probably formulated many of the same questions and thoughts. The fear exists that we are helping people to get used to homelessness and to think it's acceptable for a large part of our population to find their housing in shelters. The more that sheltering becomes specialized or institutionalized, the less focus will be put on the lack of affordable permanent housing. Kip Tiernan, founder of Rosie's Place (Boston) articulates the concern very strongly:

'... Which is more ethical? To open a shelter or to create an economic environment in which shelters are not an option? We have unfortunately put ourselves in the position of desperately needing shelters, but creating a world of shelters is different than creating a world of opportunity where people can have their own visions and dreams. I'm convinced that there has been a dangerous accommodation to homelessness, and if we don't stop it now, we will end up with a permanent American underclass for whom shelter providers will be the custodians.'"

Tess continues to point out to all of us, that each homeless guest we welcome is an individual with unique struggles, some of which will not be resolved with a decent home. But, a home is the starting point from which a person can regain control over her destiny. No matter what her personal struggle, we are reminded forcefully that permanent housing is the common denominator for all those who are homeless. It's at this point that I feel the vision for the 1990s was formulated. We were facing the challenge of going beyond shelter. Kip's quote certainly made the point that we do have the capacity to end homelessness and what we need now is the collective will to do just that. In her own quiet way, Tess ended the article with the following reflection and call to action:

"We are familiar with the fruits that a strong collective will can grow. We know that kind of steadfast rootedness that makes Abby's able to operate. Each of us is familiar with the effects that being homeless has on an individual. Make a phone call or write a letter to let your councillors and legislators know about your involvement and ask them what they are doing to encourage availability of affordable housing. Maybe we can begin to make homelessness unacceptable."

Undoubtedly, our hearts were full of new ideas. We could create safe, affordable, decent housing and we could move beyond shelter, taking steps to be part of the solution. What obstacles would lie ahead seemed, at the time, secondary considerations. How we would raise the money to fulfill that dream was a major issue any time the staff gathered. Somehow we bolstered our spirits with the thought that our supporters would back any decision that would be made to improve quality of life. The main discussion revolved around being true to our mission of offering hospitality, of empowering, of recognizing and honoring the dignity of each woman, regardless of her circumstances. There was never a time when discontinuing shelter was an option. Women and their children would need a safety net no matter what efforts Abby's might pursue in ending homelessness for our guests.

PROGRESSIVE POETRY OF STRUGGLE AND STRENGTH

by
Darleen Gadt

Darleen, poet extraordinaire

BORN TO LOVE

I was born to love, to be gentle.
I was born with a tender heart, a benevolent soul.
Love—what I was meant to be; and angel of grace,
Was soon bruised and stabbed, burned, starved and beaten.

The knife was twisted in my gentle heart again and again
with malice and hatred.
Pain turned to fear
fear to anger
anger to rage.
So I simply stopped feeling.

I was born to love
to be gentle as air itself.
Now I live inside myself,
Not able to heal or come out of my shell.
So I hide and cry inside me.

RIGHTS

Every one of us has rights.
A right to be.
But there are those
Who would deny rights
Who would rule over others.
There are those who believe
only they should have rights.

There are those who try
to buy the rights of others.
There are those who believe
they should have rights for making fights.

We are all part of this world
We all have rights.
We just have to remember
SO DO OTHERS.

Untitled

I want to learn, I want to grow.
Both are healthy, this I know.
I want to laugh, I want to cry
Or take the time to watch birds fly.
I must feel content with who I am.
If not, for me, life's all a sham.
So if I ponder, search and seek
Inside myself, way down deep
I find a friend that gives no name.
This friend is best, all for my gain.

Linda, Age 24, Guest

Night

Walking through the night
With the moon shining bright
You've finished the day
And now you're on your way
To start a new day.
The silver coin in the sky,
Is up so very high.
The purple sea so deep and strong;
When you watch it, the night seems long.
Goodnight.

Kenisha, Age 11, Guest

Samples from our Anthology

TWO MORE BY DARLEEN GADT

At Peace

See all the colors
laid down before me
The reds, the blues, the yellows.
All is a blend of artist's hues,
of the magical touch of the artist's hand.

Even the detail of the frame
One can see the care given
And the picture!
It puts me at peace.

The Carribean warmth
A day full of sun and laughter
The people laugh seemingly
flying away.

Their clothes bright
The ocean rippling through
the waves
Is joyful.

Swing and fly in the
Song
One is free here.

The joy of the day.

ABBY'S ANTHOLOGY

A collection of writings from the Guests and Staff at Abby's House.

Summer 1988

By Deidre Britt

Buddy

Pounce!
Whining again
Maybe I'll get a new mouse.

Catitude
I got plenty of that!
What?
No new litter in the box
Hope she brings something back.

Gotta have my share of the bed.
Whatever it is I bat
my paw with it.

Then comes cleaning
I wash my coat-I am
very finicky and neat.

Pounce up to the bed
So I go to sleep
shhh
This is living!

CHAPTER 9 *Hello and Goodbye*

People continue to admire the one on my coat and I've sold everyone I've worn. When I started to sell them, I decided I'd raise $4,000 and then stop. But I surpassed that so fast that I moved to $10,000. But we're almost there, so I'll keep going. My goal is to walk down the street and see everyone with a pin."

A year later when I was interviewed by the same journalist, she aptly concluded the interview on the success of the house pins with the following statement:

> "Many people made the house pin project a success. But it is to Ms. Edinberg, who started it, that Ms. Rafferty hands her highest praise: 'She's been one of our greatest blessings.' "

House pins were just the special means that Abby used to join the Edinberg energy to the mission of the house named in her honor.

Just as we were ending the 1980s on what seemed a high note that nothing could disturb, we received sad and very disturbing news. Our board of directors had met with officials from the Department of Mental Health. Those two staff positions that had been so generously financed by DMH for ten years were suddenly, without warning, eliminated. The reason advanced was a change had been made in DMH priorities. Certainly the need for shelter of the mentally ill was greater than ever. Because no facts to support their sudden shift in priorities were offered to us, the decision remained a mystery. What was clear to all of us was this: we had no intention of joining this systemic denial that women struggling with mental illness no longer needed our services. We would continue to have these women as a priority in our shelter. As recorded in the December 1989 newsletter:

> "That night of our meeting with DMH, each member of our Board moved through varying feelings of frustration and anger. Most of all, we strengthened our resolve all the more to continue to open our doors and to be a safe place for our guests. And safety doesn't come from liv-

When in late 1989, Lois Edinberg arrived at Abby's front door and met Elaine Lamoureux, who graciously gave her a tour of our shelter and explained our mission, I sensed that Abby Kelley Foster's spirit had appeared again, to provide us with an answer about financing future plans for expanded housing and improved services. In Lois' hand was a sample of Lucinda Yates' famous house pin. Lois told Elaine she had been sent our way by long-time friends and advocates, Kathy Hasegawa and Pat Johnson, who represented the Worcester Committee on Housing and Homelessness. Both women knew Abby's could use the money from a house pin fund-raiser. What nobody knew was what had been expected to be $1,000 in house pin sales has, in the past 13 years, resulted in over $250,000.

Lois brought not only her enthusiasm to Abby's House, but she actually began a campaign that definitely appealed to people interested in keeping the issue of shelter and homelessness visible. As Lois said in an interview with Allison K. Jones of the *Telegram and Gazette* on January 18, 1990:

> "One day I went to the El Morocco to eat and I was telling a friend about the pins. These people at another table overheard me and came over and said, 'What are you doing for the homeless?' And they bought some pins.

Paul Grosbeck, Sara Robertson and her sister,
Kathy Hasegawa, mid winter in Hawaii

Lois Edinberg and the House Pins.
She's been one of our greatest blessings.

Susie Sullivan, dedicated to helping women

Houses for the homeless

Pin sales used to support projects for needy here, nationwide

By Allison K. Jones
Staff Reporter

Since Dec. 1, Lois J. Edinberg has convinced 1,700 people to buy homes for the homeless.

No one's going to live in these houses, but dozens of people have received shelter from them, nonetheless.

Mrs. Edinberg's "homes" are depicted on colorful enamel pins that are being sold throughout the country in a grass-roots campaign to raise money for the homeless. The project was started last year by Lucinda Yates, a Portland, Maine, jewelry designer.

SOLD THE MOST

According to Ms. Yates, Mrs. Edinberg has sold more pins than any other person in the country.

"I'm amazed at what this woman has been able to do," said Ms. Yates.

The pins sell for $10, with $4 going to programs for the homeless. Mrs. Edinberg has raised more than $7,000 to be used by Abby's House, a shelter for women on Crown Street, to pay for renovation of its basement. The project created a children's playroom and space for homeless women to socialize and make crafts.

Nationwide, the program has raised an estimated $65,000, with more than 18,000 pins sold, Ms. Yates said. The pins are being sold by roughly 40 organizations nationwide.

Mrs. Edinberg, a dark-haired woman wearing a teal sweater, heavy silver pendant and rings, didn't plan to organize a pin sales campaign. She saw a friend wearing one of the pins and asked for eight to sell to students in a knitting class she teaches.

"I'm a jewelry freak and they're beautiful," she exclaimed.

But before she could deliver them, the pins were snatched up by her daughters and some friends.

ORDERED MORE

So she ordered 100 to sell at a Temple Emanuel craft fair. They were sold in two hours. She ordered 300 and they disappeared in two days. And Mrs. Edinberg decided she was on a roll.

"I went to Strand's Ski Shop to buy skis and someone there liked the one I had on and they told me to come back with my pins to sell them to employees and customers," she said.

"One day I went to the El

Morocco to eat and I was tel friend about the pins. These p at another table overheard m came over and said 'What ar doing for the homeless?' and bought some pins.

"People have admired the on my coat and have asked to them. I've sold every one worn."

When she started to sell th she decided she'd raise $4,000 t stop.

"But I surpassed that so f that I said I'll go to $10,000," said. "But we're almost at th now. I'll keep going.

"People say 'When is it (sale going to stop?' I don't think it My goal now is to walk down t street and see everyone with pin."

Turn to MAKING/Next Page

Elaine Lamoureux, Lois Edinberg, and I look at the pins

ing in a particular neighborhood or attending a certain school. It comes from being in a community of caring people who expect that they can live with each other respectfully and peacefully, and who are committed to working towards that way of life."

As I recall, we were all particularly saddened that elimination of these positions meant the departure of Susie Sullivan, who had begun working at Abby's in 1980, doing the morning, early evening and overnight shifts at the shelter. Susie arrived with her two-year-old daughter, Melanie, and in October of 1982 gave birth to a son, Matthew. The children were an integral part of our community. We can never say enough about this wonderful woman whose dedicated, tolerant and loving presence here continues to be felt in our home. Everything you could ever want to learn about sensitive perseverance and understanding you could learn from Susie. Shortly after her departure from Abby's, Susie began her work as a parent-child support person with the Head Start Program. We still see Susie, who has maintained her connection with Abby's and occasionally does some emergency staffing in the shelter she grew to love. She remains a living example of Adrienne Rich's words: "The most important thing one woman can do for another is to illuminate and expand her sense of actual possibilities."

Susie's Melanie and Matthew with Brenda's Alex (in middle) play in Abby's backyard–1987.

House pins help the homeless
Artist-designed broaches prove to be big sellers

SOUTH PORTLAND (AP) — A South Portland artist's sales of low-priced jewelry in the shape of houses have raised nearly $300,000 to benefit the homeless in 38 states.

The low-priced jewelry designed by Lucinda L. Yates is available from retail outlets as well as non-profit groups, all of which donate 40 percent of the price to community shelters.

Ms. Yates, who previously created high-fashion jewelry, said she came up with the idea for house pins after failing to find volunteer work in the community.

"I wanted to get involved in some capacity, other than working in a soup kitchen. And here I was offering my services but I was getting little or no response," she said.

The colorful cardboard brooches caught the imagination of local residents.

Then, the president of the Women's Council of Realtors in Portland took some of the pins to its national convention in Florida and sales started to spread to other states.

The business gained wider attention as other national groups, including foundations and a college sorority, joined the cause.

"When I wear a house pin, I get stopped by people wanting to know where I got it," said Sister Eileen Reilly of Richmond, Va.

Her church has donated $3,250 so far to the Freedom House shelter through sales of the jewelry. The money is helping start a second shelter for newly employed workers who can't afford the down payment for an apartment, she said.

In Worcester, Mass., Lois J. Edinberg discovered the jewelry when a woman visiting her weekly knitting group wore a pin.

Ms. Edinberg was so intrigued by the idea of buying and wearing designer jewelry for a social cause that she and her husband ordered several hundred.

A year later, they had raised $28,000 for Abby's House, a women's shelter in Worcester. The money is helping fund a daytime program for women and their children.

Next year, a national group will begin selling the pins. The Beta Sigma sorority voted at its Arizona convention to market the pins for its fund-raiser at college campuses in 1991.

So far, 80,000 pins — each one slightly differ- ent — have been sold. In the last three weeks, the company Ms. Yates created to manufacture the brooches has been getting 1,000 new orders a day, she said.

Ms. Yates, her family and several friends make the pins at her South Portland office. She also employs several home-based workers for a total work force of 25 people.

The 35-year-old Portland native said she is just as surprised as anyone at the popularity of her pins. "Pretty soon we'll have to have 18-wheelers come in here to pick up all the orders," she said.

In 1989, Yates formed a private company, Lucinda Inc., that sells the pins for $6 each to non-profit organizations. Buyers must first sign a contract promising to resell the jewelry for $10.

They recoup their original cost and turn the rest of the money over to homeless shelters.

LUCINDA YATES of South Portland displays house-shaped pins she has designed, the sale of which aids the homeless. (AP Photo)

Ann Marie Shea, a woman of will herself

It's 15 years for Abby House

FOR SOME Abby House founders, this Friday (4/5) night's anniversary celebrations will be an occasion for pride and an occasion for sadness.

The pride is in setting up a shelter for women that had endured all these years. The sadness, says director Tess Sneesby, is that the shelter is still needed.

"The founders of Abby's orginally had in mind five years of existence. They thought in five years there probably wouldn't be a need for a shelter. They have mixed feelings," says Sneesby. "It's too bad we have to be here in a sense.

"On the other hand, we can celebrate the fact that so many women have been helped. Between the shelter, day program and food pantry, we've had close to 20,000 who have used the services. That way we can certainly celebrate. This has been a way for women to get a sense of themselves and get empowered."

Konnie brought greetings from the City

Angela - The Valiant Woman

CHAPTER 10 *True Women of Will*

The elimination of the staff position funded by the Department of Mental Health meant that Elaine, in order to keep her salary, would be transferred to Worcester State Hospital. For several months, Abby's suffered her absence, while Elaine trained at the State Hospital for work that she didn't really like. Finally, in mid-March 1990, the board of directors took another major financial risk and hired Elaine back. She still continues to amaze all of us with her incomparable skills of advocacy and empowering. This hiring was certainly something made possible by the miraculous marketing of Lucinda's house pins. It made sense to me that when Lois first met Elaine at Abby's front door, the spirit of Abby Kelley Foster had already pre-determined these events and subsequent resolutions. In November of 1991, Lois Edinberg joined our staff as the first development coordinator.

So, as a community, we faced the new decade with courage, reciting in unison the strong poem from J. Ruth Gendler's, *The Book of Qualities*:

> "Courage has roots. She sleeps
> on a futon on the floor and lives
> close to the ground. Courage looks
> you straight in the eye. She is not
> impressed with powertrippers and she
> knows first aid. Courage is not afraid
> to weep and she is not afraid to pray,
> even when she is not sure who she
> is praying to. When she walks,
> it is clear that she has made the
> journey from loneliness to solitude.
> The people who told me she is stern
> were not lying; they just forgot to
> mention that she is kind."

Our last newsletter of 1990 repeated the call to courage in its closing paragraph:

> "There was always a hope that the day would come when there would no longer be a need for our organization. We have been struggling with the fear that our guests are expressing about the hard times ahead, as well as with the fear that Abby's will not have the financial resources to continue offering shelter, food, clothing, advocacy and support services to our guests. It takes COURAGE to face the darkness of fear. And, it takes COURAGE to move ahead in the light of faith, faith in ourselves, our guests, in each other."

And, in the 1990s there were so many events that would challenge our collective spirit, but we found the courage to move ahead. The first major hurdle was to plan for our 15th anniversary. It was hard to imagine that we had been at this work for 15 years and the prospects still remained bleak for women and their children. Another committee was formed to highlight Abby's commitment to them, but also to find someone who could, in a powerful way, show these guests as women of will. Ann Marie Shea, of the Theatre Department of Worcester State College, suggested that we try to enlist the services of the famous Tina Packer, founder of Shakespeare and Company in Lenox, who had crafted a performance following the progression of women characters in Shakespeare's plays. We didn't want to contact Tina until we had seen her do the performance. So in August of 1990, Tess, Elaine, Carol Burns and I drove to Lenox to attend a Sunday matinee performance of "Women of Will." It was the most powerful performance of women's strengths any one of us had ever seen. Tina Packer and her male counterpart interacted beautifully. We came away starstruck and convinced this performance would be just perfect for our 15th year. We quickly negotiated with Ms. Packer and she agreed to come to Worcester's Mechanics Hall to perform. We were ecstatic!

About a month prior to the performance, which had been booked for April 5, 1991, a phone call from Tina stirred up some concern. Her male partner would not be able to join her for the performance. However, Tina assured me that she would make the necessary adjustments to successfully perform "Women of Will." I thought nothing was impossible for this woman to do and so I buried my concern and only now and then wondered how she could rearrange a play written for two to become a one-woman performance.

Hindsight certainly informed me that my deepest concerns were real. The night was a glorious one. Washburn Hall was filled with staff, supporters and friends of Abby's House who had gathered to celebrate with us. I greeted everyone; City Councillor Konstantina "Konnie" Lukes brought the greetings of the city of Worcester, but the pièce de résistance was Angela Dorenkamp, Professor of English and Women's Studies at Assumption College and long-time friend of Abby's, who delivered this magnificent tribute:

> "When I was asked to say a few words here tonight to mark this auspicious occasion, the first thought that came to mind was the passage from Proverbs about the valiant woman whose price is above that of rubies. It seemed to me that term described the women who began Abby's House, all those who helped its continuance and those who were valiant enough to seek its aid and protection. When I looked at the passage, however, I knew that some alterations would have to be made. So I found myself coming up against the tradition of biblical exegesis, which led me, not to Abby Kelley Foster, but to an equally great foremother, Elizabeth Cady Stanton.

> In 1895, Stanton issued "The Woman's Bible," a series of commentaries on biblical texts which referred to women or unnecessarily excluded them. She realized the opposition which her untutored attempt to deal with these matters would arouse. In her introduction, in fact, she wrote something which sounds eerily contemporary:

> *'Others say it is not politic to rouse religious opposition. This much-lauded policy is but another word for cowardice. How can woman's position be changed from that of a subordinate to an equal, without opposition, without the broadest discussion of all the questions involved in her present degradation? For so far-reaching and momentous a reform as her complete independence, an entire revolution in all existing institutions is inevitable.'*

> Well, the purpose of my revision of the Biblical passage is not as radical as that of Stanton by any means. Nevertheless, I want to place us briefly and tremblingly on this path built by women, who, like Sojourner Truth, were able to quote the Bible at some length. Truth once reprimanded a gentleman who called upon the gospels to support women's inequality by reminding him that Christ was born of God and a woman, so man had nothing to do with it. In that spirit, let us offer this re-working of the valiant woman in honor of all the women of Abby's House."

The Valiant Women

We have found the valiant women whose price is far above rubies.

The hearts of their sisters safely trust in them, and they enrich each other;

They will do good and not evil all the days of their lives.

They provide food and shelter both day and night, working with their hands and hearts and minds.

They seek to feed the hungry, obtaining food from afar;

They rise while it is yet night and give meals to their guests.

They consider a building and get it; with the fruit of
their hands, they plant a garden.

They gird their loins with the strength of virtuous volunteers.

They perceive that their work is good, that despair is
seeded with hope.

They lay their hands to grant writing and their guests
hold the fruit of that effort;

They stretch out their hand to the poor, yea, they reach
forth their hands to the needy.

They are not afraid of the cold for their household; for
all their household are clothed by the Thrift Store.

They seek coverings and quilts; their talents are without
measure;

They are known in the city, where they sit down with the
powerful.

They gather fine house pins and sell them to buy comfort for their sisters.

Strength and hope lead them to minister to those of
weakened resolve and absent hope.

They open their mouths with wisdom; and in their
tongues is the law of kindness.

They care about their household and eat not the bread
of idleness;

Their sisters rise up and call them blessed; their brothers,
too, and they praise them in turn.

Many daughters have survived and have lived virtuously,
but those who have been mistreated and those who love
them shall be praised!

Give them the fruit of our hands; and let their own
works praise them in the city.

Angela's presentation, in my opinion, proved to be *the* highlight of that Anniversary night. The audience responded with
applause and expressions of deep appreciation. Then, the lights
dimmed and we knew "Women of Will" was about to begin in
the Great Hall.

How did the one-woman performance go? It certainly wasn't
what we had seen in Lenox last summer. Without the second
performer, it was a monologue, which failed as an art form to
achieve the powerful message of women's ability to face head on
the challenges of the male antagonist. Tina seemed to be ram-
bling, unable to bring it all to a close. I was hoping at some
point there would be a point to it all! Two women next to me
had fallen asleep. There was a growing sense of audience rest-
lessness. Oh, Tina Packer proved she knew Shakespeare's
women, but there was little evidence she had performed
"Women of Will" with the powerful gusto I had previously witnessed. The piece absolutely needed a second person to achieve
the desired effect. I can't even begin to describe how embarrassed I felt, but, as they say on Broadway, the show must go on.
To avoid an unpleasant confrontation, I chose to write to Ms.
Packer after the fact. Elaine couldn't wait. She told her directly that we had paid for one thing and received another. So, please
give us our money back! Of course, *that* didn't happen. Since
then, I concluded that when Elaine faced Tina and asked for a
return of Abby's money, I *had* witnessed Women of Will, only
this time there was no male performer, no audience, no applause,
just truth speaking to power. Richard Duckett's review of the
performance was exceedingly kind.

Having survived the evening, Abby's women of will moved
forward into the '90s with energy and conviction. We had, after
all, provided services to over 20,000 guests in those first 15 years
and the organization was expanding and envisioning new directions. By mid 1991, we had done some shifting and some hiring: Tess had become the new executive director, Elaine the
coordinator of support services, Judie Cofsky had replaced me as
the third coordinator of the Day Center, and Hilda Chasse of the
Little Franciscan Sisters was welcomed as the new house manager. As for myself, having passed through most of the "jobs" that
had needed doing, I became the contact with the donors, the
special projects person, the correspondent, and was christened
with the title "founder." I continue to envision myself as a public relations person of the organization. This was certainly a year
of new and old faces adjusting and re-adjusting. It was the best
of times and the worst of times, especially if you found change
difficult. Abby's was growing up very quickly and it seemed that

Elizabeth Stanton's home in Seneca Falls

ENTERTAINMENT

'Women of Will' is enjoyable but needs more Shakespeare

By Richard Duckett
Telegram & Gazette Reviewer

Review

Tina Packer tried to pack quite a lot in during her presentation of "Women of Will" at Mechanics Hall last night.

Included were observations on the early, middle and late phases of William Shakespeare's development as a playwright from the perspective of his depiction of women; a recounting of the Psyche/Eros myth as a springboard to exploring feminine attributes in the human psyche; a recounting of Packer's progression from a rebellious teenager in her native England to fulfillment here as artistic director of Shakespeare & Company in Lenox; and some actual readings from Shakespeare's plays.

Phew!

But if the quick ticking of the clock might make a case for Packer's trimming the material, she still came across as a thoroughly likable, intelligent and agreeably earthy guide to the subjects under discussion.

And it certainly held the interest of the approximately 600 on hand for what was a benefit performance celebrating the 15th anniversary of Abby's House — a shelter for homeless women and their children.

Packer spoke in an engaging way, holding forth informatively and amusingly. But her rendition of speeches written by Shakespeare was even better. Particularly impressive was her reading of Queen Margaret's acidic comments to the rebellious but captured Duke of York in "Henry VI."

The only pity was that there wasn't enough [...] of her prese[...] offer an an[...] what she wa[...] world, and [...] Psyche/Eros [...] as offering th[...] tionships) an[...] the poetry [...] sometimes e[...] ground.

Packer said[...] feminine ele[...] gether so th[...] can see." He[...] place, but a[...] speare would[...] flow bolder.

Judie Cofsky begins her duties at Day Center

Women welcome Judie C.

Hilda Chasse, a woman of all trades

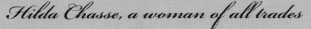

It's Official!

Angie coming down Day Center aisle in Judie's dress

Orlando places ring on Angie's finger

overnight we had become an organization requiring a great deal more structure. It was hard for me not to be doing *everything* as had been my self-appointed role for so many years. Although I welcomed new people with a genuine warmth, the division of labor that such welcoming demands was not easy for the "founder" who, of course, knew just how everyone's labor should not only be divided, but done! The next few years gave me many opportunities to learn painful, but invaluable, lessons in letting go. I will always think of Abby's House as a mother thinks of her child. That says it all.

This was also the year that an exciting event occurred in the Day Center—the wedding of Angie LeBlanc and Orlando Rodriquez. At that time, I was a Justice of the Peace, and Angie was a daily guest in the Day Center. She and Orlando had five children, but had never been officially joined in marriage. So, on a very hot summer day, Angie and Orlando, with their children as attendants and ring bearers, were joined in a civil ceremony. Angie looked beautiful, wearing one of Judie Cofsky's stylish dresses. Marie, Judie's daughter, provided the decorations; Elaine, Judie and Edie Galindo provided the Spanish delicacies and the buffet luncheon. I was not certain they would live happily ever after, but no one thought about it that festive July afternoon.

Volunteers Anne Humes and Ann Hedge, both of the Day Center, initiated a new project, announced in the September newsletter:

Dear Friends,

"Abby's By Day is looking forward to putting together an ethnic cookbook. You can help by sharing your favorite recipe with us. As you know, Abby's is extremely beneficial to our community, and in order to continue to grow, we need your support. Your participation in this fundraiser will allow our dreams of more activities to become a reality. Could you look up your favorite dishes and send them to us? We are also forming a cookbook committee. Are you interested?"

But, for one reason or another, the cookbook never materialized until 1996, our 20th anniversary year and it was certainly worth the wait.

19 Crown Street, going beyond shelter

Carol Burns

Annette Bleau

Bev Plucinski

Julie, Tess, Judy, Elaine, Eva

Judie C., Tom and Ted

CHAPTER 11 *Progress, Pain and Persistence*

eanwhile, the vision we had for going beyond shelter was taking shape. The previous December, a fire had pretty much ruined the old boarding house at 19 Crown Street. The house had been abandoned, but was being used for drug deals and probably prostitution. A deal had been botched, apparently, and in retaliation the house was torched. It left us with a terrible mess next door, but with hope in our hearts that the "mess" could be transformed into our first supportive housing unit. In our November 1991 newsletter, the good news became public information:

> "Abby's has recently been presented with an opportunity! We have learned that the rooming house next door to us (19 Crown Street) may be available to purchase. With 14 single rooms and two 1-bedroom apartments, we see this as a chance to add a permanent and long-term housing component to our work here. We can already envision the supportive living community that will evolve. We can even see the garden and picnic tables in the backyard. Our early research reveals the great challenge of raising the funds for both acquisition and rehab; it also reveals the great interest and excitement that exists for this project."

And, this was just the beginning. Lois Edinberg had arrived just in time. Her first task was to initiate a fundraising campaign to make 19 Crown Street a reality for Abby's. With enthusiasm,

Lois gave unbelievable energy to this project—no easy task in what we recognized as challenging economic times. The project was designed and planned by Judie Cofsky, Carol Burns, Eva Engel, Annette Bleau, our faithful volunteer bookkeeper, Bev Plucinski, Julie Komenos and Tess Sneesby. Within a short period of time, the committee with board approval, hired Ted Szkoda as project manager, enlisted the aid and expertise of Judy Schlosser, Tom Hand and Lorraine Fletcher of the Worcester Housing Partnership, Inc. (now known as Worcester Community Housing Resources, Inc.) and the legal eagles, Sandra Landau and Kathleen O'Connor. In March of 1992, a grant from the Federal Affordable Housing Program through Flagship Bank gave a significant boost towards rehabilitating the vacant building. We received $85,000 for the project and we remain grateful for the presence of former Flagship president, Donald McGowan, and vice president, Tom Burr who believed in our vision and stood with us as we moved beyond shelter.

An initial letter to our supporters, donors and staffers proved extremely successful. They *would* help Abby's raise the remaining $265,000 needed to complete the project. One letter that came from a couple who has been actively involved in helping the community for over 50 years said:

> "You know that cracked brick in the northwest corner of 19 Crown Street? Well, we'd like to invest in it ... and if our names were Getty or Trump, we'd invest in all your old cracked bricks!"

Another letter from a supporter whose sensitivity touched us all said:

> "I recently observed the 25th anniversary of my mother's death. I felt that I wanted to mark her passing in some meaningful way. Your newsletter provided the answer! The home at 19 Crown Street seems like the perfect next step."

Our enthusiasm continued to be fueled by letters and donations from far and near. Adding themselves to our supporters in this cause were the students of Tatnuck Magnet School. Principal Cheryl McKeon and teachers, especially Maryanne

2 TELEGRAM & GAZETTE, SATURDAY, MAY 30, 1992

STEVE LANAVA

Erin Dolan, left, and Meaghan O'Connell, anxiously await their duties as masters of cermonies at yesterday's Abby's Day program.

Pupils adopt Abby's House

Homeless people on the street
Go to Abby's House where folks are sweet.
They give you lots of care.
Nice people work there.

By Ashley Park, Grade 3, Tatnuck Magnet School

By George B. Griffin
Staff Reporter

Annette Rafferty fought back tears yesterday as Tatnuck Magnet School students presented her with a check for $230.57 and poems and stories they wrote about Abby's House.

Rafferty, who founded Abby's House, a shelter for homeless women and children, said she was overwhelmed by the outpouring of support and gifts from the children.

The gifts and poems were presented at the end of a program yesterday in Christ the King Church, 1052 Pleasant St. The program was the culmination of the school's public service project.

Nearly 380 children in kindergarten through sixth grade recited original poems and stories and sang special songs for the event.

Paula Harrity, coordinator of community learning programs for Worcester schools, said every Worcester school each year does a community service project as part of its regular curriculum.

The Tatnuck Magnet School, 1083 Pleasant St., adopted Abby's House as this year's project, she said.

During April and May, students at the school designed posters, did research, wrote stories, reports and poems, and helped collect household items to donate to the shelter. Students also raised money for the shelter by selling snacks, flowers and pussy willows.

The spring issue of Tatnuck Toucan Talk, the school's literary newspaper, was devoted to the children's poems and stories about Abby's House.

Abby's House is named in honor of Abigail Kelley Foster, an abolitionist and women's rights activist who grew up in Worcester in the 1800s.

A set back?

The school children help out

52A (Insert)

Adding themselves to our supporters in this cause were the students of Tatnuck Magnet School. Under the guidance of Principal Cheryl McKeon and teachers, especially Maryanne Gray, the students undertook an project that would integrate community service and curriculum. They decided to adopt Abby's House and to sell snacks at lunch time (pussy willows and flowers) for the benefit of our families. For two months, they designed posters, wrote stories and reports and helped collect practical household items. On Ma y 29, 1992, the school gathered at an assembly where poetry was read and special songs sung and presentations were made. This was a fabulous finish to eight weeks of a concentrated effort on behalf of the homeless. Some of the "original" poetry written for the occasion appeared in our Summer newsletter:

"The Homeless"
(Kristin Keane, Gr. 6)

The homeless are people
not things:
They can't be brushed off
to the side of the street.
They have feeling and
dreams.
People give them dirty
looks.
Sometimes people can be
so cruel.
You never know maybe in a
year or two
You could become
homeless yourself;
So remember the dirty
looks!"

"Abby's House"
(Andrew Chase, Gr. 3)

There was a house
Down by the lane
Abby's House, yeah
that's the name.
They take the
homeless from the
street
And give them a
chance so they won't
be beat.

"Abby's House"
(Angela Diaz, Gr. 4)

We lived at Abby's House
because we had a fire. My
mom, my brother and I got
in the car and we went to
Abby's. We knocked on the
door and they let us in. We
stayed at Abby's for six
weeks. Then my mom got a
job at a school.

"Abby's House"
(Ashley Park, Gr. 3)

Homeless people on the
street Go to Abby's House
where folks are sweet.
They give you lots of care.
Nice people work there.

"A Good Thing"
(Michael Goldman, Gr. 1)

In hebrew, a good
thing is called a
mitzvah. A good deed
is when you hold the
door or when you
help people in many
ways. On Crown St.
there is a place where
they help people. We
give food to Abby's
House.

"Abby's House"
(Elizabeth Haras, Gr. 5)

When people are
homeless it's sad. So
people at Abby's
House make them
glad. They bring their
children along and
learn some happy
songs.
They will learn to
depend on
themselves instead of
others for help.
Abby's House is a
great place for any
person or race.

DATEBOOK, FEBRUARY 23, 1992 17

BOOKS *A splended biography of a local treasure*

Worcester's tireless abolitionist, Abby Kelley

ABBY KELLEY AND THE POLITICS OF ANTISLAVERY
By Dorothy Sterling
W.W. Norton & Company, 436 pp., $22.95.
Reviewed by Albert B. Southwick

Any list of the most notable American women of the 19th century will include the usual names – Susan B. Anthony, Lucretia Mott, Elizabeth Cady Stanton, Lucy Stone and, possibly, Victoria Woodhull. But many people will omit Abby Kelley, perhaps the most outstanding of them all.

Although we in Worcester are somewhat familiar with her, thanks largely to the bicentennial pamphlet by Nancy H. Burkett, Abby Kelley's reputation has long been overshadowed by others.

This splendid new biography should help revive interest in a remarkable woman who, for more than 40 years, was a powerful force for the rights of blacks and for women. Her home, now known as Liberty Farm, still stands on Mower Street, a national historic landmark. It once was a stop on the Underground Railroad, where fleeing slaves were surreptitiously housed and fed on their long journey to Canada and freedom.

Abby Kelley, born in Pelham in 1811, raised in Worcester on a farm near Newton Square, became converted to the cause of Abolition when she was a schoolteacher in Lynn. By the age of 30, she already was a noted speaker on the evils of slavery. But her growing fame led to a split in the anti-slavery movement, when male abolitionists objected to giving female abolitionists equal rights and recognition. In 1840, when William Lloyd Garrison appointed her to the steering committee of the American Anti-Slavery Society, the organization split.

The women's rights issue bedeviled the Abolition movement for the next 20 years, even though Abby Kelley was the most effective speaker and fund-raiser in the field. She traveled thousands of miles, from Maine to Michigan, by way of stagecoach, wagon, canal boat and, later, railroad to spread the word to audiences sometimes friendly, but often hostile. On occasion, she traveled with other lecturers, including the former slave, Frederick Douglass. It was one of the most remarkable crusades for a principle that this country has ever seen.

Sterling does a superb job in describing the politics of Abolition. She has written several books on the era and knows the material

Abby Kelley

like the back of her hand. The anti-slavery movement included, on one hand, conservatives who wanted to send blacks back to Africa, and on the other, radicals like Garrison, who proclaimed "No Union With Slaveholders" and burned the Constitution at a public rally in Framingham.

Abby Kelley was a Garrisonian all the way. Not for her any compromises, like the Liberty Party of 1840, or the Free Soil Party of 1844. She saw such attempts to use the political system as a cop-out, an admission that the U.S. government that accepted slavery was a legitimate one. She split with Garrison only after he endorsed the new Republican Party as a possible solution to the slavery issue.

Marriage of Devotion

In 1845, Abby married Stephen Foster, another dedicated Abolitionist noted for his fevered rhetoric and implacable stands. Because the local church refused to condemn slavery, he called the clergy "thieves, adulterers, man stealers, pirates and murderers... ." He frequently interrupted church services with his denunciations. Although he added spice to many a meeting, he was less effective than Abby in opening people's minds to the abomination of slavery. But theirs was a marriage of devotion. After their daughter, Alla, was born, Stephen stayed home to tend the farm on Mower Street, while Abby continued her campaigns across the North.

sapped. Nevertheless, she continued to be involved in the struggle for women's rights, temperance and the proper treatment of former slaves in the South.

Last Protest

The Fosters' last social protest came in 1872, when they refused to pay the property tax on their Mower Street place, on the grounds that Abby was illegally being denied the right to vote. Much to their disgust, the Worcester tax collector refused to take action for more than a year. When a public auction was finally held, the property was sold to a bidder for $100. That bidder reneged on his bid when Stephen Foster angrily accosted him and declared that he would not move without a fight. The issue was finally settled in 1880, when the Fosters paid the back taxes. By then, Stephen was "frail and broken," according to Garrison. He died the next year.

Abby lived on until 1887. She had sold the farm and had been living with a relative at 100 Chat-

SUNDAY TELEGRAM, NOVEMBER 22, 1992 B1

Volunteers shine on shelter work

Continued From Page B1

renovations using volunteers and donated materials. The plumber and electrician get paid, but everybody else is here as a volunteer."

The volunteers filled the house inside and out, carrying supplies and trash in criss-cross paths, sawing, painting, nailing, cleaning and doing yard work while talking and laughing.

It all made sense to the volunteers in charge. Coordinating the work ahead of time and getting it to flow smoothly was one of the many feats accomplished by Worcester Shines! during its six weeks of planning. A complicated system of teams – safety, errand-runners, clean-up and numerous others – were kept in contact by walkie-talkies and note runners in addition to steady shouting back and forth.

"Those are the logistics," said Van Batenburg after explaining the system. "As far as the spirit, I think you can feel it."

'SPIRIT OF SERVICE'

"We did our own fund-raising separately from Abby's House, and got materials donated from a whole list of places, even down to feeding the volunteers," Parker said. "The whole point of our doing this is to bring the spirit of community service to all who volunteer and to make this kind of work more commonplace in people's lives."

Several Abby's House staff members dropped by to watch the work during the day, but no residents were on hand. In preparation for the project, the last shelter resident had left by Friday morning, Chasse said. Women in need would be welcome after the volunteers left, she said.

"It's absolutely incredible to see the outpouring of volunteers who are here because they want to be here. The best thing they did today was bring people together – people working together in harmony, some of them total strangers," said Abby's House guest advocate Elaine Lamoureux of Worcester.

Volunteers, dozens of whom showed up unexpectedly, were registered and assigned duties throughout the day.

"They came not just from Worcester but from surrounding towns and from Boston, New Hampshire, the Springfield area" and elsewhere, Parker said.

Yesterday's project, managed by Joseph LaRosa of LaRosa Conractors Inc. in Marshfield Hills, was the second for Worcester Shines! Last November, the group renovated Belmont Nursing Home.

Van Batenburg said the organization will probably undertake a new daylong project each November.

A tip of the hat

... to the Tatnuck Magnet School students who went the extra steps to support Abby's House, a shelter for homeless women and children. The 300 students from kindergarten through sixth grade studied the Abby's House mission and wrote stories and poems dedicated to the shelter and those who live there temporarily. They also raised money and donated useful articles. As a community service project and learning experience this was a moving example of those who care.

Worcester Shines

WEDNESDAY, NOVEMBER 11, 1992
TELEGRAM & GAZETTE

James Dempsey

An empty shelter, a baby's cry

When client advocate Sharon Walsh arrived at work at the Public Inebriate Program shelter a couple of Mondays ago, above the general hubbub of the clients eating breakfast and getting ready to leave she heard something she had never heard there before – a baby crying. "I thought I must be imagining things," she said.

Like a number of the guests at PIP, the baby and her mother were there because they had been evicted. The difference was that Andrea Farrow and her 10-month-old daughter, Bryanna, had been ejected, along with a number of other women, from a shelter for homeless women and children.

The dismissal of the women from Abby's House on Crown Street was on Sunday, Oct. 25. According to Farrow and another of the women, Nancy Hamilton, a total of nine women and two babies were dismissed. They said their eviction came without warning and was a sort of rough justice administered to everyone because a few women had broken rules. Tess Sneesby, director of Abby's, disagreed. She said all the women dismissed broke the shelter's rules and were warned. She wouldn't give a number other than "quite a few," but said fewer than nine were terminated.

NOT EQUIPPED FOR BABIES

The women went off in separate directions. Farrow and her baby and Nancy Hamilton, who is three months pregnant, ended up at PIP. "The mother arrived with no money, no formula and no diapers," said Buddy Brousseau, director of administrative services. "The staff called every family shelter we know, and were told no

I guess not.

Homeless families need services

T+G 12/10/92

A recent column by Jim Dempsey in the Telegram & Gazette highlighted one of the many problems faced by homeless families and those who work to help them.

Homelessness is a complex and growing problem in Worcester and throughout this country. Those families who find themselves without security of their own home deserve to be treated compassionately.

Homelessness does not free persons from acting responsibly and with accountability for their behavior. At the same time shelters such as Abby's House have the responsibility to ensure the safety and confidentiality of their guests.

These two issues apparently came into conflict recently at Abby's House. The staff, in order to ensure the safety of others, asked several women to leave. Abby's has been delivering quality services to homeless women and children in Worcester for the past 16 years. We are confident that this decision was a painful but necessary one.

A further problem that this incident points out is the need for a variety of services on a 24-hour emergency basis, such as counseling, medical services, child care etc. to meet the unique needs of homeless families.

JAMES F. MURPHY
Director
Homeless Outreach and Advocacy Program
Worcester

B6 TELEGRAM & GAZETTE, THURSDAY, NOVEMBER 19, 1992

Volunteers to shape up Abby's House

By Maria Bunnewith
Correspondent

WORCESTER – Volunteers from all over the community will be rising with the sun at 6:38 a.m. Saturday to put in a full day of hammering, sawing, painting and raking at Abby's House, a shelter for battered and homeless women and their children.

A community service group called Worcester Shines! is organizing the project, which will include building an office, painting walls and doors, insulating a garage for food storage, replacing a suspended ceiling, painting the front porch, and working in the yard at Abby's House.

Craig Van Batenburg, founder of Worcester Shines!, said the group's philosophy is that community service should be a way of life. "We do it for fun, because it's a great thing to do," he said.

SISTER HILDA

Van Batenburg stressed that the choice of Abby's House for its project did not come about because it was more worthy than any other charitable organization in need, it was rather the influence of Sister Hilda, a volunteer at Abby's House.

"We fell in love with Sister Hilda and she with us," he said. "The whole project is based on relationships. It's not a project FOR the house, it's a project WITH the house."

Worcester Shines! was founded last year and did its first renovation project at Belmont Nursing Home last November. Van Batenburg said that $25,000 worth of work was done in 10 hours by about 200 volunteers.

Joseph LaRosa of LaRosa Contractors Inc., who volunteered at last year's project, has been chosen by the group as this year's project manager. He is a full-service general contractor and builder/remodeler in Marshfield Hills. LaRosa will lend tools and equipment to the project and bring along members of his staff.

Rosa LaRosa, who owns the company with her husband, said they think this is a particularly worthwhile project. "Why does he (Joseph) do it? Because he has the opportunity to," she said.

Abby's House, which is run on grants and donations, has been providing refuge for homeless or battered women and their children for the past 16 years.

Project volunteers are asked to bring paint brushes, gloves, plastic covers, window cleaner, paper towels, rags, hammers, carpentry tools, rakes, trash bags, brooms, small ladders and energy with them. Work will continue until sundown, and, according to members of Worcester Shines, "fun will be provided!"

Contributions for project supplies and the operation of Abby's House can be sent to Abby's House, 23 Crown St., Worcester, 01602. For more information, contact project leaders Craig Van Batenburg at 753-2431 (days) or 852-7840 (home), or Joan Parker 869-6703, or Sister Hilda at 756-5486.

Support continued to pour in.

Gray, provided the needed guidance and the students undertook a project that integrated community service and curriculum. They decided to adopt Abby's House and to sell pussy willows and flowers and snacks at lunchtime for the benefit of our families. For two months, they designed posters, wrote stories and reports and helped collect practical household items. On May 29, 1992, the school gathered at an assembly. Students read poetry, sang songs and made presentations. This was a fabulous finish to eight weeks of a concentrated effort on behalf of the homeless. Some of the original poetry written for the occasion appeared in our summer newsletter.

We felt confident that we would reach our goal. Abby's was well on its way to providing permanent housing for some women so they won't have to pick up their valuables in shopping bags and carry them around from place to place—"from bus stop to all night cafeterias, from phone booths to libraries, to alleys, to emergency wards, to yet another shelter." (Kip Tiernan, "The Gleaners" Newsletter, 1984). And Kip reminded us that permanent housing would mean never having to ask: "Have you got a bed for me tonight?"

By coincidence that same year, Dorothy Sterling published her new book, *Ahead of Her Time: Abby Kelley and the Politics of Anti-Slavery*. It brought unexpected attention to the wonderful woman after whom we had named the shelter and in another stroke of good fortune, it was splendidly reviewed by our friend Albert Southwick. Schools, civic groups, churches, and individuals joined us in the effort to restore 19 Crown Street.

We were enjoying the progress and the publicity, when, out of the blue, an incident in the shelter that should never have been made public, appeared in the November 11th Jim Dempsey column in the *Telegram and Gazette*. The headline was inflammatory, the contents one-sided, provided by two former guests who had presented an inaccurate report. Mr. Dempsey had given us an opportunity to present "our side of the story." But, we were not able to break the sacred rule of confidentiality:

> "Our policy is this: we don't talk about our guests, past, present or future ... the bottom line is the house rules were broken and when that happens, people are terminated. We try to keep a safe space here."

This couldn't have happened at a worse time: solicitation for the new house was well underway. We had planned fundraisers for the future and Worcester Shines, an organization of volunteers, was about to announce its intent to shape up the shelter and was asking for contributions of project supplies and bodies to do the necessary work. We were very upset by the betrayal of the two women who broke the rules in a very serious manner and then chose to turn their anger on the shelter providers. Of course, we were more upset that a respected journalist decided to run a story, the whole truth of which could not be spoken. I guess an understanding of the need to protect all the women in a homeless shelter didn't seem as important as a sensational headline: "An Empty Shelter, A Baby's Cry."

Well, Abby's House did survive the crisis, thanks to friends like Jim Murphy (the former Director of the Homeless Outreach and Advocacy Program or HOAP) who wrote a strong letter of support on our behalf. The letter reenforced the difficulty of delivering quality and safe services to homeless women and their children. In spite of the unfortunate publicity, Worcester Shines was completely successful in its efforts to spruce up the shelter. Nearly 200 volunteers showed up at 6:30 in the morning of November 21st and by sundown, the face of Abby's original building was lifted! Sister Hilda, our house manager, was, in her own words, "on cloud nine." The work done was amazing to behold: there was new lighting, a dropped ceiling and fresh paint everywhere. They created new office space, the doors were insulated and the food pantry space in the garage was expanded. Leaders Craig Van Batenburg and Joan Parker, along with the dedicated volunteers, gave us more than we had anticipated. They restored our somewhat shattered spirits and provided the needed push forward in the cause of standing with our guests through thick and thin. The month of November, a time when Mother Nature's summer beauty slowly dies, proved to be a time of death, dying and coming back to a stronger sense of our life in the community. The integrity of the organization was, and always will be, intact. Anyone who followed the 1992 fall publicity of Abby's House was forever impressed with the price one pays to say nothing. It was a powerful message to guests of Abby's that clearly stated: You can say what you want—but no matter the circumstances, confidentiality is our policy and always will be as long as our doors are open. By the beginning of

December, we were all singing the lines from the Nova Scotian singer, Rita McNeil's song, "Everybody":

"Everybody needs to know a little peace
A little luck when the morning comes.
Now, you will meet on your way
The hands that keep and the ones that take.
But just remember in the heart
There is light and there is dark.
All of this will come to you
As you see and as you do...."

Salons That Care ...

& Dinner Fashion Show

to benefit abused women
and children, through
Abby's House

Thurs., Nov. 5, 1992
Marriott Hotel
Worcester

5:30 cocktails
6:30 dinner

SALONS THAT CARE

. GIL'S FAMILY CARE, HUDSON

. PAUL CONZO HAIR AND SKIN, WORCESTER

. RUSSELL BLAINE SALON LTD., AUBURN

. SALON ESTIQUE, WORCESTER

. STREAKS HAIR DESIGN, WORCESTER

Under wraps *Thursday, Dec. 17, 1992*

CHRIS CHRISTO

WORCESTER — Lisa Hastings, left, and Sandra MacIntyre prepare to bring packages into Abby's House, the shelter for women, yesterday. The gift-wrapped packages contain personal care items for women and were prepared by members of the Women in Development organization.

Elks raise funds for homeless shelter

WORCESTER — More than 100 people danced the night away last night at the Worcester Elks Club to raise money for Abby's House, a shelter for homeless women and children.

Chairman Lisa Todd said by the time the money is counted, they expect to raise $1,000 for Abby's House. The ball, sponsored by the Emblem Club, was held at the Elks Lodge, 233 Mill St. The money came from sales of tickets, special pins and a number of raffles conducted at the ball.

CHAPTER 12

Is Not Now the Accepted Time?

On March 8, 1993, Abby's was ready to announce the opening of the campaign for the Crown Street home. The committee had specifically selected March 8th since it was International Women's Day and in her address to the press assembled in our Day Center, Tess made the connection:

"We open our campaign on International Women's Day because this place, named after Abby Kelley Foster, came about because women across race and class, from all around Worcester County worked hard to raise the money to open and to operate it and to interest others in staffing and supporting Abby's to keep it going and growing. Today, 17 years later, the energy put into this amazing effort bears new fruit in symbolically breaking ground for a permanent home. This dream of ours is expressed in the words of a former guest of our shelter:

'Abby, if I never see your doorstep again, or a bench or a sidewalk; if I stop being homeless it'll be a miracle. There is something called home, and it ain't the streets. It's a place just special for you. Maybe someday I'll have my own special place I can call home.'"

The next speaker was Judie Cofsky who had assumed the position of housing coordinator at 19 Crown Street. (Judie's job as Day Center coordinator was now in the hands of Holy Cross graduate Karen Staropoli and Terri Griffin, an intern from Salem State.) Judie proceeded to outline the rehab plan for 19 Crown Street:

"We will be providing 16 units of decent, safe and affordable housing to homeless women whose extremely low income makes market rate housing inaccessible. Each room will be decoratively furnished with a bed, bureau, night table, chair and refrigerator. Residents will share common areas: 7 bathrooms, 3 laundry areas, living room, kitchens with individual cupboard space and a landscaped yard. A homey and clean physical space is vital, since our environment plays such an important part in how we perceive ourselves."

Lois, who had opened the press conference, then ended it by introducing Julie Komenos, president of our board of directors. Julie announced that we had just received two sizeable contributions to kick off the campaign—one from the Little Franciscans and the other from the Digital Women's Basketball League headed up by Sue Mallard. We were definitely off and running.

March proved to be a month of gathering more support for Abby's House and of continuing our efforts to go beyond shelter. On the 14th, we received word that once again the Greater Worcester Community Foundation had awarded Abby's House $10,000 for continuation of services. This was one of our largest monetary allotments from the Foundation and, of course, we were excited and grateful. That connection with the Foundation, begun under Kay Marquet and continued under the direction of Ann Lisi, will always be honored as a major part of Abby's history. Every move this organization has made is, in some special way, connected to someone, some place, some group, some church, some business in this community. This can never be overstated. Abby's is at the heart of Worcester's own magnificent history.

And didn't this prove a truism when Richard Jones, then education coordinator of the Worcester Historical Museum, asked to have one of their programs held at Abby's House on March 28th of that important year? Under the broader title of "In Diverse Places," Abby's would host a presentation called, "To See the World Grow Better: Abby Kelley Foster's

Judy Schlosser (c) facilitates the purchase of 19 Crown Street

Channel 3 begins the press conference

ABBY'S HOUSE

A Multi-Service Organization
for Homeless Women and Children

PRESS RELEASE
For immediate release

DATE/TIME: MONDAY, MARCH 8, 1993 at 11AM
PLACE: 19 CROWN ST., WORCESTER, MA
CONTACT: LOIS EDINBERG/TESS SNEESBY 508-756-5486

EVENT

On Monday, March 8, 1993, International Women's Day, Abby's House will host a ceremony and luncheon at 11am to mark the beginning of rehab construction at the site of 19 Crown St., which will provide permanent, affordable housing. International Women's Day provides a meaningful framework in which to celebrate the expansion of our services to homeless women. As women struggle towards creating a world free from the oppression of poverty, violence and inequality, the need for safe and supportive living space is critical. The instability and degradation of homelessness must not be an acceptable part of our society, and Abby's is excited to be able to restore dignity and opportunity to women's lives.

DESCRIPTION OF PROJECT

The 19 Crown St. project involves the purchase and rehabilitation of a vacant, fire damaged building into permanent, affordable, supportive housing for homeless women. Through this project, Abby's will provide 16 units of housing for women whose extremely low incomes make market rate housing inaccessible, and, who would benefit from supportive services. The Worcester Housing Partnership, Inc. is acting as the development consultant for the project. The cooperation of the community will enable this project to be a success. We are very excited to fulfill our dream of providing supportive, affordable, permanent housing for our guests.

DESCRIPTION OF ABBY'S HOUSE

Abby's House is a grassroots organization that provides emergency shelter to homeless women with or without children who are struggling with domestic violence, eviction, unemployment, emotional crisis, recovery from substance abuse and lack of decent, affordable housing. Supportive services such as meals, food distribution, clothing, and advocacy are available to present and former guests of our shelter. Abby's has been operating since 1976 through volunteer hours and financial donations given by hundreds of groups and individuals.

Karen (c) with Milly Silverberg and Dell Marone of Whitefield Methodist Church, West Brookfield

IN DIVERSE PLACES

"To See the World Grow Better"
Abby Kelley Foster's Worcester

Sunday, March 28, 1:30 p.m.
Abby's House, 21-27 Crown Street, Worcester

Nineteenth century Worcester was home to Abby Kelley Foster, a leading abolitionist and ardent supporter of women's rights. Albert B. Southwick, historian and journalist, interprets the life of this remarkable woman against the backdrop of a city often receptive to her progressive ideas. Annette Rafferty, a founder of Abby's House, describes the work of this transitional shelter for homeless women and children. Abby's House opens its doors to the public, by special arrangement, to honor Foster in celebration of International Women's History Month. Free.

Funded in part by the Worcester Cultural Commission with funds allocated by the Massachusetts Cultural Council.

SUPPER IN THE SQUARE
Change and Challenge in "New Worcester"
Monday, May 17, 6:30 p.m.
Webster House Restaurant, Webster Square, Worcester

In Diverse Places moves to the Webster House, where the colorful history of "New Worcester" is recounted by Main South historian Arthur Longwell. David Forsberg, Worcester's chief development officer, evaluates the area's current developments. Members $12.50; non-members $15 (includes dinner). Proceeds benefit Worcester Historical Museum.

Il Southwick and his wife, the late Shirley Southwick

Lisa (c) with daughters Catherine and Alice

Lucy Stone of West Brookfield

TELEGRAM & GAZETTE   SATURDAY, OCTOBER 24, 1998

Plaque honors women's rights fight of 1850

Tony Vigliotti donated the plaque

Nancy Kane in front of plaque

Worcester." Albert Southwick, historian and journalist, and I would combine our talents and present both an interpretation of the life and work of this 19th century activist, and the work of the shelter that honors Foster. I remember the Day Center room being filled with people who had come to learn as much as they could about this woman, Abby, and about whom Al Southwick had said:

> "I would say that she (Foster) was probably the most outstanding woman that ever came from Worcester.... She did probably as much as any single person in breaking down barriers and convincing people that abolition's time had come."

Among the women attending that afternoon's presentation was Lisa Connelly Cook who became in 1995 the first president of Worcester Women's History Project, an organization dedicated to raising awareness and creating recognition of the history of the women's rights movement in Worcester. One of the first tasks of the Project would be to plan and execute a re-enactment of the First National Woman's Rights Convention held in October, 1850 at Worcester's Brinley Hall (340 Main Street, made public in 1998 by an official plaque donated by attorney Anthony Vigliotti). The October 23-24, 1850 convention was specifically held to consider the rights, duties and relations of women, and among the organizers were Abby Kelley Foster, Lucy Stone and Paulina Wright Davis of Providence. In October of 2000, we would be invited to revisit those same issues to determine whether anything had changed in 150 years or was it business as usual.

Like Abby, Lisa was single-minded in her vision of what the Worcester Women's History Project would and could accomplish. On May 12, 1994, she brought this vision to the first meeting of women held at the YWCA, asking us to examine the history of Worcester women and to establish a way to keep their memories alive for generations to come. The rest is history. An organization was born, officers elected, bylaws written, and plans slowly emerged shaping Women 2000 (the name selected for commemoration of the 150th Anniversary of the first national convention). One woman had initiated all this activity which has brought many talented women into the organization. All praise to Lisa for giving us a call to action, for providing the push forward. Like our sister Lucy Stone of West Brookfield, Lisa answered the two questions posed by Abby Kelley Foster to Lucy, then a young student at Oberlin College in Ohio. Having been denied a platform at Oberlin (which, incidentally, was strongly antislavery) because of her radical reform ideas, Abby held her lectures in a nearby town, Elyria. Lucy Stone traveled there to hear Abby and was influenced by this dynamic woman who nudged Lucy into increased antislavery action at Oberlin. Hesitant at first, Lucy finally decided to do something about Abby's questions: "Why delay? Is not now the accepted time?"

Those two questions affected both Lucy's and Lisa's responses to life. I thank Lisa for not delaying and I thank Abby Kelley Foster for continuing to roam around the neighborhood, around the city and the county asking those same two questions and for reminding us that so many women are in the thick of some struggle, trying in their own way to see the world grow better.

A celebration, attended by more than 400 people Wednesday at Mechanics Hall, kicked off the fourth year of the Telegram & Gazette Visions 2000 community improvement program.

Six area residents were honored for achievement and excellence. The Citizen of the Year Award went to Annette A. Rafferty, founder of Abby's House, a shelter for battered women and their children.

VISIONS 2000

A very special day for Abby's

A House Standing on the Edge of Glory

Spring always brought to my mind that famous Robert Browning line, "Oh, to be in England, now that April's there." But in April of 1993 I was glad to be in Worcester! Would you ever think that an article appearing in the April 25, 1993 *Sunday Telegram*, entitled "Agencies Pay Top Leaders Executive Salaries," would advance Abby's cause in raising the needed money to complete 19 Crown Street? Well, it had the same effect as the headlines that appeared in the 1872 edition of the *Woman's Journal* when Liberty Farms was being auctioned off because Abby and Stephen refused to pay taxes until women had the right to vote. The headline read: "Abby Kelley Foster is Homeless." Help came from every imaginable source to buy the farm for $69.60 plus interest and costs and to give it back to the Fosters. The buyer, Osgood Plummer, backed down finally when Stephen looked him squarely in the eye and shouted, "[I will] rely on the force of inertia ... there's power in the eye of an honest patriotic woman (Abby)." And so there was. Abby herself declared, "If I am turned out of the house which we have built, which is hallowed to me by joy and sorrow, by life and death, no roof shall ever shelter me. I will go up and down the streets of Worcester and upbraid every man I meet with his sin against justice (preventing women's suffrage)." (*Ahead of Her Time*)

When Worcesterites of 1993 read the special report of that day and the follow-up which appeared in the April 26th *Telegram*, the help Abby Kelley Foster received from her friends came one hundred fold from the supporters of Abby's House. The report indicated that 92.5% of our revenue went into direct

services and that our executive director was at the bottom of the pay scale ladder. One could argue that salary needed improvement (and didn't those of us working there know that), but it certainly demonstrated the organization's commitment to its mission, its willingness to risk moving forward and its trust in the community to recognize Abby's accountability for dollars given. Tess was, as I imagine all the other executives were, embarrassed at highlighting her salary, but it served its purpose for Abby's House. The reconstruction of 19 Crown Street was underway. Ted Szkoda, architect and contractor, had hired his "subs" and each day, we noted the changes. Would it be done by September? Ted was confident—Tom Hand absolutely certain—and so, Lois and the committee reached out to more and more groups who liked the idea of contributing money in exchange for having a room dedicated to them or to someone important in their lives. Within a short period of time, all of those units Judie Cofsky mentioned at the press conference in March were accounted for in that dedication plan. Today, the door of each room bears a plaque with the name of the person, persons or group sponsoring the furnishings within; Nan Rubens put her artistic touch on the plaque with her honeysuckle stenciling.

Within that short period of time, all of us had moved from humming the healing song of Rita McNeil to singing out-loud Joan Baez's words, describing what 19 Crown Street would be:

> "My house stands at the edge of glory.
> Steady as the seasons change.
> Dreams of grace arise before me,
> And they call me home again."

The June newsletter provided everyone with the update and introduced Paula Sleeper who would be living in as the resident manager of the new home. Paula was no stranger to Abby's, having worked many months as a very competent shelter staffer. Now, as a college student, she needed a place to both live and work and we could think of no one with better qualifications to fill this new assignment.

That spring also brought some special surprises for those of us still working at Abby's House. The League of Women Voters invited Elaine Lamoureux, to address their membership at the 1993 annual meeting on the topic of domestic violence. She

Bottom line is money and lives

By Bob Kievra
Telegram & Gazette Staff

'You can do numbers, but you also have to measure how you're changing someone's life. And that's very difficult.'
Tess Sneesby

The bottom line is more personal than financial

"Abby Kelley Foster is homeless."

Molly Del Howe and Lizzie Fussell o... Liberty Farms, 116 Mower St. as it is to...

Liberty Farms - up for sale in 1872!

Could this be reconstructed?

Ted (seated-r) and his crew

Nan Rubens and the honeysuckle at 19 Crown

shared the bill with Sarah M. Buel, Director of the Domestic Violence Unit of the Suffolk County District Attorney's Office. This was such an honor for Abby's.

Three of us, Elaine, Tess and I, were also honored by the membership of the Unitarian Universalist Church of Worcester, and were presented with the prestigious Beacon Award. In that same month, I was singularly honored by Worcester State College with the presentation of their Community Service Medallion. All of this honoring reflects the respect the community at large has for Abby's House. Any medal, or plaque or medallion, goes directly to the heart of the matter. Abby's exists and provides its services because the community owns this place! A way of claiming ownership in an organization often translates into honoring someone connected to it. I think everyone would agree with that statement. The homage paid comes directly from the heart because an investment of concern has been made by those who honor. This is authentic mutuality in my way of thinking!

In late June, Elaine received a phone call from a former guest, Elsa Luffborough Mensah, who lived at Abby's with her three boys in 1984. Elsa was bubbling over with the good news that the oldest boy, Doug, a graduate of Doherty High School, would be delivering the valedictory address at Northeastern University's 1993 graduation. Doug Luffborough drew national attention with a speech (and a song) that riveted the Boston Garden crowd of 14,000. Did it have anything to do with the other speaker, President Clinton, who was so impressed with Doug that he invited him and his mother to the White House? What impressed us, however, was not the speakers or the song, but the reason why Elsa called: "I called to let you make sure that women with children know there is hope. Tell them not to get discouraged." Elaine had the following commentary on Elsa and Doug: "Women who are going through hard times don't have role models. They always hear put downs. She (Elsa) made her kids believe in themselves. No matter what the financial conditions, good mothering gets results. He (Doug) got the degree, but she worked for it."

Fundraisers galore and articles in the local media helped push Abby's towards the completion of the new house. People came from everywhere to participate in the final drive. We were thrilled to have Paul Rogers (yes, the King of the Green Thumb), come to give us ideas on how a backyard could be both beautiful and practical. Having followed his lead, the backyard is home to a thriving vegetable garden, thanks to the hard work of Maggie Wain. Today the yard has been further beautified with a meditation corner and a flower garden of remembrance. When Julie Komenos' mother, Elaine Razzana died, Julie wished to create a place where plants, bushes, and flowers would be planted on a regular basis as memorials to deceased guests, friends and supporters of Abby's House. The remembrance garden was dedicated on Women's Equality Day, held in 2000 on August 24. A side-of-the-house flower garden has been developed over the past years by Wachusett Regional High School students, Marion Twining, Ellen Grimm and former guest, Emma Flores.

Worcester schoolchildren continued their commitment to Abby's through the PEAK program, headed up by our long-time friend, Don Moran. Sixty-two students from West Tatnuck, Nelson Place, Elm Park, Roosevelt and Wawecus Road schools designed five colonial cabinets, sold raffle tickets and were able to present us with a check of $1,100. Judie Cofsky (not Joan Kosky as indicated in the newspaper article) received the money from Don. This was not the first time the PEAK program came to the aid of Abby's. I know Midland Street, Flagg Street, Francis McGrath and Chandler Street Schools were involved in the same project in previous years when another check of $2,400 was also presented to Abby's. We can never thank Don Moran and all those schools and students enough for that dedication which moved us closer to the opening of 19 Crown Street. If I have omitted any school, I apologize.

Body and Soul, a fitness center for women, held an "aerobathon" fundraiser. One of the participants was Carolyn Sheldon, who volunteered at our Day Center. Within the next five years, Carolyn brought another terrific group into Abby's community: Ladies of Harley, women bikers who, along with their men friends, rode their motorcycles for the benefit of Abby's, raising money for children's camperships. Yes, Carolyn and her husband own N.F. Sheldon, Harley-Davidson headquarters!

The Greater Worcester Jaycees sponsored a Las Vegas Night and JMK Productions had partial proceeds from the staging of MASS APPEAL come our way, through the help of Laura

THE LEAGUE OF WOMEN VOTERS OF
THE WORCESTER AREA

requests the pleasure of your company
at the

1993 ANNUAL MEETING

Monday, May
Higgins Hou
Worcester Polytechni

Elaine Lamor
Abby's Hou

Sarah M. Bi
Director, Domestic Vi
Suffolk County District At

DOMESTIC VI

Business Meeting
Buffet Dinner
Speaker

Guests welco
Come hear the speakers even if y

**WORCESTER
STATE
COLLEGE**

486 Chandler Street   Worcester, MA 01602-2597

Office of the President

March 16, 1993

Ms. Annette A. Rafferty
25 Elmwood Street
Worcester, MA 01602

Dear Ms. Rafferty:

It brings me great pleasure to inform you that the Worcester
State College Board of Trustees unanimously approved the
recommendation of the All College Committee to award you this
year's Community Service Medallion for your outstanding
contributions to society through community service. Worcester
is very fortunate to have you as a member of its community.

This award will be presented to you at our Commencement exercises
scheduled for Saturday, May 22, 1993 at 10:00 a.m. Additional
information will be sent to you regarding the details for
this event.

Again, thank you for allowing us to honor you. By so doing,
we bring great distinction to the Worcester State College
campus.

Sincerely,

Kalyan Ghosh

Kalyan K. Ghosh
President

KKG/jas

Growing commitment

WORCESTER — Molly Ahearn, 16, of Paxton, and Liz Perola, 15 of Sterling, plant flowers at Abby's House on Crown Street yesterday. The Wachusett Regional High School sophomores, along with other classmates, "adopted" Abby's House in their freshman year, and will volunteer to help all four years they are in high school.

Wachusett students

CENTRAL MASS DIGEST

ment returned last Thursday of 18 counts of bankruptcy fraud involving his March 15, 1990, bankruptcy filing in U.S. Bankruptcy Court.

Harrington said he will schedule a new trial date.

PEAK classes put skills to use

WORCESTER — Sixty-two students from West Tatnuck, Nelson Place, Elm Park, Roosevelt and Wawecus Road schools in Donald Moran's computer/math/science PEAK classes held an open house recently at Nelson Place School.

During the past semester, students have been using their computer skills to send E-mail, conduct teleconferencing and exchange pen-pal letters, databases, school newspaper articles and graphic designs.

One course project involved using computers to design five Colonial cabinets. Word processing was also used to make raffle tickets that were sold to raise money for Abby's House. A $1,100 check was presented to Joan Kosky, a director of Abby's House. During the past two years, Moran's PEAK students have raised $3,450 for charity.

D.C.-BOUND: Elsa Luffborough Mensah and her son Douglas Edward Luffborough III await their flight from Logan Airport to Washington D.C. last night as they set off on a visit to the White House on a personal presidential invitation.   *Staff photo by Mark Garfinkel*

A tale of inspiration sends
mom & son to White House

Paul Rogers (l) giving garden advice

Ladies (and gents) of Harley honored by Julie Komenos (r)

Elaine Razzana

STAGE *by Richard Duckett*   DATEBOOK, MAY 30, 1993   7

JMK's leading couple relishes
their theater life together

Laura Scarborough doesn't usually put theater programs of productions she has attended in her lingerie drawer after the show is over.

But she did in 1986 after attending a performance of "The Good Doctor" at the former Marian High School in Southbridge that was directed by Michael Knych.

There must have been some sort of undercover prescience at work — although it didn't necessarily reveal itself right away.

Scarborough, who was born and raised in Worcester, was attending "The Good Doctor" on a date with a co-worker of Knych. She was briefly introduced to Knych a

'MASS APPEAL'

■ **When:** 8 p.m. Thursday, Friday, Saturday, and June 11 and 12
■ **Where:** Notre Dame Hall, Salem Square, Worcester
■ **How Much:** $7

Parish hall, which has a stage, could be a good venue for a theater. Marian's ex-headmaster is the Rev. Norman Jalbert, now pastor of Notre Dame-St. Joseph's. Furthermore, it was Father Jalbert who married Scarborough and Knych at the church in 1989.

If a story that began with lingerie

learned how something could be accomplished by focusing on a goal."

With that in mind, JMK Productions was formed (the company is named after his daughter from his previous marriage, Julianne Mae Knych, who lives with her mother in Southbridge).

"I knew I had the ability, but wondered if I had the energy to produce community theater," Knych said.

"But with me, you had twice as much energy to achieve that goal, together," added his wife.

Commendable

JMK Productions has always put unique posi-... art Play-... similar and ...de) of being a ...hat goes out of ...community.

...d in Webster, ...Henry Slota ... Bartlett High ...ed $1,600 for a ... town of Web-

...establish our ...company that ... the stage and ... community,"

Laura Scarborough and Michael Knych.   STEVE LANAVA

Scarborough who dedicated the production to her late uncle Bill Scarborough, whose favorite charity was Abby's House. The year ended with a beautiful Day in the Park sponsored by Paul Conzo Hair and Skin, Simply Victorian, and Worcester Publishing.

Abby's was finally ready for the Big Day—the dedication of 19 Crown Street—on Sunday, September 26, 1993. A Najavo chant had been thoughtfully selected for the blessing, one that described the beauty of the finished product and the deep hope that the women who would become its residents would be filled with its spirit:

> "House made of dawn. House made of evening
> light. House made of dark cloud. House made of
> male rain. House made of dark mist.
> House made of female rain. House made of
> pollen. House made of grasshoppers.
>
> Happily may I walk. Happily, with abundant
> dark clouds, may I walk. Happily, with abundant
> showers, may I walk. Happily with
> abundant plants, may I walk. Happily, on a
> trail of pollen, may I walk.
>
> Happily, may I walk.
> May it be beautiful before me.
> May it be beautiful behind me.
> May it be beautiful below me.
> May it be beautiful above me.
> May it be beautiful all around me.
> In beauty it is finished.
> In beauty it is finished."

The morning came with rain, but by early afternoon only sprinkles were coming down on a crowd that had gathered outside 19 Crown Street. No one there seemed conscious of the misting. There was electricity in the air. You could feel the excitement and touch the pride that everyone was exhibiting with hugs and handshakes. It didn't matter whether those in attendance had been involved with the project. Today belonged to all of us. I find it difficult to put into words just what I was feeling, nearly 18 years after the spirit of Abby Kelley Foster had

led us to this street, to this historic neighborhood, to this community of people. In my mind, I was trying to visualize that day when Mary Matthew Labunski and I walked onto the porch at 23 Crown Street. It had become a landmark of women's efforts on behalf of other women, all in the name of that remarkable woman (Abby) who surely, using a phrase popular in the mid-1990s, talked the talk and walked the walk! My thoughts were interrupted by Tess' voice as she asked the crowd, "Isn't it a beautiful home?"

Tess then proceeded to thank all of those involved in the project and to remind us:

> "Abby's House is that space for so many of us, in different ways, at different times in our lives. 19 Crown Street ... will be a home, a space of inner discovery for the women who will reside here. Surrounded by space that is safety, stability, peace and beauty, we hope that women will come to know their own beauty and experience a sense of wholeness. ... Your presence here today clearly declares your own belief that everyone deserves a home."

The hours of celebration were followed by a few days of sadness, as we all said our good-byes to Karen Staropoli, our Jesuit volunteer worker, who had completed her year with us and was on her way to graduate school in her home town. She was shuffling off to Buffalo! Karen left the following reflection:

> "As my year at Abby's draws to a close, many people have asked me, 'So, how was your experience?' The truth is, I have gained so much that I can hardly put it into words. I have witnessed the pain and struggle that women of all backgrounds have had to deal with. I have seen women pull through situations with an inner strength that has amazed me. I have watched women support each other and encourage each other through the darkest times of their lives. I have seen women finally come to the realization that they are important, that their life truly matters. I have watched a dream unfold into a reality with the work on 19 Crown Street. I have seen unconditional acceptance and incredible patience

Celebration at 19 Crown St.

Kay Kroyak cuts the ribbon

*Liz Mullany,
Crown Hill President*

Janice Nadeau, district councillor

The crowd cheers!

Mary and Joan dance under the tent

9-27-93

May It Be Beautiful All Around
Beyond Shelter
Supportive Affordable Housing

Our New Home!

*"House Made of Dawn
House Made of Evening light"*

*Celebration of the
Opening of
19 Crown St.
Sunday, Sept. 26, 1993
1 - 5 p.m.*

The finished product - 19 Crown Street

from women who have dedicated their lives to a cause they believe in so strongly.

It is difficult to express all that I have learned and experienced during my year at Abby's. It is also difficult to express how grateful I am to everyone who was a part of my time here. I will not forget the strength and love I felt at Abby's."

By October of that eventful year, Terri Griffin, the Salem State intern, now a graduate, stayed on at Abby's as Day Center coordinator. Terri had been a shelter intern while in her senior year at Salem State College, so she came into the job well-trained and prepared. One of the first tasks Terri designed and implemented was a city outreach project, in an effort to locate former guests with whom we had lost contact. As a result of her work, new-old faces began to appear in the Center.

At the end of the year all of us reviewed the growth of Abby's House. Not only had we successfully moved beyond shelter, but our services had expanded with the opening of a Women's Health Clinic, co-sponsored with the Worcester Department of Public Health and H.O.A.P. (Homeless Outreach and Advocacy Project). The clinic continues today providing information and referrals on women's health issues, TB screening, tetanus immunization and HIV testing and counseling. These services are still free of charge in our women-only space at the Day Center. Additionally, we had expanded our Thrift Shop hours, with dedicated volunteers working hard to create a clean, attractive and fun shopping experience. Their efforts enable us even today to provide access to the shop six days a week. Everyone of them realizes that proceeds from every sale are used to operate our shelter, with our guests receiving gift certificates to shop for their needs, without having to be identified as shelter guests. We had truly seen the world grow better. Denise Levertov's words were ringing loud and clear for Abby's:

"...How could we tire of hope?
— so much in bud.
How can desire fail?
— we have only begun
to imagine justice and mercy.

Only begun to envision
how it might be to live as siblings
with beast and flower,
not as oppressors.
...We have only begun to know
the power that is in us if we would join
our solitudes in the communion of struggle...
So much is unfolding that must
complete its gesture,
so much is in bud."

The "kids" and Karen Stevens say goodbye to Karen (center)

Terri Griffin

Brenda Kartheiser, Abby's HOAP nurse

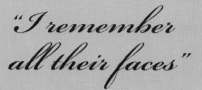

"*I remember all their faces*"

*Lorraine Fletcher—
new housing coordinator*

Joan Filipe told her story.

In the late 1980s, she made up her mind to leave an abusive husband. After a three-month temporary living situation with a married couple dissolved, she was left with nowhere to go.

"I came home from work one day and she had all my stuff packed up. Now what do I do?"

She went down to Bergson's, in the old Galleria, and called Abby's.

"I told them I couldn't be with my husband, that I had a restraining order against him for very valid reasons. Where could I go and what could I do?"

Abby's gave her shelter and more.

A few years ago, Filipe moved into 19 Crown St., Abby's permanent rooming house for women without children. This June, Abby's is planning to open a third house at 77 Chatham St., which will offer permanent shelter to mothers in need.

"It's been a very supportive and safe home," said Filipe of the rooming house. "I like the fact that men can't live in the building. I'm just very grateful for safety of the house and the rapport we have. ... We can feel safe about sharing our past. It's like a home, not a rooming house."

Joan Filipe at Abby's House.

1994 Silver Hammer Awards

World Grinding Technology Center, Norton Company, Worcester

High tech abrasive product testing and development is underway at one of Norton Company's oldest manufacturing buildings. Located at the company's New Bond Street complex, the 30,000 square-foot World Grinding Technology Center was once a Norton grinding machine tool plant and for many years an abrasives grain factory. Today, following a multi-million dollar rehabilitation, the facility contains the world's most advanced machinery, tooling and instrumentation. The center offers Norton's abrasives and grinding technology expertise to help customers and machine tool builders develop new products of the highest quality at the lowest possible cost. It represents a first-of-its-kind industry initiative among Norton Company, its customers, and leading machine tool builders.

Dr. Franklin M. Loew Veterinary Medical Education Center, Grafton

Several years of planning and a successful $2.4 million fundraising campaign have transformed an empty brick building into the centerpiece of academic and student life at the Tufts University School of Veterinary Medicine. The center, which originally served as the auditorium/gymnasium at the former Grafton State Hospital, was renovated exclusively with private funds. It contains the school's library, a 170-seat auditorium, a 20-station computer room, a 76-seat teaching laboratory and study and lounge areas. Many of the rooms, like the Webster Family Library, are named for the building's benefactors. Architect for the project were Finegold Alexander & Associates, Inc. of Boston, and the contractor was Granger Corporation of Worcester.

Abby's House, 19 Crown Street, Worcester

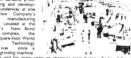

Abby's House, a multi-service organization for homeless women and children, has a new facility to assist the needy. Built in the 1800's as a rooming house, 19 Crown Street was then an established, reputable address. However, by 1991, it became a place of neglect with ongoing drug activity and was finally burned in a suspicious fire. Located in a historic neighborhood with large Victorian homes and some of the city's best views, resides Abby's House. Next to Abby's stands the recently renovated 19 Crown Street, completed at a cost of $185,000, below the anticipated budget, thanks largely to the talent and ability of design-build contractor Ted Szkoda. Today, 19 Crown Street provides permanent, supportive and affordable housing for women with very low incomes.

Worcester Common Fashion Outlets

Amidst much fanfare, the former Worcester Galleria has been transformed into the nation's first enclosed urban outlet mall, Worcester Common Fashion Outlets. The $60 million renovation by mall owners New England Development, CIGNA Investment Management and S.R. Weiner & Associates, represents the completion of the first of several major developments now underway destined to redefine the region. The mall features more than 100 designer outlets and a 700-seat food court. Highlighting its variety of retailers is the first Saks Clearinghouse in New England. There's also New England's first Barney's New York Outlet and Karl Lagerfeld. And, designer outlet stores like Donna Karan, Colours by Alexander Julian, Polo, a newly enlarged Filene's Basement and Worcester's own Sharfmans are scattered among others in this 1-million square feet of shopping nirvana.

CHAPTER 14 *Settling and Searching*

The New Year, 1994, brought a few changes in our staff. Lorraine Fletcher joined Abby's House as housing coordinator, having worked for many years with what was then Worcester Housing Partnership. Judie Cofsky returned to her work as Day Center coordinator and Terry Griffin moved on to a social work position in a northern Maine agency. I've come to think of this particular year as one of settling and searching. The settling was happening at 19 Crown Street as we busied ourselves every day with both shelter guests, Day Center visitors, phone referrals and requests for information, but most of our energy was centered on making the new residence a real home—a very safe home for single women. We had become "landladies" and that new title brought with it new challenges for both staff and residents, some of whom are still with us.

As I write about these women, I see their faces and recall their names: MaryBeth, Renee, Kathleen, Wanda, Gloria, Michelle, Maria, Sheila, Shirley, Laurie, Barbara, Jeanne, Cynthia, Sue, Colleen, Susan, Debbie, Emma, Karen, Jackie, Myriam, Cecilia, Mary, Cheryl, Paula, Janice, Celia, Jody, Norma, Joan, Maggie, Sheryl, Tina, Lourdes, Folu, Terri, Gina, Yolanda, Marion, Lucinda, Janet, Nicole, Pat, Gwen, Maybelle, Epiphania. Each one contributed (contributes) something special to the community of Abby's House.

Later that same year, the Worcester Area Chamber of Commerce awarded us the coveted 1994 Silver Hammer Award for our efforts at 19 Crown Street. In the account of the restoration provided in the Chamber's program, it stated:

"Next to Abby's stands the recently renovated 19 Crown Street, completed at a cost of $185,000, below the anticipated budget, thanks largely to the talent and ability of design-builder-contractor, Ted Szkoda. Today, 19 Crown Street provides permanent, supportive and affordable housing for women with very low incomes."

The award plaque is hanging proudly in the front hall of 19 Crown Street, next to framed photos of what the house looked like just after it was nearly destroyed by a suspicious fire. I never fail to point them out to visitors or to stop and admire that absolutely gorgeous staircase, so beautifully restored by Diony VanGerven of Brookfield. And the house is as well-kept today by the women who live there as it was on the dedication day. I consider *that* a tribute both to the women and to the craftspeople who gave them such a magnificent home sweet home!

And the year of searching? How could we be looking while nesting? Easily. A phone call to Tess gave us new information: the property at 77 Chatham Street might be available, and wouldn't Abby's be interested in "investigating" its availability possibly for restoration as a facility for women and their children? The search had begun and we were ready, floating into the unknown on the cloud of our success at 19 Crown Street. If anyone of us thought the "search" idiotic, not a word was spoken by any of us. I'm sure we all had our own thoughts about the searching, the looking into, the gathering of information for yet another house. This may have been the first time that I harbored some doubts as to whether this was a wise move. We had just finished a magnificent home and I thought we might need the time to settle it and to evaluate. And, after all, that house at 77 Chatham Street was in such shambles. How could we even imagine transforming it into something useful? Besides, Tess and I had just met with local, feminist playwright Jane Dutton and actress Susan Nest at the Broadway, where, over coffee, they agreed to do a 20th anniversary play based on the life of Abby Kelley Foster. Jane would write and direct the production and Susan would play the lead with a possible third actor (who, as it turned out, was Victor Kruczynski as Stephen Symonds Foster). Plans for this event would have to begin now.

77 Chatham Street

Lucy Barton's Boardinghouse, 100 Chatham St.

Auctioneers with Hilda, Lorraine and Tess

Daily S.U. 15 th of 1874.1.21.

Mr. Willard Jones' obituary

Our lawyer, Kathleen O'Connor, examines the documents

A few days after the meeting with Jane and Susan, I took a walk over to 77 Chatham Street where I stood on the sidewalk contemplating the building. How could this be done? "Abby Kelley Foster, if this is to happen, give me a positive sign," was the thought running through my mind. I have to confess that Dorothy Sterling's book, *Ahead of Her Time*, had become the source of my private inspirations, a kind of new feminist bible, replacing Elizabeth Cady Stanton's *Woman's Bible*. So, back at my desk, I began to re-read the final chapter of Abby's life which was spent at her sister Lucy Barton's boardinghouse, located at 100 Chatham Street. Here, I read, Abby found some contentment living with the other boarders, who, by the way, considered her eccentric. Abby's days were spent reading the long, interesting letters of her daughter, Alla, who was involved in many activities in Boston. And, she also found the time to take carriage rides: "I pay only a dollar and a half for a good carriage and go, then, for a five mile ride...." Carriage rides—possibly up and down Chatham Street, past the Willard house at number 77? It had to have been the carriage rides that finally carried me back into my usual positive state of thinking. Why certainly Abby had passed this old mansard-roofed house, the home of Mr. and Mrs. Willard Jones, many a time on that five mile ride. And I am as certain now as I was then that Abby had entertained thoughts that this old home would have made a far better site for a boardinghouse because of its size. She would have had more space and would not have to deal with complaining boarders. She'd no longer have to do all her business in a small room with the door shut! Perhaps none of this had really happened, but it was the turning point in my own consideration of the use of 77 Chatham Street. In her memory, I thought, this would become a house with more than a room of one's own. It would become apartments for women and their children, each woman with five or six rooms of her own! Thanks to Dorothy Sterling's account of those carriage rides, my equilibrium was restored and my eagerness to support the search stimulated. Onward and upward into another adventure!

The core staff met in March and discussed the final stages of the "search." There were many questions: Were we really prepared to face this challenge, financially and emotionally? Was anyone investigating other organizations that had begun family housing? If this proposed housing was to accommodate women and their children, had we considered how we would deal with an invited male guest who might become a permanent fixture? Would it be realistic to expect a female tenant with children not to have a live-in boyfriend? These concerns prompted visits to other organizations in Boston, Hartford and Providence where Tess, Elaine and Lorraine were quickly apprised of both the difficulties and the rewards of attempting single-family housing. Since such housing had been attempted by their organizations in spite of the difficulties, Abby's staff recommended that the board of directors proceed and pursue on an informational basis the purchase of the house. Board members discussed many "what ifs" and finally concluded that had "what ifs" directed Abby's course of action, there would be no shelter and no 19 Crown Street! Emily Rothschild came into the search as consultant and a design committee formed, consisting of one core staffer, one board member, the architect and Emily. The costs would be covered by a CEDAC grant designated for pre-development work. In the board minutes of April 1994, it states the following:

> "At this time, the plan [we envision] for the house would include 8 apartments. Seven of them would be 2 bedrooms and 1 apartment would be a 4 bedroom unit. There would be a community room on the first floor. There would be no residential manager, but support services would be provided."

Certainly this initial plan was revised as the architect looked more closely at the structure. By June of 1994, we discovered that the Resolution Trust Corporation had placed 77 Chatham Street on what they called an "N-Series List," meaning that such properties are routinely scheduled to be auctioned to for-profit developers. That was enough to send the design committee into fast forward in an effort to have 77 removed from the list. Lorraine and Tess literally flew to Boston to attend a national oversight board meeting of the Resolution Trust Corporation (RTC). Their flight paid off. They met with the national director, Steve Allen, and discussed their proposal with him, discovering that Steve had worked with low-income housing in the Crown Hill/Piedmont neighborhood during the early 1970s. Lorraine and Tess also made personal appeals to Senator Ted Kennedy, State Senator Arthur Chase and House Representative

Peter Blute to help in whatever way they could. All three were tremendously helpful and in no time, we received the good news that 77 Chatham Street was removed from the for-profit auction list. The property would eventually go to auction, of course, but Abby's as a non-profit could bid. Our dedicated lawyers, Kathleen O'Connor and Sandra Landau, made the path to this auction smooth.

In mid-July, Tess began meeting with the Crown Hill Neighborhood Association, the neighbors, Whittier Terrace, with District Councillor, Janice Nadeau and with the Director of Spring Valley Convalescent Home. Newsletter mailings to our supporters and donors included all the necessary information gathered to date on this latest "search." The response was unusually positive and enthusiastic. Backing for this latest project was strong. What else could we expect from the community? Nearly 20 years of commitment to the mission of Abby's was evident. "Don't stop now," "Go for it," and "We're with you every step of the way," were the messages from our supporters. Such backing was certainly a vote of confidence. By the end of the month, the design committee hired Gorham, Richardson and Associates, a firm with an excellent track record with the "architect-contractor" model, one that has a separate designer and builder. Funding sources were nearly in place, but the total development cost would necessitate a capital campaign at some point in the very near future. Still, we forged ahead with that same deep faith characteristic of Abby's and with the knowledge that "it would happen." Events snowballed, even in late summer, beginning with the auction that took place outside 77 Chatham.

Sandra and Kathleen, the legal eagles, were working day and night to get paperwork in place for the foreclosure on 77 Chatham Street. The architect, Scott, was designing and re-designing, preparing the papers for final approval. Our brave committee was meeting nearly twice a week, overseeing every step of the acquisition and adding more than two cents' worth of ideas. There was ongoing discussion about a capital campaign that would not only help with construction costs, but also with a maintenance fund. This would be Abby's opportunity to enhance our reputation with evidence of self-sufficiency. Our Flagship friend, Kevin Kane, was very helpful in shaping the eventual board decision to initiate a 20th anniversary capital campaign, but more on that decision later in this journey of 25 years.

Go for it!

CHAPTER 15 *Jumping into Work Headfirst*

The excitement of acquiring the 77 property was temporarily interrupted by the death of Bessie. After 10 years and 160,000 miles the Toyota Tercel expired! The silver "bullet" had left us high and dry, but she had lived a very good life, serving Abby's with steady delivery of goods from the Worcester County Food Bank and the daily transportation of guests. Yes, Bessie was gone, but she'll not be forgotten.

Also, the circle of involvement with community and school groups continued to expand during this settling and searching year. Again the PEAK program, under the direction of Don Moran, held another successful raffle for Abby's. Fundraisers were also held by the Bancroft School students and by classes from the North Middlesex Regional High School.

Venerini Academy presented the shelter with quilts; the CCD classes of St. Mary's in Grafton did a walk-a-thon for the women and children and Wachusett Regional High School freshman class "adopted" Abby's for their four years and worked to beautify the grounds along with our friends from the Tatnuck Garden Club. Perhaps the dearest contribution that year resulted from the untimely death of seven-year old Jack Peairs, beloved son of Marge and Herve and grandson of long-time supporter, Loretta Peairs of Westboro. At the time of his sudden death from Henson's disease, Jack was a student at Thorndyke Elementary School and together with Principal Matt Ryan, teachers and Jack's parents, all memorial gifts came to Abby's House. Marge and Herve wrote (of these donations): "Our beloved son, Jack, always had a place to shelter him, so we

donate these gifts to help women and children in need." Jack's life and death became a source of hope to the children here. Loretta wrote and forwarded to us a copy of Jack's Maxims: Life as he lived it, from a beloved grandmother's point of view:

"Know what you love and do it with all your heart.

Seek out what challenges, and when you have mastered one challenge, look for the next.

Give generously of the strengths and crafts with which you have been blessed, not for thanks, but for the joy of sharing.

Don't spend time on things you don't enjoy (except sometimes to make someone happy).

Think. Think about everything—how machines work, about strategies to win games, mysteries of time and the universe.

Love laughter."

The sorrow that we all experienced from Jack Peair's death has changed into a lasting relationship with his parents who adopted two children, a brother and sister, a few years ago. Life is different for them now. Jack will always be their precious child, but, courageously, they have moved forward as adoptive parents and are providing love, shelter and support to their new family members. And I have no doubt that Jack's Maxims are still a family cornerstone.

Loretta LaRoche, doctor of mirth, now a famous PBS Channel 2 star, came to help us reclaim our happier selves with a benefit event held at Holden Hills Center. "How to prevent hardening of the arteries" did the trick for the staff. Loretta cer-

PEAK is paying community back

By Clive McFarlane
Telegram & Gazette Staff

WORCESTER — Three years ago, Providing Equity for Able Kids, a program to supplement the education of Worcester public schools' brightest and most talented pupils, was nearly felled by the budget ax.

The program was spared, however, when Worcester — one of the few communities in the commonwealth to do so — passed a Proposition 2½ override to secure additional school funding.

Since the override, pupils in the PEAK program have been trying to "pay back the community," according to Donald Moran, one of eight teachers involved with the program.

In Moran's 13-week computer/math/science class, for example, the pupils have been building and raffling Colonial-style cabinets, and turning the proceeds over to Abby's House, a shelter for homeless women and children.

Last week Abby's House was presented a

> **"T**hey are learning so much. You can see their self-esteem rising every day.'
>
> NANCY COTTER,
> MOTHER OF PEAK PUPIL

$1,325 check from the raffling of five cabinets made by Moran's PEAK class, which includes pupils from Flagg Street, Rice Square, Nelson Place and Lake View schools.

The check brings to $4,700 the amount of money pupils have raised since they instituted the cabinet-making project as part of their PEAK activities.

"The students came up with the idea," Moran said. "They see it as a way to give something back to the community, because

the override saved a program they all enjoy very much."

The PEAK program, which has been in operation for 16 years in the public schools, offers supplemental instruction to 421 pupils in grades 4-6. The classes are offered in all the elementary schools. Pupils usually work with a PEAK teacher one day each week, and are required to keep up with their regular classroom work.

While the pupils are bent on paying the community back for supporting their program, their parents say the biggest payback is the impact the program is having on their children.

"They are learning so much," said Nancy Cotter, whose daughter Kathy, a sixth-grader, is one of Moran's pupils. "You can see their self-esteem rising everyday."

Moran said he has been amazed by the pupils' high level

Tess says goodbye to Bessie

Jack Peairs

Local News

Angela G. Dorenkamp, left, and Veronica Griffin join in singing "We Shall Overcome."

BETTY JENEWIN

TELEGRAM & GAZETTE

THURSDAY, AUGUST 25, 1994   **C9**

COMMEMORATION

BEST BET *Abby's House will sponsor a Women's Equality Day program at 6 p.m. Friday at the site of Abby Kelley Foster's grave, Hope Cemetery, 119 Webster St., Worcester.*

Abby's House

Afforable housing projects in Worcester and Marlboro are among those in New England that have received a total of $4.3 million in grants and below-market loans approved by the **Federal Home Loan Bank of Boston.**

A $70,000 direct grant and $110,000 20-year advance was made through **Flagship Bank & Trust Co.** for **Abby's House** acquisition and renovation of a building at 77 Chatham St., Worcester, that will provide rental units for families with very low income.

In Marlboro, a $73,898 direct grant was made through **Framingham Savings Bank** to **Advocates Inc.** for the renovation of rental units at Prospect Street Apartments for disabled, very low-income people.

Laughing off the stress

Loretta LaRoche

tainly demonstrated that failing to deal with stress and unproductive behavior does "sabotage happiness and success."

As in the past, the year ended with our now-annual events, the celebration of Women's Equality Day on August 26th and the tag sale, always held on the Saturday after Labor Day. Both events require a great deal of planning and preparation, but after each one of those days is over, everyone realizes that community and volunteer participation is well worth the effort involved. It is obvious to me, while reviewing my memories of these years, that Abby's House is special not only in its delivery of services, its commitment to the mission, the incredible volunteers, but especially because we are a community of very positive, upbeat people whose spirit is "catching." This is not a "pollyanna" musing, but a very accurate assessment of a group who sees, hears and faces the overwhelming problems of Abby's guests, but doesn't succumb to despair. I believe that this attitude of concentrating on the positive is one of the reasons why so many individuals have become involved here. I believe this because 25 years have passed and I still feel hopeful even when social policies toward poor women are no kinder now than they were in 1976. In fact, they are increasingly cruel and punitive. I believe this because I have all of our newsletters, by Editor Tess Sneesby, as an invaluable resource to read and re-read. The women's stories that Tess told have been simultaneously heartrending and heartwarming. Would I ever have the fortitude to face some of their days? I doubt it. But I found, page after page, year after year, true stories that inspired me, kept me hoping for better days, working for solutions, befriending these women, keeping their memories alive and keeping me humbled. Abby Kelley Foster, I know, envies me those resources. Dorothy Sterling's biography, in a chapter entitled, "A Lonely Rocket in a Dark Sky," included the following:

> "In addition to the letters to Alla (her daughter), Abby sometimes attempted longer pieces of writing. So many people had asked for her reminiscences that in 1885 she started to put them down. The task was difficult, because she had little material to jog her memory. [She wrote] ... 'I never kept a diary, or any incidental notes of my life. I never kept any articles from newspapers either commendatory, or condemnatory, and seldom kept a letter,' she explained."

Sterling continues in this chapter to tell us that at age 75, Abby finally sat down at her writing table and recalled for a new generation the barriers that women had faced 50 years earlier. It is through these personal remembrances of my years at Abby's House that Worcester and Worcester County residents will remember forever what they did to support women supporting other women and their children who face the same barriers as their predecessors did in Abby's time.

Just two days short of Abby Kelley Foster's 184th birthday, we awoke on January 13, 1995 to read in the business section of the *Worcester Telegram and Gazette* the following:

> "Affordable housing projects in Worcester and Marlboro are among those in New England that have received a total of $4.3 million in grants and below-market loans approved by the Federal Home Loan Bank of Boston.
>
> A $70,000 direct grant and $110,000 twenty year advance was made through Flagship Bank and Trust Co. for Abby's House acquisition and renovation of a building at 77 Chatham Street, Worcester, that will provide rental units for families with very low income...."

Abby had delivered a big present, as usual, ahead of her time! My heart was beating fiercely because this surely signaled an unusually busy, productive year. Being just another year older, I wondered if I could keep up with the pace. The house at 77 Chatham Street became a reality sooner than I had imagined. I can't remember just when I picked up a book of Marge Piercy's poetry, but I did and found reassurance in this woman's words, entitled, "To Be of Use":

> "The people I love best
> jump into work head first
> without dallying in the shallows
> and swim off with sure strokes almost out of sight ...
>
> I want to be with people who submerge
> in the task, who go into fields to harvest
> and work in a row and pass the bags along ...
> who are not parlor generals and field deserters

B2 TELEGRAM & GAZETTE TUESDAY, MARCH 7, 1995

Beechwood Inn boosts Abby's House campaign

WORCESTER — Abby's House, a shelter for women and children, is the recipient of a gift of 5,000 hotel-sized toiletries from the Beechwood Inn in an initial move to kick off development of a property at 77 Chatham St.

Sara J. Robertson, former Worcester mayor and supporter of Abby's House, said the Chatham Street project, which would provide safe, affordable housing for low-income women and children who would otherwise be homeless, is expected to get off the ground this spring.

The contribution from the Beechwood Inn is a step in that direction, Robertson said. The toiletries are to be distributed to clients of the shelter.

"We're hoping other companies will recognize the need," Robertson said.

The Chatham _____
seven two-bedro_____
cluding replacem_____

Abby's House _____
the project. Busi_____
asked to make do_____

ABBY'S HOUSE
A Multi-Service Organization
for Homeless Women and Children

20th ANNIVERSARY FUND PLEDGE FORM

Yes, I/we would like to make a pledge of $ _____ to the Abby's House 20th Anniversary Fund, to be paid as follows:

1995: $ _____   1996: $ _____   1997: $ _____   Other: $ _____

A check is enclosed in the amount of $ _____ (payable to *Abby's House 20th Anniversary Fund*)

Name _____
Address _____ Zip _____
Phone (_____) _____
Signature _____ Date _____

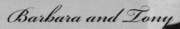

Barbara and Tony

Juanita and Clint

Terri Priest

Larry and Gloria with Annette

Joan Cassidy

Mary Lou Anderson

Monnie Rockwell

*Sunburst's
Sylvia Jane*

Frank Cassidy (at work!)

Anne Humes

but move in a common rhythm
when the food must come in or the fire be put out."

Well, of course I could keep up the pace. I might even out-distance my co-workers in our efforts to complete this next phase of growth at Abby's House. Perhaps I would qualify as matriarchal, but I was no parlor general and definitely not a field deserter. The new year had begun and we were already moving in a common rhythm, because another affordable, decent, safe house was coming into existence. By the end of January 1995, the board signed a nine month contract with Callahan and MacIntyre Associates, who would help us set up the mechanics of a capital campaign. We quickly formed a committee to move the campaign forward into the community, with the following women offering their services: Janet Amorello, Mary Donovan, Julie Komenos, Claudia Russo, Meg Savage, Tess Sneesby, Sharon Smith Viles and Mary Spahr.

By mid-February, activity at Abby's House had moved from fast forward to near whirlwind. Sid Callahan and Sandra MacIntyre had quickly organized the capital campaign commit-tee, which would be known as the 20th anniversary committee. The campaign took on an urgency and an excitement that was challenging and demanding. We met every week and outlined the tasks: businesses and major donors to be contacted, in the hopes of strengthening our ties and our partnership in establish-ing yet another safe, affordable house. Publicity was critical. Every move would have to be highlighted, attracting attention to our 20th anniversary goal. We would have to make new con-tacts, carefully formulate grants, and plan events beyond our usual fundraisers. We needed to compose a letter to our sup-porters and donors under the signatures of the chair of the cam-paign. Chairing the campaign required someone well known in the Worcester community. Time commitment would be essen-tial, and with everyone living on the fast track, it proved to be very difficult, almost impossible, to find a chairperson. At long last, we found two women willing to be co-chairs. These women had known each other for over 25 years, and were still involved in the mission of Abby's House: Frances (Fran) O'Connell and Annette! There was no turning back now; the die was cast. Upward was over. Onward was the key to success now.

As expected, groups everywhere in the city, the county, and across the country responded eagerly. The fondest memory I have of that special year is of the house parties. And what are they? A group of neighbors and friends would be invited into a particular home where refreshments were served and some member of the capital campaign committee would then make a presentation with the hopes of soliciting financial support for the 77 Chatham Street project. I was honored to have been invited into the home of Barbara and Tony Athy, my cousin, to do the first party. Sandra MacIntyre and Claudia Russo were with me for encouragement and support, but I would do the presenting. In delivering my talk on the history and future plans of Abby's House, I recognized how precious both were to me. It was so easy to speak about the early years and the development of Abby's into a multi-service organization. This had been my life for more than 23 years. These house parties were nothing more than a continuation of the same format the original women pio-neers had used to promote the need for a shelter. If I had enter-tained any doubts about my ability to convince others of joining this new housing initiative, they all vanished as I proceeded to address the Athy guests. Pardon my moment of pride, but was there anyone more qualified than I to do this job? I had taken ownership of this project. So, go for it! And I did, choosing to end my party talk with amusing stories of Abby Kelley Foster's spirit roaming the neighborhood, bringing new people into our community and guiding us to and through new efforts on behalf of poor women and their children. I never did find out what the monetary results of that April 20th house party were, but by then everyone was either impressed with my personal spiritual affiliation with Abby or befuddled by my conviction that she was our spiritual companion. Anyway, the evening was a social suc-cess. The seed was planted and proved, in the long run, to bring us closer to our set goal of $500,000.

House parties continued to take place throughout the year at the following homes: Veronica Griffin, Joan and Frank Cassidy, Ann Carlson, Angela Dorenkamp, Holly Heggie, Konnie Lukes, Joan Masseo, Fran O'Connell, Terri Priest, Mary Taft, Michalene Evans, Cathy Gusha, Sarah Lenis, Carrie Mulrein, Sara Robertson, Mary Lou Anderson, and Monnie Rockwell. Church gatherings were sponsored in the same vein at Federated Church of Sturbridge, organized by Clint and Juanita Beuscher, Congregation B'Nai Shalom, called by Rabbi

ple

Features/2
Entertainment/3
Comics/4
Television/5

C

FACES of ABBY'S HOUSE

TEXT BY ALLISON K. JONES, PHOTOS BY BETTY JENEWIN

Text by ALLISON K. JONES, photos by BETTY JENEWIN

They arrive scared, crying and, often, carrying a child. They wonder how they'll survive with no home, few belongings and little money.

They are greeted at Abby's House in Worcester by a warm hug and a staff that is willing to listen.

Abby's House is a program for women, by women.

For 19 years, the 10-bed emergency shelter on Crown Street has been helping women made homeless by poverty, domestic violence, drug addiction or other problems. It pulls them into its embrace with the promise of a warm meal, room to rest and a welcoming heart.

Named after Abby Kelley Foster, a 19th-century Worcester abolitionist and feminist, the shelter houses an estimated 425 women and children each year. Another 9,600 women participate in the agency's day program, health program and other services annually.

Women staff the shelter and a long-term residence nearby. And it is women who ensure the agency's survival.

"We have marvelous men supporters, and I can't underestimate their contribution," said founder Annette A. Rafferty. But "it was a groundswell of support from women" that established Abby's in 1976. "This

movement of women's energy has been so strong that we've grown from just an overnight shelter" to a full-service agency.

Volunteers, 110 of them, are the backbone of Abby's operation, according to Rafferty. Most are women. The agency's $230,000 budget is funded by private donations from men, women, churches, civic groups and community foundations.

"This is a place where women can find common ground," Rafferty said. "We have women here of all faiths and political viewpoints. Abby's House cuts through all that because our mission is clear: The empowerment of women to shape their own future."

Genevieve

Haitian women are taught to endure. Haitian men, Genevieve said, are taught that beating women is acceptable.

"Beating a woman is nothing there," she said. "I know a man who had a woman and he was so jealous that one day, he took a _____ _____ her face. He didn't want other men to see her because she was so pretty."

Police, she said, looked the other way.

Nonetheless, Genevieve, 36, divorced her first husband because he was unfaithful, and she came to the United States. She left her second husband because he beat her. She recently left her longtime boyfriend in Worcester, because, three months ago, he began to use drugs and beat her, too.

"He banged my head against

the wall. He said he was going to find a gun, and they were not going to arrest him because he was going to kill me and then he was going to kill himself.

"That's when I left."

Abby's House helped Genevieve and her three children find new housing. Genevieve, who asked that only her first name be used, has worked as a nurse's aide and is training to become a licensed practical nurse.

Her father was a gentle man, Genevieve said. She was shocked that the men she met were not.

Many Haitian women stay with abusive husbands. "They always say, 'That's your man. What else are you going to find?'

"I originally thought I couldn't make it on my own. I always cried because sometimes you need the company. Now, I swear off men. I don't want nobody to abuse me or my kids."

Sonia Elmore

Drunk and in a rage, Sonia Elmore's father plunged into the house and charged toward the bathroom, a knife in his hand. Her mother was in the shower. He pounded on the bathroom door, screaming, "I'm going to kill you."

Sonia's little sister, then about age 5, stopped him.

"She was always Daddy's little girl," said Sonia, now 24. "She sat him down and got the knife away from him."

Sonia Elmore vowed never to re-enact that violent scene in her own life. Her mother divorced soon after it, and the man her mother later married was "the greatest," Elmore said. "He gave me the first birthday party I ever had."

Yet when Elmore married and her own husband cursed her, when he grabbed her by the neck and pushed her to the ground, she didn't recognize it as spousal abuse.

"I didn't know yelling and pushing your wife was abuse, or even that forcing your wife to have sex is rape," Elmore said. "I thought you had to hit someone or give them a black eye."

Elmore, a mother of two, worked full time as a customer service representative. But she didn't think she could survive without her husband.

"Part of my thinking was I couldn't do anything." She had neither a high school diploma nor a driver's license. "I didn't know what excise taxes were or pay any attention to politics. I didn't know anything. That's why I put up with abuse so long, because I didn't know how to (live) on my own."

However, last fall, as she watched her 2-year-old son grab a glass and hurl it in anger like his father, she realized she had to act. After a violent fight with her husband Nov. 18, she left with the children. She turned to Abby's House, where the staff helped her file for divorce.

"I can make it on my own," she says now. "I'm never going back."

Annette A. Rafferty

Domestic violence leaves many people confused.

They consider batterers criminals. But they also consider victims too weak or too foolish to walk out on the men who give them black eyes and bruises.

Annette A. Rafferty, 65, a former nun who co-founded Abby's House, disagrees.

"When you have the privilege of working with the homeless and abused, you discover parts of them that no one else has had the ability to see," she said. "There's beauty. There's strength. There are things we can learn from women (whom) society sees as wasted lives."

Often, "we don't see how far they have struggled and how much courage they have.

Instead of just seeing where they are, see where they've come from.

"In the face of these women, I am overwhelmed with awe."

Joan M. Liggons

It should have been an exhilarating event. Instead, after her daughter's birth, Joan M. Liggons' life collapsed.

In 1960, she fell into a postpartum depression so deep she couldn't pull herself out, even to fill a baby bottle. She was hospitalized, and there she

stayed three years.

"That was the end of my life," she said. "There was no more me."

By the time she was released, she said, her husband had divorced her and married a teen-age neighbor. He demanded permanent custody of their child. Faced with few options, she consented.

Turn to DESPITE/Next Page

Betty Jenewin

Abby's House report praised

Congratulations to Betty Jenewin and Allison K. Jones. Their March 14 portrait of Abby's House was exceptional. The photographs were beautiful and the text deeply moving. We can learn from poor women, women who work with very little and the strong women worthy of this tribute.

LISA CONNELLY COOK
Millbury

---

admission and unlimited rides. $1-off coupons available at area merchants. Green Hill Park. Call (800) 831-9847.

Abby's House Fund-raiser, Team O'Sullivan joins WXLO to raise funds for Abby's House, a home for women in need of shelter. Enjoy billiards, food and games. $15. 5:30-8 p.m. Jillan's, 315 Grove St. Call 793-2929.

Despite abuse, marriage did have bright spots

Continued From Previous Page

Guilt ridden and alone, she was hospitalized repeatedly in the years that followed. It would be decades before she was diagnosed and treated as a manic depressive.

Liggons became an alcoholic. She married unwisely.

"Joe was 29 when I met him. He was very handsome. He was tall. He had a beautiful personality. Joe could do a lot of good."

But Joe also abused drugs. When he was high, "Joe beat the living hell out of me," she said.

"People say, 'Why don't women leave them'" she said. "Well, God help us if we do, because they'll kill you. There were times we went fist-to-fist in the later years. I usually won most of those. (By then) he was drunk most of the time. He got very weak.

"There were good parts to him. Abusive relationships are not always bad. He never forgot my anniversary. He never forgot my birthday. We traveled a lot. ... He always cared about people. He'd invite people home and he'd say, 'Babe, put on a pot.'"

When times were bad, Liggons fled to Abby's House and to Worcester, where she grew up. But, eventually, she'd return to Joe. He died in 1985 at age 49.

Liggons, 59, has been sober now five years. She doesn't waste time on regrets. But she remembers childhood visions of a life of fame. She remembers thinking she'd become a movie star.

"But most of all, I wanted to be married," she said. "I wanted to wear white and (then) have two or three kids of my own.

"I never got it. All the most important things I wanted were right there, but they slipped through my fingers."

Jeanne C. Rosenblatt

'The issue of poverty is not understood or accepted," said Jeanne C. Rosenblatt. "There's contempt for people in poverty."

Rosenblatt spent 25 years in social work. But she said she didn't understand poverty until she volunteered at Abby's House.

"We need to understand that if you're born in poverty, you're likely to remain there," she said. "It's not possible for everyone to pull themselves up by the bootstraps.

"There has to be a real understanding of what it is to be without resources — meaning, did you have a decent place to live growing up and decent meals and health care and encouragement? Was your family without serious problems of poverty or addiction? We need to be aware of the vast differences between having some comfort ..."

And struggling to shape a life from nothing.

Debbie Hachen and at a Strawberry Festival at Christ the King Church, with Anne Humes at the helm. Long-time supporters Larry and Gloria Abramoff hosted a "store-party" at Tatnuck Booksellers where a quilt I made was raffled and won by Dr. Cheryl Houston. Jean Dahler and Sylvia Jane of the Sunburst Restaurant in Sturbridge held an event in May and by mid-summer, Joe O'Brien had pulled team O'Sullivan (those who had supported Kevin in his run for State Representative) into Jillian's, a local billiard parlor, where a party was also held. The list of house-store-restaurant parties was endless. Meanwhile, we were all waiting to learn the plans of the Crown Hill Neighborhood Association for the 20th anniversary.

In the midst of all this anniversary activity, we continued to plan and carry out daily, usual activities. International Women's Day on March 8th was observed with a benefit by Aubrey Atwater, a Rhode Island folk singer/multi-instrumentalist, at the Student Lounge of Worcester State College. Aubrey focused her presentation on the contributions women have made to Irish and American folk music. What a beautiful respite in the hurried, flurried pace we were keeping, to hear the music of this skilled dulcimer, tin whistle and banjo playing singer. The evening refreshed our souls and we were prepared to begin another week of "upward" which began with a truly engaging and educational piece in the March 14, 1995 edition of the *Worcester Telegram and Gazette*. The text had been thoughtfully prepared by Allison Jones and the photos taken by our dear friend Betty Jenewin. No party, no appeal could have done more for Abby's and the 20th anniversary project of restoring 77 Chatham Street than this true-to-life account, "Faces of Abby's House." The article and pictures of "Faces" captured so well the mission of the organization. Especially compelling were the true stories of Genevieve, Sonia and Joan, all extremely brave, courageous women and, for me, Jeanne Rosenblatt's observation touched the heart of the matter:

> "We need to understand that if you're born in poverty, you're likely to remain there. ... It's not possible for everyone to pull themselves up by the bootstraps... There needs to be a real understanding of what it is to be without resources ... did you have a decent place to live in growing up ... decent meals and health care and encouragement ... was your family without serious problems of addiction? We need to be aware of the vast differences between having some comfort and struggling to shape a life from nothing."

That's why we exist—to be the comfort, to be the decent place, to help women shape something meaningful from absolutely nothing, to offer resources and much needed understanding. I continually reflect on that statement, because like Jeanne who felt she didn't understand poverty until she volunteered at Abby's, neither did I. And after all of these years, I'm still straining to understand the varied faces and shapes of poverty in that common quest to end it for as many women and children as is possible in one lifetime.

"We need to be aware of the vast differences between having some comfort and struggling to shape a life from nothing."

News

Walk in counseling now available at Abby's House

By Sarah Corkum

To become more accessible to the homeless and battered women it has served for almost 20 years, Abby's House, located at 23 Crown St., has established a new walk-in service.

The service is funded by a $10,000 grant from the Greater Worcester Community Foundation. Walk-in hours are 9 a.m. to noon Wednesday, noon to 3 p.m. Thursday or by appointment.

Since Abby's House opened its doors in 1976, its staff and volunteers have offered a wide variety of services, including an emergency shelter, support groups, medical care and educational and cultural programs.

"The walk-in service actually originated from the women who have come through the shelter requesting the need for some sort of support system after they have left," explained Elaine Lamoureux, the guest advocate running the walk-in service along with other advocates.

The program is open to all women who have experienced or are experiencing domestic violence, as well as to family and friends of battered women. The aim of the program is to provide information, emotional support, court advocacy, peer counseling and crisis intervention.

The women are able to meet one on one with a counselor or in a group setting with other women.

"We hope the women will shape the self-help program themselves with a leader present," said Lamoureux. "Since most abused women have been controlled for so long, we hope this program will provide them with a new feeling that what they have to say is valid."

For the first year, the emphasis of the program will be on outreach and group work, with a variety of support groups and educational programs.

"What's so unique about this particular program," emphasized Lamoureux, "is the fact that it is the only one of its kind offered in the city. While most support groups require initial contact, an interview and usually a long waiting list, our program bypasses the waiting process."

And in cases of domestic violence, time is crucial. "We hope women will always have this service in the back of their minds — a place to go in a crisis situation," Lamoureux said. "In shelter situations, women frequently make appointments and for one reason or another they cancel or don't follow through. This only serves to compound their feelings of guilt — and we hope to eliminate this problem by offering 'spur of the moment' support." ●

TELEGRAM & GAZETTE

WORCESTEI

WEDNESDAY, APRIL 12, 1995

New life for Crown Hill site

Annette A. Rafferty of Abby's House passes through the entrance — half boarded-up — at 77 Chatham St., which will be rehabbed into apartments for women and children.

CHRIS CHRISTO

Abby's House sets rehab

By Emilie Astell
Telegram & Gazette Staff

WORCESTER — It won't be long before boarded-up windows and peeling paint at 77 Chatham St. give way to hammers and nails as a renovation crew starts its work.

The 2½-story mansard-roofed building is to be converted to seven, two-bedroom apartments for low-income, homeless mothers and their children.

Abby's House, an agency that helps homeless and battered women with and without children, is the owner of the building and developer of the project. A fund-raising effort was kicked off yesterday at a press conference at the Chatham Street address.

Ground-breaking at the property, which has been vacant five years, is scheduled for June 7, with construction to start soon afterward. Renovations should be completed by January.

The project cost is approximately $500,000. Abby's House hopes to raise money through individual donations and contributions from churches, civic groups, corporations and foundations.

Patricia A. Conzo, president of the board of directors of Abby's House, said the project helps both the neighborhood and the women who will live in the renovated building.

Tess Sneesby, executive director of Abby's House, said Flagship Bank is offering the agency a federally backed loan for an unspecified amount.

The building is in the Crown Hill Historic District. The Preservation Society of Worcester and the Worcester Historical Commission support the project.

Patti Conzo announces rehab plans

Love, Laughter, Lasagna fans with Loretta (center

CHAPTER 16 *Walking in and Stumbling-Dirt and Humbug*

W ithin a few weeks after this in-depth report was published, Abby's was able to make another public announcement of our effort to offer that comfort and support with the formal establishment of a walk-in counseling service funded by the Greater Worcester Community Foundation. As Elaine Lamoureux explained, "The walk-in service actually originated with the women who have come through the shelter, requesting some sort of support system after they have left."

After much consideration of what this service could offer, we decided that the walk-in would be open to all women who have experienced or are experiencing domestic violence, as well as to family and friends of battered women. So, the final goal of the program would be to provide information, emotional support, court advocacy, peer counseling and crisis information. Elaine further noted that the program was unique in the area since it would bypass an initial contact, an interview, and a long waiting list. Walk-in hours continue to be Wednesdays and Thursdays at the main office at 23 Crown Street. We all know that in cases of domestic violence, time is critical, but it takes this program to remind us that women need to have this service in their minds—a place to go in a crisis situation:

> "In shelter situations, women frequently make appointments and for one reason or another, they cancel or don't follow through. This only serves to compound their feelings of guilt and we hope to eliminate this

problem by offering 'spur of the moment support.' " (Elaine Lamoureux)

In an unending chain of public events, there came the official announcement of the capital campaign to rehab 77 Chatham Street into apartments for very low-income women and their children. This took place on Tuesday, April 11, 1995 at 11 a.m. at the site of the Willard Jones home. It was a fairly simple announcement with board president Patricia A. Conzo stressing the need and reminding all of us that this project would help both the neighborhood and the women who would eventually live in the renovated building. We also announced that a groundbreaking at the property was scheduled for June 7th, the beginning of our 20th year. Construction would start in the early summer and all, hopefully, would be completed by January 1996. (This date for completion was a pie-in-the-sky wish. An unmerciful winter delayed completion until spring of 1996.) Nevertheless, it was a thrilling moment to announce this news with hopeful hearts and to know, once again, that we had the backing of Flagship Bank, the Preservation Society of Worcester, the Worcester Historical Commission, the Crown Hill Neighborhood Association, and the community. The business of raising that $500,000 was pressing and, so, encouraged by Callahan, MacIntyre and Associates, the 20th anniversary committee, the core staff and the chairs, like Piercy's favorite friends, jumped into the work headfirst without dallying in the shallows and [nervously] swam off with sure strokes almost, but not quite, out of sight!

During April and May we held more house parties and fundraisers, including a "Today's Business Woman" luncheon and fashion show presented in conjunction with Secretaries Week for our benefit. It was held at Center Court of the Worcester Common Fashion Outlets and once again we were all treated to another round of "Love, Laughter and Lasagna," performed by Loretta LaRoche. By this time, all of us needed the healing touch of laughter. No matter how noble our cause, it was impossible not to experience the tension and the pressure of fundraising, and, at the same time, continue to do the daily work and the extra assignments required of a capital campaign. An evening at Temple Emanuel with Loretta provided once again the right prescription for curing the anxieties, easing the tensions

Groundbreaking Ceremony
at
77 Chatham Street
June 7, 1995
4:00 p.m.

Open House
at 19 Crown Street Facility
and at our shelter, 23 Crown Street
following the ceremony.

Refreshments to be served.

The crowd gathers for the June 7th ground-breaking

B6 TELEGRAM & GAZETTE   THURSDAY, JUNE 8, 1995

Abby's House breaks ground

By John J. O'Connor
Telegram & Gazette Staff

WORCESTER — Kathleen Luthman called herself "one of the lucky ones" yesterday during Abby's House groundbreaking at 77 Chatham St.

Abby's House hopes to refurbish the building, abandoned for five years, to create seven two-bedroom apartments for low-income mothers and their children.

Abby's House helps homeless and battered women with and without children. It has a shelter at 21-23 Crown St. and a supportive housing unit at 19 Crown St.

Luthman was one of those women.

She told about 75 people at the groundbreaking that "two years ago I was being evicted from my apartment. There was a lot of drinking going on. I had heard of Abby's House. They took a chance on me. Everyone there encouraged me to go to my therapy and to keep my doctor's appointments.

"They gave me back something I had lost. They were all so supportive," she said.

Luthman lived at Abby's House for nine months. "When I moved into my own apartment, I felt lonesome. When I was feeling down I would visit Abby's House and they would talk with me. I am getting my self-esteem back and I don't feel I have to hide my face anymore. My own sisters have always shown me support and one of my sisters drove up from New York today to hear me give this speech," she said.

"Women who are mistreated don't know they don't have to live that way," she said.

Luthman was one of several speakers at yesterday's ceremonies.

The cost of the project is about $500,000. Abby's House hopes to raise money through individual donations and contributions from churches, civic groups, corporations and foundations.

Patricia A. Conzo, president of the board of directors of Abby's House, said the agency is starting its 20th year by preparing 77 Chatham St.

She said 21-23 Crown St. was open to provide shelter and service the needs of homeless and battered women with children. Conzo said 19 Crown St. was opened for single women.

"We want to open this building (77 Chatham St.) as permanent housing for low-income women and children."

"It is easy to help someone you know," Conzo said. "It is difficult to reach out and help a stranger."

Let it rain,

Let it rain,

Let it rain!

and lifting the drooping spirits. Here's to a daily dose of Loretta's brand of humor. I often wondered if Abby K. F., whose presence in the public forum boasted of outcries, denunciations, soul-searing statements against slavery, had ever laughed out loud, with tears streaming down her face. It's hard to visualize Abby doubled over with laughter, but I am convinced if anyone could have brought at least a smile to that wonderfully stern but beautiful face, it would have been Loretta LaRoche.

By early June, Fran O'Connell and I signed the final letter that would circulate everywhere announcing the 20th anniversary project. There wouldn't be a single soul in the community who would not know of this progressive and daring move and, as usual, we knew the response would be positive. This official announcement was followed posthaste by invitations to the June 7, 1995 groundbreaking ceremony. As a child, I remember my Irish-Catholic relatives speaking all kinds of folklore, such as "happy the corpse the rain falls on" when someone was buried. So, when June 7th dawned in a steady downpour, those words flashed warning signs in my head. We had no corpse, but one look at this 77 Chatham Street shambles, decorated with all kinds of graffiti and sheltering, no doubt, a good share of deceased rodents, I envisioned it as a corpse, about to be resurrected, and I silently prayed for the rain to continue. Guess what? It did. Indeed, in my estimation the house had already been blessed. People came from as far as Boston to participate in the 4 p.m. event. There was Dave Bancroft, representing Mary Padula, from the Office of Community Development; John Eller of Federal Home Loan Bank, and State Representative Harriette Chandler. Locally, representatives included: our district councillor Janice Nadeau; city councillor and vice mayor John Anderson; Mary McAdams (Dean) of Flagship Bank and Trust; Rosamond Rockwell of Preservation Worcester; and Marge Purves, president of the Crown Hill Neighborhood Association.

Representing our guests was Kathleen Luthman, and our volunteers were represented by musician of the day, Ellen Laverdure. Joan Felipe, a 19 Crown Street resident, Genevieve Georges and her children, formerly of the shelter, Lorraine Fletcher, housing coordinator and Emily Rothschild, housing consultant all turned over shovels of earth. Some of us had a few words to speak to the assembled crowd, but it was our director,

who summed up everything with the following powerful reminder of our rootedness:

> "... Those who were involved in the founding of Abby's were outraged that no safe haven existed for women and they channeled that anger into a focused, persistent and steady action. They, along with each of us throughout these years, created a place of gentle hospitality, a place where, in belonging, in being 'home,' we could find our own beauty and discover the power within ourselves. I recently read a quote by Herman Hesse that reminded me of our mission as an organization both yesterday and today as we stand here on this property:
>
> *'We have to stumble through so much dirt and humbug before we reach home. And we have no one to guide us. Our only guide is our homesickness.'*
>
> Let's continue to move to a time when everyone has a stable, permanent home."

Nothing could have been added to that tribute, to that challenge, to that stark reality involving dirt and humbug and the constant, daily struggle to find our own way "home." The day ended with refreshments and conversation at the shelter and the 19 Crown Street home. A huge notch had been carved into the onward pole that groundbreaking day by the staff, the volunteers, the funders, the supporters, the guests and residents. The rest of the notches would be skillfully carved by the contractor, the subcontractors, the architect, and the carving would begin the very moment a contract with Roman Mazurek of Rodan Construction Company had been signed, sealed and delivered.

We were extremely busy during the summer of '95 with weekly events for the cause of 77 Chatham Street, and we were occasionally delighted by unexpected publicity appearing in the wider community newspapers. Mary Donovan, one of the 20th anniversary committee members and former editor of *The Voice*, did a splendid piece on Karen Nunley, an Abby's House volunteer, and Mary Liebe, one of our shelter guests. The article paid not only well-deserved tribute to the work of Abby's, but also effectively highlighted how positively one volunteer can affect

Artist brightens the life at Abby's

By Mary Donovan
Record Staff

WESTBORO — When Karen Nunley volunteers at the Day Center at Abby's House, she runs bingo games, shows movies, serves lunch and helps run other activities. But the most important thing she does is just be there.

The Day Center is at Abby's House on Crown Street in Worcester. Abby's is a shelter for women and their children who are homeless for whatever reason. Next door is the supported housing that is run by Abby's. The Day

Center is a place for women and children from the shelter and the housing to get together in a way their daily lives often can't provide. Women from the neighborhood are also welcome.

Nunley volunteers at the center twice a month. "I really enjoy doing it," she said. "You feel like you're doing positive stuff."

The positive stuff is filled with variety. On a recent Monday, Nunley sat in a comfortable chair chatting with two women and occasionally casting an eye at early

ABBY'S, PAGE 14

Record photo by Mary Donovan

KAREN NUNLEY (left), a Westboro artist, puts her arm around Mary Liebe who is currently staying at Abby's House shelter where Nunley volunteers.

It's official! 77 Chatham is Abby's House

Roman Mazurek

◆Abby's House Capital Campaign◆

Issue 1   July 1995

GIVE ABBY'S A FOOT UP

Abby's House is raising $500,000 to renovate 77 Chatham Street in Worcester into seven two-bedroom apartments for low- income families. These families will have a permanent home, thanks to the generosity of you, the Friends of Abby's House.

This project celebrates twenty years of Abby's service to the community. YOU CAN HELP!!!

Abby's House wants everyone in the community to save at least one square foot of pennies. There are 256 pennies in a square foot, and the Abby's House project is a total of 23,954 square feet, so Abby's House needs a total of 6,132,224 pennies.

Please save your pennies and give Abby's House a FOOT UP to success. The total of this activity, $61,322.24, will help Abby's House reach its goal. Of course, you can contribute to Abby's House in many other ways: pledging a gift over three years (or more), a check in any denomination, in-kind gifts of new or nearly new furniture and appliances, or by volunteering assistance in the shelter or thrift shop. Everyone can be a part of the Abby's experience — people helping people.

Won't you help? Either pick up a container from Abby's House or use one of your own containers to collect your pennies for Abby's. Everyone can contribute in their own way. When your container is full, please drop it off at Abby's House, 19 Crown Street, or call an Abby's House volunteer to have your donation picked up. Tax-deductible receipts for the amount donated will be given when you turn in your container.

CALL ABBY'S HOUSE FOR MORE INFORMATION ON THIS EXCITING PROJECT, BUT IN THE MEANTIME, START SAVING YOUR PENNIES FOR ABBY'S TODAY.

Abby's House is renovating 77 Chatham Street into seven two-bedroom apartments for low-income families.

President
Patricia Conzo

Treasurer
Annette Bleau

Clerk
Virginia Mischitelli

Directors
Pat Albrecht
Ann Carlson
Lucelia Delenus
Maddy Entel
Patty Falcone
Jane Grady
Martha Hosey
Suzanne Howart
Nancy Nobert
Frances O'Connell
Jeanne Rosenblatt

Thanks to Our Hosts

House Parties:
Barbara Athy   (4-20-95)
Joan Cassidy   (5-11-95)
Ann Carlson   (4-18-95)
Angela Dorenkamp (6-8-95)
Veronica Griffin   (4-30-95)
Holly Heggie   (6-7-95)
Konnie Lukes   (5-6-95)
Joan Mazzeo   (5-3-95)
Fran O'Connell   (5-7-95)
Terri Priest   (4-30-95)
Mary Taft   (5-7-95)

Church Gatherings:
Federated Church of Sturbridge
- Clint & Juanita Beuscher   (5-31-95)

Templ - Rabbi Dabble Hachen
- Congregation B'Nai Shalom   (6-29-95)

Strawberry Festival - Christ the King Church -
Anne Humes, Chair   (6-22-95)

Events:
Tatnuck Bookseller & Sons
- Larry & Gloria Abramoff, hosts   (6-21-95)

Sunburst Cafe, Sturbridge
- Jean & Sylvia   (5-18-95)

Jillian's
- Joe O'Brien, host (7-26-95/ 5:30-8pm)

Penny campaigners give Abby's a foot up!

New Ludlow School donates books

lives in so many different ways. Karen had an ability to forge relationships and to "teach" her craft of watercolor to someone who had no idea she was artistic. Watercolors, such as Karen Nunley brought to Abby's, proved a powerful way to cut through Hesse's "dirt and humbug and homesickness" of life. Like Loretta's laughter, Karen's paintings helped to keep attitudes positive and to open new doors of possibility to our women.

Meanwhile, the anniversary committee took some very big steps. Our consultants, Sandra and Sid, introduced the idea of a Penny Campaign that would give "Abby's a Foot Up." The idea was warmly and enthusiastically received, and Julie Komenos assumed the job of coordinating the location and distribution of over 1,000 penny containers. Goldstar Branch of Flagship Bank was the point of return of each and every container. Since each square foot of pennies equaled $2.52 and Abby's needed over 21 thousand square feet of pennies to cover the entire property, this type of fundraising effort would raise $66,000! The best part of the penny project was Abby's opportunity to involve children who reached out to help other children. It also offered golden opportunities to others who wanted to help us out but felt unable to do something on-site or to donate significant sums to achieve the final goal. Another way of connecting with the mission was born, and we thank our consultants for opening this door. Little did we realize as this portion of the campaign kicked off that by the following February, Abby's, WXLO and the Worcester Ice Cats' mascot, Scratch, would team up for the drive at the Greendale Mall! I might add that the penny campaign is still going, resulting to date in contributions totaling $23,000. The 20th anniversary committee had literally and successfully stuck its foot into it.

Assumption College students preparing Thanksgiving dinner

Worcester Academy students help Santa

Apple-A-Day children pay a visit

St. Peter-Marian students helping Abby's children

What great kids

The Crown Hill Neighborhood candlelight stroll

THE CATHOLIC FREE PRESS
July 14, 1995

Hich schoolers pitch in for Abby House

By: Michael Cox

They could have spent the week swimming, playing Nintendo or going to the mall.

Instead, four high school students from the St. Joseph's and St. Pius X parishes spent the week landscaping at Abby's House in Worcester and holding a cook-out

for the elderly at the Main Street Apartments in Leicester.

The volunteers, Lisa Laconto, Amy Marinello, Christina Bauer and Brian Hippert, all of Leicester, said they wanted to do it because it feels good to help other people.

According to Carol Cornacchioli, pastoral associate at St. Jos-

eph's Parish, "We offered it as a ministry experience to the students so they would feel like they have done something special to help other people."

Ms. Cornacchioli said all of the young adults have volunteered their time on their own as a life enriching experience separate from any

other pastoral or civic obligations.

She said they chose Abby's House, a shelter for battered woman, because, "We wanted to spruce up the place so there is an obvious sense of hospitality for the families who are staying here."

Continued on Page 6

Brian Hippert is one of four students working at Abby House as part of a summer ministry program. PHOTO BY MICHAEL COX

High School students donate time

Continued from Page 1

The landscaping project resulted in the creation of two new flower gardens in the front yard.

According to Ms. Cornacchioli, the project took nearly two days. "First, we had to dig out all the grass in the front yard. Then, we had to sift the loom, plant the plants and mulch the area."

The plants, which made the whole project possible, were a gift from an anonymous donor.

In addition to the landscaping work the group also helped with a major clean-up inside Abby House.

On Tuesday, the students had a chance to meet and have lunch with the women at Abby House.

Ms. Cornacchioli said this was the second year a group from St. Joseph's and St. Pius have gone to work at Abby House. Last year, the students painted the fence in the backyard.

Cristina Bauer, a student who was involved in both projects, said, "People deserve it to have a nice home to live in just like everyone else."

Sr. Hilda Chasse, house manager, was very grateful for the help.

She said, "I find it so beautiful for young people to do something good for someone else. It's life giving."

Ms. Cornacchioli said, "We like to end each day with a prayer."

The week began on Monday with an orientation and reflection on ministry.

On Thursday, the group held a cook-out for the elderly at the Main Street Apartments in Leicester and concluded the week with a Mass and supper at St. Joseph's Rectory.

Barbara Herman
welcomes you to tonight's gala for the Benefit of

Abby's House

November 8, 1995

Goddard House
1199 Main Street
Worcester, MA

7:00 - 9:30 p.m.

Entertainment by David Witt and Drumbhodi

ABBY'S HOUSE
21-27 CROWN STREET
WORCESTER, MA 01609

Jewels IN THE Crown

YOU ARE CORDIALLY INVITED TO STEP BACK IN TIME AT A

Candlelight Stroll and Progressive Cocktail Party

OCTOBER 15, 1995, 5 TO 7 PM
HORS D'OEUVRES AND COCKTAILS
$25 PER PERSON

Stroll from house to house, as you meander through five jewels in Worcester's historic Crown Hill neighborhood, a neighborhood created in the 1850s and recreated beginning in the early 1970s. Proceeds from this party will benefit the Abby's House 20th Anniversary Capital Campaign and the restoration of another Crown Hill jewel, 77 Chatham Street.

FOLLOWING THE PROGRESSIVE COCKTAILS, YOU ARE INVITED TO

A Private Sunday Supper

prepared by Struddale's renowned Executive Chef, Georges Marisult, at Mulcan's, 592 Main Street, a lovely restored 19th century commercial building (with convenient parking next door).

SEATING IS VERY LIMITED.
$50 PER PERSON FOR BOTH PROGRESSIVE COCKTAILS AND PRIVATE SUPPER.

RSVP BY OCTOBER 10, 1995.

Yes, I (we) was (were) stepping back in time Sunday, October 15

_____ TICKETS FOR THE PROGRESSIVE COCKTAIL PARTY @ $25 PER PERSON
_____ TICKETS FOR BOTH THE PROGRESSIVE COCKTAIL PARTY AND PRIVATE SUPPER @ $50 PER PERSON
$_____ TOTAL ENCLOSED

SORRY, I (WE) CANNOT ATTEND BUT WOULD LIKE TO DONATE TO THE RENOVATION OF 77 CHATHAM.
$_____ TOTAL ENCLOSED

(CHECKS CAN BE MADE TO ABBY'S HOUSE CAPITAL CAMPAIGN.)

TICKETS AND THE ADDRESSES OF YOUR PROGRESSIVE COCKTAIL SITES WILL BE MAILED TO YOU UPON RECEIPT OF YOUR RESERVATIONS.

RESERVATIONS ARE LIMITED SO PLEASE RESPOND EARLY.

NON-PROFIT ORG
US POSTAGE
PAID
WORCESTER, MA
PERMIT NO. 337

Tag Sale

What a wonderful evening

TELEGRAM & GAZETTE   Page B3

Holden

■ A Halloween Hoe-Down, featuring country line dancing with music from Mickey Chapman and the Music Express and instruction from Chuck Harter, will be held from 7 p.m. to midnight tomorrow at the Holden Hills Conference Center. The event will benefit Abby House of Worcester, a multiservice organization for homeless and battered women with or without children, and the Holden Chamber of Commerce.

For ticket information, call Abby House at 756-5476, the Holden Chamber of Commerce at 829-9220 or Oriol Health Care at 829-7383. Tickets, at $15 per person, will be available at the door. A taco bar and prizes will be featured. Costumes are optional.

THURSDAY, OCTOBER 26, 1995

The Holden Hoe-down!

Wise Women holiday cards about to debut

By Dolores Courtemanche
Telegram & Gazette Staff

WORCESTER – The Three Wise Men no longer have a monopoly on holiday greeting cards.

This year, you'll have the option of buying cards featuring the Three Wise Women.

The fanciful, yet sophisticated cards were created by Barbara Herman, a Worcester interior decorator. For several years, she has designed and assembled the handmade cards for friends and clients during the holiday season.

The idea evolved, Herman said, because she hated to throw away wallpaper books that contained many beautiful patterns. So each year, she pored through the books looking for suitable papers for her cards.

Her theme has always been the Three Wise Women. One year her card had three Indian women shown from the back. This year, because wallpaper with an African motif is so popular, the Wise Women are dressed in colors patterned in earth colors. Next year, Herman said her theme will be stick figure "divas" dressed in gowns. "I think of them as all women, which is why I make them with no features," she said.

Several months ago, members of Abby's House board of directors met at a home where a couple of Wise Women cards were framed. There, it was suggested that Herman have the cards published.

Herman said she didn't want the cards printed just for profit, so she decided that proceeds would be shared with Abby's House, a shelter for abused women and their families. Abby's House will receive 50 percent of the profits and the remainder will be used for expenses and to get a start on next year's cards.

The Three Wise Women will be introduced at a gala from 7 to 9:30 p.m. Nov. 8 at the Goddard House, 1199 Main St.

The cards are processed with four-color printing. Each will be decorated with feathers, shells and sequins for earrings. It will take some time and the joint effort of many people – friends of Herman's and Abby's House – to prepare the cards for sale. Herman said 3,000 were printed, and it took her 18 minutes to glue a feather, pearls and sequins on just one. "We'll have some workshops to put them together," she said.

The cards and envelopes measure 9-by-7½ inches and are not folded, so they may be framed. Packages of five cards will sell for $15. A single card may be purchased for $3. Cards will be available for purchase, following the gala, at Barbara Herman Interiors, Abby's House, YWCA, Monahan Pharmacies, Webster House, Picnic on Park, Early & Clark Florists and the Sturbridge Senior Center.

There will be entertainment and refreshments. The celebration is by invitation only, but the public will be welcome as space allows.

Barbara Herman, an interior decorator, is making Three Wise Women cards, foreground, to benefit Abby's House. JIM COLLINS

TELEGRAM & GAZETTE TUESDAY, OCTOBER 24, 1995 C1

B2 SUNDAY TELEGRAM SEPTEMBER 17, 1995

Uplifting experience

WORCESTER — Edna L. Sexton of Holden takes the high road with her and table as she negotiates through the parked crowd yesterday at the 14th annual tag sale to benefit Abby's House. More than $12,000 was raised, said Toni Snersby, executive director of the shelter for homeless and battered women on Crown Street.

CHAPTER 17 *The Queens Came Late*

Abby's House, it seemed to me, was appearing almost daily in the newspapers with stories and pictures of events and activities, ranging from Jillian's fundraiser to pictures of Leicester High School students sprucing up the property around the shelter and 19 Crown Street. According to Carol Cornacchioli, the students offered to do the exterior work "so that there would be an obvious sense of hospitality for the families staying [at Abby's]." Announcements about the annual Women's Equality Day, the amazing tag sale, and Pat Nedoroscik's intentions to prepare for the Holy Cross Craft Fair popped up in our own newsletter, along with the news that volunteer Dorrie Hutchins wanted help and recipes to (finally) publish a cookbook for the 20th anniversary. At long last, the Crown Hill Neighborhood Association announced its anxiously awaited plans to promote the 77 Chatham Street project. On October 15 there would be a candlelight stroll through the neighborhood and a progressive cocktail party from 5 to 7 p.m. The invitation read:

> "Stroll from house to house, as you meander through five jewels in Worcester's historic Crown Hill neighborhood created in the 1850s and recreated beginning in the early 1970s. Proceeds from this party will benefit the Abby's House 20th Anniversary Capital Campaign and the restoration of another Crown Hill jewel, 77 Chatham Street."

The stroll was a huge success. Many came into the neighborhood for the first time, and it was an eye-opener, indeed, to see the interiors of these beautifully restored homes. The hospitality extended by the homeowners, as well as by the residents of 19 Crown Street, was warm and characteristically gracious. For anyone interested in extending their day in the neighborhood, a private Sunday supper was prepared by Stendahl's renowned chef, George Marjault, at Milano's, a lovely restored 19th century commercial building at 592 Main Street. Both the stroll and the supper remain memorable moments in the life of Abby's.

There was no stopping this onward thrust! The following weekend, a Halloween hoe down was held at Holden Hills Banquet Center with a portion of the proceeds going to Abby's capital campaign. On the heels of the hoedown came the unforgettable gala on November 8th when creative Worcester interior decorator Barbara Herman introduced her new line of wise women holiday cards at the Goddard House. Not wanting the cards printed for profit, Barbara decided proceeds would benefit Abby's House in its efforts to convert the newly acquired building on Chatham Street into apartments. This was an unforgettable evening. The gala attracted crowds of new and interested people. The cards were an overnight hit and within a few days were available for purchase at seven different locations. Barbara had struck the right holiday note, but not for everyone. I received a letter from an unhappy donor who was mightily upset that we were disturbing the accepted tradition of the Christmas story, by "ousting" the men from their rightful position. This was something no one had anticipated. From her perspective, the cards challenged theological conclusions. We were being scolded for our outrageous feminism. The honest truth was this: creativity, not theological tampering, had been the intention of this theme. Being the artist she was, Barbara used her ingenuity and recycling commitment to develop a new art form. Was it possible that use of old wallpaper books to create these colorful cards could be perceived as an attack on tradition? Evidently. The letter concluded with a veiled threat to discontinue the writer's financial support of the organization. I answered the letter assuring her that the cards were a creative venture, not a statement of feminist revisionism. Further, I expressed my hope that she would reconsider withdrawing support from the women who would gain help from the sale of the cards. (By the way, my

BULLETIN BOARD

Area

■ **Citizens Energy Corp.** announced a 20 percent increase in its annual Shelter Winter Assistance Program.

Citizen Energy will spend $300,000 this winter, up from $250,000 last year, to pay the heating bills of 140 homeless shelters in the region.

Twenty-five thousand dollars has been targeted to 13 shelters in Central Massachusetts to purchase roughly 7,000 gallons of oil and pay more than $20,000 in utility heating bills during the winter months.

Worcester shelters include PIP, Jeremiah's Inn, Channing House, the Central Mass Shelter for Homeless Veterans, Shepherd's Place, the Linda Fay Griffin House and the Abby Kelly Foster House.

Other area shelters benefiting from the program include: Horizon House and Our Father's House, both in Fitchburg; Pathways and Turning Point Shelters, Framingham; the Marlboro Shelter; and Winter Haven, Milford.

Starting in 1987, the Citizens Energy Shelter Winter Assistance Program has provided 671,000 gallons of heating oil free of charge and spent more than $1.2 million on oil and utility heating bills.

The Numbers

Drawn Friday, Dec. 22

MASS MILLIONS

TELEGRAM & GAZETTE

TIME OUT

THURSDAY, DECEMBER 7, 1995

▶

HOLIDAY BENEFIT PARTY

Mocha Java, above, Slip Knot and Cross the Water will play Saturday at a benefit for Abby's House, a shelter for homeless or battered women and their children. 3 p.m. to closing, G. Willickers, Route 20, Shrewsbury. Children's entertainment, 3 to 5 p.m. Tickets, $10. Proceeds will be used to buy toys for children residing at the shelter.

MARK C. IDE

Ellen Laverdure speaks at Abby Kelley Foster's grave in Hope Cemetery during Friday's Women's Equality Day program, an event sponsored by Abby's House.

SUNDAY, AUGUST 27, 1995   158 PAGES
WORCESTER, MASSACHUSETTS

Women recall the long fight

Suffrage war was won 75 years ago

By Jennifer Greaney
Telegram & Gazette Staff

Worcester's record for the number of voter registrations in one day was shattered as women rushed City Hall to put their names on the voting rolls.

The Evening Gazette unabashedly proclaimed in a subheading on a front page story that the "majority of those who have their names put on voting lists today are married and of housewife type that were thought not to be interested in politics."

The date was Aug. 25, 1920, just one week after Tennessee became the 36th state, the last of the two-thirds necessary, to ratify the federal amendment granting women the right to vote.

Yesterday marked the 75th anniversary of the day the amendment, the 19th to the U.S. Constitution,

Turn to WINNING/Page A10

Abby-The play was nearing completion

TELEGRAM & GAZETTE   SATURDAY, DECEMBER 23, 1995   A3

Hillary may be back in '96

Hillary Rodham Clinton, maybe. John F. Kennedy Jr., no.

Mrs. Clinton could be returning to Worcester in April to help celebrate the 20th anniversary of Abby's House. The first lady wowed an overflow crowd at Mechanics Hall last year during a campaign stop for congressional candidate Kevin O'Sullivan.

Coming back to Worcester would be part of her husband's re-election campaign. It would give Clinton a chance to shine a spotlight on the problem of domestic violence. Abby's House, founded in 1976, is dedicated to helping homeless women and battered women.

It looks like a pretty good bet, but the visit is still four months away. A lot can happen between now and then. First ladies can get busy.

Timothy J. Connolly

Politically Speaking

Women's Equality Day

The rumor mills were busy

letter worked!) Secondly, Barbara found the following poem that cleverly expressed what probably was the case that first Christmas Day. Surely, women would understand and, hopefully, a wonderful work of art would not be "banned."

The Three Queens Were There

The Queens came late, but the Queens were there
with gifts in their hands and crowns on their hair.
They'd come, these three, like the Kings, from far,
following, yes, that guiding star.
They'd left their ladles, linens, looms,
their children playing in nursery rooms,
and told their sitters: "Take charge!
For this is a marvelous sight we must not miss!"

The Queens came late, but not too late to see
the animals small and great,
feathered and furred, domestic and wild,
gathered to gaze at a mother and child.
And rather than frankincense and myrrh
and gold for the babe,
they brought for her who held him,
a homespun gown of blue, and chicken soup ...
with noodles, too ... and a lingering, lasting cradlesong.

The Queens came late and stayed not long,
for their thoughts already were straining far—
past manger and mother and guiding star
and child a-glow as a morning sun ...
toward home and children and chores undone.

—Written by Norma Farber

December brought all of us home for the holidays. The shelter opened to the public for purchase of the 20th anniversary house pins, especially designed for us by Lucinda, and the Three Wise Women cards and tee shirts. Barbara was on hand to sign those cards, which were definitely first editions. The next evening a holiday benefit party, sponsored by Mocha Java, Slip Knot and Cross the Water, was held at G. Willickers in Shrewsbury. And just before Christmas Day, Citizens Energy Corporation announced a 20% increase in its annual shelter winter assistance program. What good news and what a great gift! On Saturday morning, December 23rd, Tim Connolly's *Telegram and Gazette* column had our hearts beating. Could it be possible that Hillary Clinton would be back in Worcester to help us celebrate the 20th anniversary? Is it any wonder that I kept reading and reading "Bright Morning Stars" (Traditional) that appeared in our last 1995 Newsletter:

> "Bright morning stars are rising
> The night is almost gone
> The sycamores are bending
> Their branches to the dawn
> The wind sighs on the river
> The willows bend to pray
> And dawn is breaking gently
> Upon the brand new day
> Day is breaking in my soul..."

Abby's House had completed another year and there was so much more to come on this fascinating onward journey. We were at the dawn of the 20th anniversary and the play about the life of Abby Kelley Foster was nearing completion. Before the hanging of her portrait, Abby's name would forever be carved into the minds of those who would attend the Mechanics Hall production of "Abby," Jane Dutton's masterpiece, crafted for this brand new day.

You are cordially invited to be our guest
at the Premiere Performance of:

ABBY

Written by local playwright Jane Dutton,
starring Susan Nest and Victor Kruczynski.
All proceeds benefit Abby's House,
a multi-service organization serving the needs of
homeless / battered women, with or without children.

Mechanics Hall
Saturday, April 27, 1996
Reception-7 P.M.
ABBY -8 P.M.

Gala Celebration
following in
Washburn Hall

Please present this
Card for
Admission of Two.

Rich Ardizzone and his musicians

WORCESTER'S INDEPENDENT VOICE SINCE 1976

worcester magazine

April 17-23, 1996

FREE

ABBY'S HOUSE IS HOME

Twenty years on a mission

Peter Blute on environmental extremists, p. 6

Scratch makes the playoffs

ARTSWorcester's female shriners

TELEGRAM & GAZETTE TUESDAY, APRIL 23, 1996 B3

Women's services expanded

Jeanne Mattson of Worcester, left, looks at a dress she might purchase at Abby's Thrift Shop, which is part of Abby's House. Assisting her is Marilyn Crandell, a volunteer, also of Worcester.

Abby's House is celebrating 20th anniversary this week

By Kathleen A. Shaw
Telegram & Gazette Staff

WORCESTER — Abby Kelley Foster, during her 19th-century sojourns to promote women's rights and the abolition of slavery, spent more than one night sleeping in the open because she had no shelter.

It was fitting in 1976 that a new shelter for homeless women and children be named in her honor. Abby's House on Crown Street is celebrating its 20th anniversary this week.

The mission has expanded. The staff provides immediate shelter to homeless women, but now offers low-cost housing to women. Many women stay with Abby's House until they can afford to move into their own apartments. With properties at 19, 21 and 23 Crown Street, Abby's House is currently renovating a formerly vacant building on nearby Chatham Street into affordable apartments for women and children.

Abby's House held a public open house at its Crown Street properties yesterday so people could see what 20 years of effort has accomplished. The week will conclude Saturday at Mechanics Hall with a premiere per-

The play about Worcester's well-known abolitionist and feminist is written by Jane Dutton, local playwright and director. The evening begins with a reception at 7 p.m., the play begins at 8; and a celebration will follow.

"We have had success stories," said Sister Hilda Chasse of the Little Franciscan Sisters of Mercy, who handles overall maintenance of the properties. She said she is particularly pleased with the generosity of many people throughout the area who support their work in a myriad of ways.

"People are so inventive," she said. She recalled elders who have rapped on the door to donate rolls of paper towels, or the man who gave them canisters of change. He told her they started a family tradition of dumping all their change into a canister each Friday night, with proceeds going to Abby's House when it was full.

Many people choose to donate their women's and children's clothes to the thrift shop. Julie Komenos, development coordinator, said the thrift shop nets $25,000 to $30,000 a year for Abby's House.

Worcester Cultural Commission
EXECUTIVE OFFICE OF CITY MANAGER THOMAS R. HOOVER
418 Main Street, Suite 400
Worcester, Massachusetts 01608-1885
Telephone: (508) 799-1400

Lee R. Morin
Chair

Debra M. Lockwood

December 7, 1995

Annette Rafferty
Abby's House Inc.
23 Crown Street
Worcester, MA 01609

Dear Ms. Rafferty:

The Worcester Cultural Commission is pleased to inform you that your Arts Lottery Grant application for "ABBY" has been approved for funding in the amount of $4,000.00 pending the Massachusetts Cultural Council's (MCC) final review. Please be aware that final approval of your application by the MCC may not occur until the spring of 1996, while funding may not be made available until the summer of 1996.

Enclosed, please find an evaluation form and a reimbursement form, both of which must be completed and returned to the Worcester Cultural Commission within 60 days of the completion of the approved project. It requests for reimbursement which are received after the sixty day reimbursement period will not be processed by the Cultural Commission. If the approved project is a PASS Grant, an events notification form must also be completed and submitted to the MCC 30 days prior to the scheduled event. Do not submit any forms until you have received notification from the Worcester Cultural Commission of final approval of your application by the MCC.

In addition, cancelled checks and invoices must be used to document your project's expenses. Copies of checks or invoices must be submitted along with the evaluation and reimbursement forms upon completion of your project. A signed contract is only required in the case that this project has been funded for an amount greater or equal to $2,000.

If you have any questions, please contact Greg Ryan at the Office of Planning and Community Development at (508) 799-1400. Best of luck in the successful completion of your project.

Sincerely,

Lee Morin
Chair

/gr

Geneva E. Brown
Geoffrey L. Lamphere
Linda A. Okobro

Susan Gotz

Brice Plimmer

Homer A. Hess
Erwin H. Miller
Anthony Vigoa

Jane Dutton, Abby (Susan Nest) and Stephen (Victor Kruczynski)

CHAPTER 18 A Premiere Performance- the 20th Anniversary

O ur staff holiday party was barely concluded when the 20th anniversary ad hoc committee met on January 16, 1996 to put the plans for "Abby" into fast forward. The date had been set with Mechanics Hall: April 27th, a Saturday evening that proved to be, undoubtedly, the social event of the season. We distributed tickets to a variety of sites; set in motion an ad campaign for the program, and carefully examined the menus of several caterers (we eventually selected the Boynton). Entertainment was a major concern because we wanted only background music for the reception in Washburn Hall and upbeat notes for the post-performance moment. We were fortunate to obtain the services of Rich Ardizonne and his musicians for both receptions—just a perfect musical memory! We also needed extensive media coverage and we were successful in promoting the anniversary, as well as the stellar production through both the *Worcester Magazine* (which dedicated its April 17-23 issue to the remarkable history of Abby's House) and to the "Time Out" section of the *Telegram and Gazette* the same week.

Of course, life went on within and without the organization, although we were definitely acting as though nothing else on earth mattered. Supporters continued to hold benefits for the 77 Chatham Street project and the pennies rolled in daily. Slowly, but surely, Abby's was arriving at its designated goal of $500,000. Invitations had been mailed along with the brochure describing the event and the play and the level of sponsorship in promoting the 20th anniversary project. The committee was delighted to announce that the program would be supported in part by a grant we had received from the Worcester Cultural Commission, a local agency of the Massachusetts Cultural Commission. Everyone was being asked to "help us blow out the candles on our cake." Nervously, we awaited responses and tried to assuage Jane Dutton's anxiety as she, Susan, and Victor worked late into the night putting the finishing touches on "Abby." Could we believe it? "Abby," an original play, would be performed for the first time in beautiful Mechanics Hall to benefit the restoration of another safe home for women and their children. On Broadway, this would be a premiere performance, so why not advertise "Abby" as Worcester's premiere performance? It hardly seemed possible that two years of research, script writing and rewriting, nuancing lines and finessing language and gestures had come to an end. It was the end on paper and in preparation perhaps, but not in the heart of Jane Dutton who remembered every minute of this masterpiece. For me in particular, who spent many years reading and re-reading the life of Abby Kelley Foster, this would be an unforgettable evening. Henceforth, I would always think of Susan mounting those steps on the Mechanics Hall stage to deliver her Bloody Feet, Sisters speech, as *my* Abby Kelley Foster. And Victor, no matter how many other great roles he would interpret, would always be the romantic, but fiery, Stephen Symonds Foster, Abby's soul mate, the social conscience of the churches and the advocate for elimination of any kind of human slavery. No wonder they needed an entire day to inhabit the Mechanics Hall stage—just to become comfortable and to feel at home. I couldn't begin to imagine how much energy it would take for two people to hold the attention and the interest of a full house of theater-goers. But they would and they did! Our friend, Ann Marie Shea, forwarded to us at Abby's a review of the play written by Kirsten Person, a 1996 graduate of WSC. It had this to say of the two actors:

> "Miss Nest quickly won the audience's heart. Her physical gestures emphasized her agitation at finding herself struggling with a loyalty to her church and a conviction that slavery was an evil that must end immediately...."

TELEGRAM & GAZETTE

TIME OUT

OMICS
ELEVISION
THURSDAY, APRIL 25, 1996

SECTION
C

Dear 'Abby'

Playwright Dutton fashions love story with principle

TELEGRAM & GAZETTE   MONDAY, APRIL 29, 1996   **C3**

'Abby' captures social pioneer's spirit

By Jim Keogh
Telegram & Gazette Reviewer

Theater review

ABBY: written and directed by Jane Dutton. At Mechanics Hall. With Susan Nest and Victor Kruczynski.

WORCESTER — The towering portrait of Abraham Lincoln seemed to peer down upon the Mechanics Hall stage Saturday night as the portrait of another warrior for racial justice was being fashioned.

Abby Kelley Foster, abolitionist, feminist, wife, mother, came to spirited, textured life in the sure-handed, tightly-crafted play "Abby," which traced her public works and private passions over the course of 50 volatile years.

ABBY'S HOUSE BENEFIT

The proceeds from the evening — about 1,000 attended the performance — will go to benefit Abby's House, the Worcester shelter for homeless and battered women.

Written and directed by local playwright Jane Dutton, "Abby" stars Susan Nest as the 19th-century social pioneer, a woman who early on knew she burned with an undoubtable conviction that slaves should be free, that women should vote and that she was irrefutably right on both counts. She sets the tone early in the play, describing how the phrase "Abby Kelleyian" came to mean "a woman who does not know her place."

"But I do know my place," Abby

protests, "alongside the white man and the slave."

Abby obeys only the "still, small voice within" that inspires the vital, voluminous outward voice that decried the tyranny of hatred as she lectured across New England and into New York and Ohio. She also wasn't alone in her quest. Dutton was wise to make "Abby" a two-character play, focusing on her relationship with her equally committed abolitionist husband, Stephen Foster (Victor Kruczynski). Stephen first woos the reluctant Abby through a letter-writing campaign, their epistolary romance eventually blossoming into the real thing.

SHARP, FUNNY

Her unpopular views harden Abby, but the marriage humanizes her. (Abby's fear that wedded bliss would weaken her abolitionist resolve is unfounded.) Nest and Kruc-

zynski, abetted by Dutton's sharp, often very funny script, do a fine job of creating a tender love story between two unrepentant hardheads. Both deliver sometimes harrowing accounts of their beatings, arrests and near lynchings at the hands of pro-slavery zealots. Yet interspersed between the bursts of thunder and fury, they return to their quiet Worcester farm to re-energize and raise their daughter in their own enlightened image.

Despite the historical setting, "Abby" remains thematically current. Using Abby's own words, Dutton manages to illustrate how farthinking this heroine was. At one point she scolds women for complaining about being held down in a patriarchal society, urging them to gain control of their lives by becoming more responsible for their own finances. Though not militia-minded, Abby and Stephen also had a bone to pick with the government, refusing to pay taxes on their farm until women were allowed to vote.

The dollars raised by Saturday night's performance of "Abby" are intended to make a few more women stronger, braver and more independent — Abby Kelleyians in the best sense of the words.

Mayor Mariano

Gail Swain

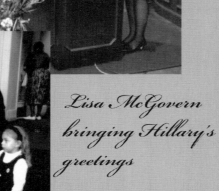

Lisa McGovern bringing Hillary's greetings

Leah Duszak honoring the life of Michelle

Doherty High students

Rep. McGovern greets Betsy Krovitz, Vida Maczyk and their children

The crowd gathers in Washburn Hall

And of Victor:

> "Mr. Kruczynski in the role of Stephen Foster firmly established himself ... his confident stage presence exuded a masculinity that served to play up Abby's femininity in a relationship where, unexpectedly, the man was the more romantic!"

Jim Keogh, who reviewed the play, had something further to add in his article, entitled: "Abby Captures Social Pioneer's Spirit," which appeared in the Monday, April 29, 1996 edition of the *Telegram and Gazette*:

> "Her unpopular views harden Abby, but the marriage humanizes her. Abby's fear that wedded bliss would weaken her abolitionist resolve is unfounded. Nest and Kruczynski, abetted by Dutton's sharp, often very funny script, do a fine job of creating a tender love story between two unrepentant hardheads. ... Using Abby's own words, Dutton manages to illustrate how far-thinking this heroine was."

Keogh concluded a similar review that appeared in the April 28, 1996 edition of the *Sunday Telegram* with this final compliment:

> "The dollars raised by last night's performance of "Abby" are intended to make a few more women stronger, braver and more independent ... Abby Kelleyians in the best sense of the word."

My memories of that evening are vivid. The hall was absolutely packed. Washburn Hall buzzed with anticipation. The atmosphere was charged with the electricity as Patti Conzo, our board president and Tess Sneesby, executive director, paid tribute to donors, supporters, staff and friends. Co-chairs of the event, Julie Komenos and I represented the brave women who, together with me, founded Abby's House. Gail Swain read Angela Dorenkamp's "Valiant Women," first delivered at our 15th anniversary celebration; Leah Duszak, representing Women in Business, presented Abby's with the Michelle Bouthiller Memorial Plaque; and women from the County Line Quilters of Southboro unveiled their striking, handmade 20th anniversary commemorative quilt. Mayor Raymond Mariano read a proclamation from the City of Worcester, and Lisa McGovern was honored to read First Lady Hillary Clinton's letter of praise addressed to Abby's House on this wonderful occasion. At approximately 7:45, the lights dimmed, signaling us to take our seats upstairs in the Great Hall. Just a little after 8 p.m. what we had been anticipating for years, happened. Abby Kelley Foster walked onto the stage. The play began—the rest is history. Laughter, silence, tears, more laughter, expressions of disbelief and wonderment that Worcester had actually played such a major role in abolition were obvious responses to Jane's interpretation of this woman's life. As the ending neared, there were several moments of stillness as Abby recalled the love and tenderness of her marriage to Stephen and the lights faded. Silence still, but then a thundering burst of applause filled the Hall. It seemed unending. Cheers resounded and bounced off the walls. Everyone was standing! I then had the honor of joining Jane, Susan and Victor on stage and, using Lucy Stone's favorite words of admiration for Abby, I blurted out:

> "With a kiss for the hem of your garment—Jane, Susan and Victor. What a success ... what a wonderful performance ... what a theatrical coup, Jane. You are the best."

There were flowers and hugs and more cheers and more hugs and still the clamor continued, down the stairs from the Great Hall back to Washburn Hall where the party continued. "Abby" had been the success we had all hoped it would be. I think it was more than that. It had raised this woman's life to the MAIN stage of Worcester's history. Anyone who didn't know about Abby Kelley Foster surely knew her now. It was that very night that the Worcester community began to think about Abby's portrait hanging in the Great Hall alongside other notable Worcester women and the men who have inhabited the Hall since its beginning.

On April 27, 1996, everyone who had witnessed the spectacular production was proclaiming Abby as their very own. Tonight, I knew that Abby Kelley Foster had come into her own. The hanging of a portrait would prove to be the frosting on this

20th anniversary cake and I could hardly wait! Just looking at the numerous photos we took that night and re-reading the many articles written before and after the play is enough for me to re-live every single minute of that experience. I am so grateful that our organization had been instrumental in reclaiming the life of Abby Kelley Foster, certainly a woman for all seasons. Thank you, Amy Gaiennie, for writing that 1974 article on Abby. Thank you, *Worcester Recorder*, for publishing the article that caught my eye and sparked an interest that will be with me forever.

Beautiful 20th Anniversary quilt presented by County Line Quilters

Jeanne Mattson, Dorrie Hutchins, and Fran Keller at Cookbook table

CHAPTER 19

Reconstructing the World: 77 Chatham Street

The realization that we had only six weeks separating us from the dedication of 77 Chatham Street was what finally brought us back to earth from the euphoria of cloud nine. Our 20th anniversary consultants, Sid and Sandra, had taught us well. That is, there is no rest, no taking time off, no opportunity to be missed if we wanted to accomplish the goal. Wheels began to turn by the end of the first week of May 1996. Tasks very similar to those accomplished in planning the April 27th event began: program design, invitations, acknowledgments, caterers, music, ribbon cutting and the blessing of the building and tours provided. Major donors were invited for an on-site sneak preview of the restoration of 77 Chatham on May 9, 1996. Work orders were given: wear low shoes, dress casually and supper would be served construction style. We still don't know what that meant, except to add that those who ate were fortunate if sawdust wasn't an unwelcome condiment in the sandwiches and salad provided. In the midst of the whirlwind of activities, an anonymous donor contacted us, wanting to finance whatever expenses there would be for the celebration.

June 6th dawned and the weather was just beautiful—warm and sunny. It would be a perfect day for an outdoor dedication. By 3:30 p.m. the back yard was filled with people. By 4 p.m. there was standing room only. Ellen Laverdure, recently hired as Day Center coordinator, began with an opening rendition. Speeches were plentiful and positive and, as the blessing was recited in unison, everyone was hoping that:

"For as long as the families live here, may our heartbeats, our dreams and our breath be joined together. May we embrace this home and its inhabitants with our loving hearts and hopeful spirit. We welcome this home, 77 Chatham Street, into Abby's family and hope it will be a place of safety and of renewal, where every sense will be nourished and each soul will find rest."

Because finishing touches were needed in some of the apartments, we decided to set mid-August as the time for occupancy of the new units. Meantime, applications for the apartments would be reviewed and interviews held with women interested in going through the process with us. At the end of June, another fundraiser was held to help put the capital campaign closer to its goal. This time, a dear old friend, Ed Goggins, gathered together The Coyotes, a rock n' roll band from the '60s and '70s, to perform at the VFW Post for an Abby's House benefit on June 19th. This event was particularly meaningful to me personally. Elaine and I knew Ed well. He was involved years ago with Abby's House, having designed and worked on a new shelter kitchen at 23 Crown Street as an employee of the Worcester Labor Council. His support and concern were with us from the beginning and, now many years later, Ed, who had been diagnosed with a rare form of cancer, was dying and he had come back to do yet another kind act for Abby's House. On October 10th, Ed was buried from Christ the King Church. We will always remember him as a gentle man with a big, big heart that held a special place for Abby's.

The big October news had to be the relocation of the Day Center from the original building at 21-23 Crown Street to the more spacious and sunny community room at 77 Chatham Street. On October 2nd, we packed up the old center and moved it all over to the newly renovated building where there was more room and lots of light. It took a few weeks to get adjusted to locating kitchen utensils, but we were all convinced it was a very small price to pay for such an upbeat, inviting new home.

On October 23rd, we were treated to samplings from Abby's 20th anniversary cookbook, prepared and served by the chefs at Tatnuck Bookseller & Marketplace. I remember spending two hours enjoying and tasting the delicious items selected

WORK ORDERS:
1. Wear low, comfortable shoes.
2. Dress very casually.

Please join us for an on-site sneak preview of the restoration of 77 Chatham Street on Thursday, May 9, 1996 from 5 to 7 p.m....

See first-hand what has been accomplished!

Supper served, construction style!

Regrets only:
(508) 756-5486
by May 2, 1996

You are cordially invited to attend The Dedication Ceremony of 77 Chatham Street on Thursday, June 6, 1996 at 4:30 p.m.

• • • ❤ • • •

The ceremony will be followed by
OPEN HOUSE
and Supper, until 7 p.m.

Some members of the long range planning committee

Myriam Plunerge

Karen Nunley

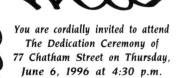

Sue Topalian

Lauri Johnson

Ellen Laverdure, Co-chairs Annette Rafferty and Fran O'Connell

Carmen Negron

Pat Nedoroszik preparing for Craft Fair

'Porch light is always on'

Women, children welcome at new Abby's House

By Mark Melady
Telegram & Gazette Staff

Fernando and Rose Rodriquez prepare to cut the ribbon at the opening of a third Abby's House residence.

STEVE LANAVA

WORCESTER — Annette Rafferty, who founded Abby's House 20 years ago hoping homelessness would be eradicated in five years, surveyed the three-story manse at 77 Chatham St. that will soon be the third Abby's residence for homeless women — the first for families.

For all its restored Civil War-era beauty and the admiring crowd wandering through the seven two-bedroom apartments at yesterday's dedication, something was missing for Rafferty.

"I can't wait to see people living there," she said. "That's when it goes from being a house to a home."

MEMORIES

The house, with its tiled mansard roof and scalloped fascia, will become home to seven women and their children in about six weeks. It's around the block from the original Abby's House on Crown Street, a neighborhood that evoked old memories for one of the 200 or so guests yesterday.

"When I saw the invitation I thought it might be near where I lived when I was first married," said John Kilcoyne of Worcester, a long-time supporter of Abby's House. His support is spurred by the memory of his sister, Dr. Margaret M. Kilcoyne, a prominent medical researcher who disappeared 26 years ago on Nantucket.

Turn to NEW/Page A6

New home dedicated

Continued From Page One

While sitting under the canopy listening to the dedication speech yesterday, it came to Kilcoyne that it was this very house he had moved into with his bride in 1946 after he had returned home from World War II.

"We only stayed a few months, but it was a wonderful time," said Kilcoyne, 72, a retired tool engineer. "I had survived the war. We had found a place to live — not an easy thing to do after the war — and we were newlyweds. I have very happy memories of this place."

Kilcoyne said his sister, who was suffering severe emotional distress when she disappeared on a bitter cold January night in 1980, was an ardent supporter of women's issues. "She would have really endorsed the kind of work Abby's House does," Kilcoyne said, "so we've supported it in her name over the years."

Though his sister's body was never recovered and for a time investigators considered foul play or that she might still be alive, her brother believes she walked into the ocean and drowned.

$500,000 PROJECT

The $500,000 Abby's House project was financed with two federal grants totaling $225,000 and through fund-raising. The grants are funneled from the Federal Home Loan bank in Boston through Flagship Bank, in a program that allows local agencies and banks to identify worthwhile renovation projects.

"Everyone gets to do what they do best," said Jon Rudzinski, a home loan bank representative. "We give away money, the local banks decide what projects are worth underwriting and Abby's House takes care of

O'Neill cited Janet Nadeau, District 4 Councilor and chairwoman of the council's housing committee, for her efforts on behalf of the project and Abby's House.

Marge Purves, president of the Crown Hill Neighborhood Association, welcomed the house to the neighborhood, saying it had been neglected and abused much as the women who will occupy it.

"Like this house, the women are still standing," said Purves, who

women."

The restoration, designed by the architectural firm of Gorman Richardson and done by Rodan Construction Co., both of Ashland, is about three weeks from completion.

The first residents are expected to move in about mid-July, said Lorraine Fletcher, housing coordinator for Abby's House. Applications will be mailed to homeless shelters and welfare agencies by mid-June.

The women cannot have more than two children, the only other condition of acceptance is being without a home. "Everybody deserves better than nothing," said Fletcher, who served as clerk of the works for the restoration.

It's not a role entirely unfamiliar to her. She worked five years as an office manager for a Northboro construction company.

"I really enjoy working with the contractor and the workers," she said.

'CLEAN, DECENT'

Mary L. Padula, secretary of the state Executive Office of Communities and Development, said the restoration would provide "a clean, decent, safe, place to live" for homeless women and children.

"The porch light is always on at Abby's House," Padula said.

She also lauded the project for helping to spark revitalization of the Crown Hill neighborhood, a theme addressed by Stephen O'Neill, director of Worcester's Office of Planning and Community Development.

The house will anchor efforts to bring back Crown Hill, O'Neill said. "By coming together we make our neighborhoods better places to live."

grew up in Hartford, near the late 19th century home of writer Mark Twain. She quoted Twain's remarks about the house he had built for his family.

"He found a sense of peace and benediction," she said and quoted Twain: "It was of us and we were in its confidence."

Purves said she hoped the women who lived there would find "happiness and confidence within its walls."

Outside the new residence, Tess Sneesby, right, executive direc... Abby's House, shares a laugh with Lois Herman of Insurance Ma... Agency, the company that insures Abby's House.

STEVE...

The new 77 Chatham st. house

Ed Goggins
1947-1996

Ed and his family spent time in Ireland,
and he embodied the best of what he loved
about the Irish spirit.
An artist and an artisan,
he worked with his hands,
wrote stories, made music
and entertained those lucky enough to know him
with his wit.
Like the best of the Irish,
he counted his wealth in his friends,
and he was a rich man.

New location of Day Center

by the chefs and listening at the same time to the rave reviews given in particular to the bread pudding dessert submitted by former Day Center participant Edie Galindo. Since that time, the bread pudding has become a favorite of other guests who come to the daily meals at the Day Center. Special thanks are due to Larry and Gloria Abramoff, executive chef Jack Corey, Steve Husson and Laura Benis for all their efforts to promote the cookbook. It was worth waiting for; the idea began some years before with Ann Hedge and Anne Humes.

November was a busy month. Two successful craft fairs, one at Holy Cross College headed once again by Pat Nedoroszik, Norma Decoteau and Karen Stevens, added nearly $1,500 to the capital campaign and because of the efforts of Helen McLaughlin, the Shrewsbury Ecumenical Council Fair, held traditionally on November 11th, netted a similar amount. As the rest of the world continued to downsize, we continued to dream BIG dreams about improved and expanded services for women with or without children. To aid in this process of future growth, a long range planning committee was established. Tess asked me to chair the committee and I asked Sharon Smith Viles, with whom I had staffed the shelter in the early years of Abby's, to be my co-chair. Two heads are always better than one. The two heads turned into eight by the middle of November, when we met for the second time in the new office space (which was left behind when our Day Center moved across the street to 77 Chatham Street). Other committee members included the following women: Carmen Negron, Karen Nunley, Myriam Pluverge, Sue Topalian, Sr. Anna Marie Kane and Lauri Johnson. Each of these individuals had long-time ties with the organization. Two of them were residents or former residents of our supportive housing units. Lauri, who was on the present fundraising committee and Anna Marie, who was responsible for initiating Abby's Friends while she served as Chaplain at Holy Cross College in 1976, agreed to serve as consultants in gathering and analyzing data collected from questionnaires that were sent to staff, volunteers, donors and supporters. This long range committee had a very good idea by mid-February 1997 on how Abby's House would plan for the new century, and knew how this grassroots organization was perceived by those involved directly or indirectly in the daily operations. This was more than long range planning; it was an evaluation of 21 years of service.

As we mailed newsletters with the questionnaire enclosed, I remember thinking that it was the next step, but a risky one for the organization. Were we in a position to dream this big? Oh well, the deed was done and we would face the facts soon enough. I felt a little like Adrienne Rich must have felt when she wrote:

> "My heart is moved by all I cannot save
> so much has been destroyed...
> I have to cast my lot with those
> who age after age, perversely,
> with no extraordinary power,
> reconstitute the world."

Let come what may!

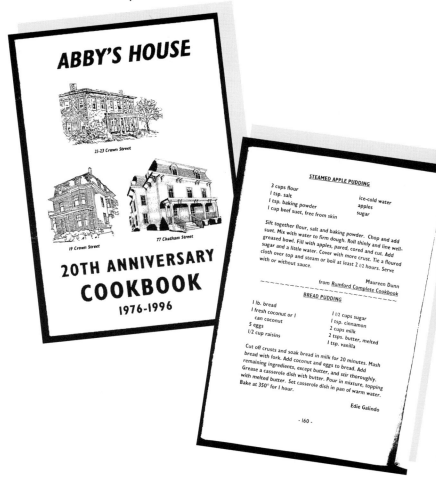

CHAPTER 20

Our Lives Are Our Speeches

There was an unusual number of gift-givers to Abby's new office. People's generosity seemed unending and it was heartwarming that we were successful in making our donors aware that our mothers and single women need remembrance at the holiday time as well as the children. Our office was transformed into gifts central. It was the best holiday season for all of us. New families moved into 77 Chatham Street and they reveled in gifts galore. For us, the best gift had already been given—this magnificent new home, made possible by so many in the community. Just saying "thank you" seemed this year to be very inadequate, but I tried in the December newsletter to express the impossible:

> "It seems appropriate to express our collective thanks to all who, in 1996, have brought such diverse elements into such a remarkable harmony at 21-23 Crown, 19 Crown and at 77 Chatham Street, where seven new, delightful families are now living. Let me say a special word of gratitude to YOU who made possible this place where the young are nourished in beautiful, decent and safe housing. Our capital campaign was a success because of you. Your pledges keep coming without reminders, and we know you'll respond in the same generous spirit to our annual appeal. What greater evidence is there that you are sharing equally, 'caring for the weak, cherishing life's creatures and shaping a twisted world into one that exemplifies compassion wedded to power;

> a world where the needs of the many come first.' Without YOU, the world would indeed remain harsh and unkind. Thank You!"
> (And thanks to Judy Chicago for her thoughts.)

As responses to the long range planning committee's questionnaire began to pour into the office, we realized that, without a great deal of analysis, Abby's was truly on the right road and that the organization was being encouraged, indeed mandated, to "stay focused" by continuing "to do what you're doing." Then we received two concrete signs which, of course, I attribute to Abby Kelley Foster. The first occurred on January 20th when, in the business section of the *Telegram and Gazette,* there appeared an article on Vida J. Mazyck! Vida and her son Ashton had been guests at Abby's where she shared her story of journeying to Worcester to sell tee shirts at the 1995 Martin Luther King Breakfast, having lost her home in South Carolina. However, she never lost her dreams. Abby's staff and volunteers truly rejoiced in Vida's success today as the winner of the Worcester Common Outlets' "Outlet for Success" contest, earning her a year's free rental space in the mall to launch her business, "Imprints and Engravings," selling customized goods and services. As the *Telegram and Gazette's* Elizabeth Cooney remarked in her article, "Any aspiring business owner would welcome a prize worth $100,000 in rent, but for Mazyck a trip to the winner's circle means a chance to reclaim her financial independence." That simple sentence confirmed my belief that Abby had been Vida's inspiration. She had heard Susan Nest as Abby speak the very words that startled women and men to the realization that economic freedom for their daughters was the key to true emancipation. Abby's words rekindled the spark that always burned within this powerful woman's heart. After she moved from the shelter, Vida found her way to the Martin Luther King, Jr. Empowerment Center where she worked day and night to begin her business that had been wiped out by Hurricane Hugo in her hometown of Moncks, South Carolina. According to Robert Thomas, executive director of the MLK Center:

> "She touched all the bases ... this lady has worked hard. She's jumped all the hurdles ... let's help her fulfill the dream, as a community that's supposed to be inclusive.

MONDAY, FEBRUARY 17, 1997 E1

TELEGRAM & GAZETTE
BUSINESS
SECTION E

Employer encourages economic independence

Home Grown produces hope

Ellen Kirkemo-Sautter sees opportunity where some might see only hardship.

The president and treasurer of Home Grown Originals Inc. in Westboro manages a specialty food business committed to hiring and sustaining disadvantaged workers. She looks for prospective employees through state agencies, welfare-to-work programs and in shelters. Her research and recruiting has taken her to the Pine Street Inn and Rosie's Place in Boston and Abby's House and the Central Massachusetts Shelter for Homeless Veterans in Worcester.

If some turn their eyes away from joblessness, homelessness or the welfare system, that is where Kirkemo-Sautter is looking, and not from a distance. After contacting the Public Inebriate Program in Worcester, for example, she investigated possibilities there by volunteering at the site.

Home Grown Originals develops and sells a line of condiments called KR's Naturelle, but their real end-product is hope.

FRIEND'S RECIPES

It was in early 1995, before state welfare reform created incentives for employers to hire people receiving assistance, when Kirkemo-Sautter's dream of a socially responsible business meshed with her friend Keith Rutherford's desire to bring his recipes to market. Home Grown Originals was incor-

Home Grown Originals kitchen supervisor Bob Sylvester helps chef Keith Rutherford and President Ellen Kirkemo-Sautter pack Zickles, pickled zucchini.

BETTY JENEWIN

Elizabeth Cooney
Small Business

in Colorado and Massachusetts, directs the food side of the busi-

one of multiple steps that need to be taken." Necessary supports are child care, transportation and language training for non-English speakers.

Kirkemo-Sautter is seeking transportation solutions and exploring with lawyers the idea of a collaborative child care arrangement. Employees might look after one another's children on-site, if parents agree and liability allows.

STOCK OPTIONS

Magnificent Maggie Wain

MONDAY, JANUARY 20, 1997 E1

TELEGRAM & GAZETTE
BUSINESS
SECTION E

Future of her own design

Prize-winner hopes to help others realize their dreams

WORCESTER — Two years ago today, Vida J. Mazyck came north to Worcester to help an old friend from South Carolina sell T-shirts at that year's Martin Luther King Jr. Community Breakfast. When she heard speakers at the event describe their hopes for Worcester's growth and renewal, she decided to move here to pursue her entrepreneurial vision.

Now, as winner of the Worcester Common Outlets' "Outlet for Success" contest, Mazyck, 35, is preparing to move into free retail space for a year where she will launch her business, Imprints & Engravings, which sells customized goods and services.

Any aspiring business owner would welcome a prize worth $100,000 in rent, but for Mazyck a trip to the winner's circle means a chance to reclaim her financial independence.

Mazyck's journey from the King breakfast to the mall included stays at two shelters in Worcester — Youville House and Abby's House. But while Mazyck and her young son had lost their home, she never lost sight of her dream.

"We had lots of adversity," she said last week during an interview in the mall's food court. "I find that it either strengthens a person or weakens them. It made me stronger."

Mazyck's experiences have imbued her with self-knowledge, a determination to succeed and a commitment to inspire others through her own achievement. Her business plan won her the 1,583-square-foot store lease next to Tahari when she'd been applying only for pushcart space. But her resolve to redeem that promise now requires $50,000 in financing.

OWN DESIGN

Adversity struck her first retail business in the form of Hurricane Hugo. At age 25 in her hometown of Moncks, S.C., she had established Creative Expressions, a precursor to her current endeavor. As a promotional-products distributor and special-events planner, she employed two people. But lacking the proper in-

Vida J. Mazyck, winner of the "Outlet for Success" contest, and Anthony L. Kalinowski, general manager of the Worcester Common Outlets.

BETTY JENEWIN

Amazing Vida!

It will be 'shame on us' to have her come this far and not be able to execute it."

Having won the prize, it became Vida's dream to employ people receiving AFDC benefits. As she said in her own words:

"I've seen life from both ends of the spectrum, but when I had my personal struggles I've known what it's like not knowing where to stay next. I'm partial to the disadvantaged, the people who've lost sight of their dreams. I'd like to let them know how you can dream again."

Once again, Vida echoed in her own fashion the "Bloody Feet, Sisters" of our spiritual guide: "My life has been my speech ... bloody feet, sisters, have worn smooth the path by which you have come hither."

The second sign came when Maggie, a 19 Crown Street resident, responded to an opportunity to work in a specialty food business committed to hiring and sustaining disadvantaged workers. This was a major move for Maggie, who had lost confidence in her ability to work after a lifetime of holding low-paying jobs. It was certainly worth the try, and after a couple of interviews, Maggie was hired! I thought at the time how delighted Abby would have been to hold a conversation with Vida and Maggie. They were her kind of women. Both of them were living out the struggle to be economically independent. Both of them were trying to create a stable, safe atmosphere that would guarantee future employment. What kind of advice would Abby have imparted? First, she'd applaud their efforts, encouraging them to move forward and then she'd issue the inevitable warning: "Let us not be too confident. I want you to remember that nothing is done while anything remains to be done."

Two years later, Vida Mazyck accepted an invitation to become a member of Abby's House board of directors and Maggie W. moved out of 19 Crown into her own apartment. Both women are inspirations. There will never be a fall, a jump, a catastrophe or a hurdle that will destroy their spirits. Under the most trying circumstances they have carved out their own places in the community.

Our Lives are Our Speeches

They are sisters and strong women

Tracy

Parlee and her children

III. KEY CONCLUSIONS

1. **"Keep doing what you're doing!"**

• Abby's role of providing a "safe haven" of shelter and support for women and children in need was overwhelmingly supported as successful, invaluable and the primary direction to continue for the future

• "Stay focused". Respondents strongly advised staying focused on a primary mission and expressed concern that spreading existing resources too thin would reduce the quality of programs offered.

2. **Provide Educational Programs**

• 82% of the respondents believed Abby's House should be a center for women's information, parenting workshops, support groups, education and job training resources.

• Respondents recognized an urgent need to address the root causes of crisis situations: viz.; poverty, domestic violence, substance abuse and low self-esteem.

• Job training is key to enabling women to become self sufficient and improving self-esteem.

• Parenting workshops would address a skill deficit observed in guests and a void of programs in the community.

III. Key Conclusions (continued)

3. **Develop safe, affordable, housing**

• 73% of respondents believed Abby's House should concentrate mainly on safe, affordable, housing development.

• Safe housing is a fundamental need which must be met before other personal growth areas can be addressed.

• Housing is typically the largest, single expense in one's budget.

• There are limited options for safe, affordable housing for women available in the greater Worcester community.

IV. IMPLICATIONS FOR FUTURE DIRECTIONS

• **Affordable housing and educational programs are both closely aligned with Abby's mission and current role and are both overwhelmingly supported by Abby's base of donors and supporters.** Given equal fit and support, the Long-Range Planning Committee evaluated Abby's internal strengths and weaknesses and the external environment to prioritize these options.

• **The core staff is small. Given this fact, valid concerns exist regarding the possible dilution of focus adversely affecting program quality.**

• **A safe, affordable place to live is first in the list of most women's needs.** Without that foundation, women cannot take advantage of resources available for job training, parenting skills, etc.

• **Many of the women in Abby's programs are in some level of crisis or transition.** The guest advocate and the day center currently provide information, support and coordination of available services to address acute needs. Until all immediate needs are met, women are not able to focus on longer term educational options.

• **The greater Worcester community has other resources available for educational programs**: local colleges, the YWCA, Daybreak and the Women's Center at MedCenter Central Mass.

• **There is a lack of safe, affordable housing for women and children in greater Worcester.**

V. RECOMMENDATIONS

Taking into consideration the Abby's House mission, its internal capabilities and the external environment, the Long-Range Planning Committee believes that:

- **Abby's primary future direction should be to maintain the high quality level of its existing programs. In terms of growth, the primary focus should be on the development of safe, affordable housing.**

Since educational programs clearly add value for the women of Abby's, but may be available elsewhere in the community, we offer:

- **a secondary recommendation, that Abby's staff, both core and volunteer, develop a targeted plan to network with other programs and community resources to ensure that women are aware of, and able to participate in, programs on job training, parenting, and other women's issues.**

'Abby' re-emerges to a full house

Play about activist benefits city shelter

By Mary Anne Magiera
Telegram & Gazette Staff

WORCESTER — But for the play "Abby," an important ingredient of Worcester's past as a safe haven for abolitionists and women's rights activists would be lost to all but the most diligent history buffs.

Instead, this weekend, for the second year in a row, the play delighted sold-out audiences and financially benefited its namesake, Abby's House, a shelter and multiservice organization for women and children on Crown and Chatham streets.

Set in the 1800s, the work chronicles the life of Abby Kelley Foster and her husband, Stephen Foster, who traveled for years from their farm in Worcester's Tatnuck section throughout the country to speak out against slavery and for women's rights. "Abby" premiered last April in Mechanics Hall, highlighting the 20th anniversary observance of Abby's House. This year the play was performed at 8 p.m. Saturday and 2 p.m. yesterday.

BETTY JENEWIN

Playwright Jane Dutton, left, acknowledges audience applause after a performance of "Abby" on Saturday. With her are actors Susan Next and Victor Kruczynski.

Turn to 'ABBY'/Back Page

Production was 'electric' history

What can we say about a truly wonderful play written by Worcester's own Jane Dutton and performed to perfection by Susan Nest and Victor Kruczyski? If you haven't seen "Abby," you've missed a real treasure on stage.

They bring history to life with humor and grace and take us back in time to the 1800s of Worcester and our country, a time when it wasn't popular to stand up and be heard and, for a woman, a double no-no. Abby made such a contribution to overcome injustice and show compassion for an unpopular cause.

Go see "Abby" and share in it next time. Don't miss it when, and if, it plays again because you will be sorry. It's really electric.

FRANK and SHIRLEY MUSCI
Auburn

A12 TELEGRAM & GAZETTE THURSDAY, APRIL 17, 1997

'Abby' revival wins raves

Continued From Page One

The play was the idea of Abby House founder Annette Rafferty, who sought out Worcester playwright and director Jane Dutton in 1994 to write a play about the woman for whom the organization was named. Rafferty got the hesitant Dutton to agree to finish the work in time for the 20th anniversary observance.

NEW PLAY POSSIBLE

Yesterday afternoon, Dutton greeted people as they flowed into the 525-seat Hebert Auditorium at Quinsigamond Community College for the play's third performance.

"I'm very happy," she said, surveying the audience of mostly women. "The response has been better than we ever expected it would be."

Susan Nest and Victor Kruczynski, who played Abby and Stephen, and Dutton received standing ovations after all performances.

Will "Abby" become an annual April event?

Dutton hesitated, "Oh, I don't know ... I'm working on a new play."

There were no commitments from Abby House principals yesterday because details have yet to be worked out, but the organization, they said, does not plan to give up the idea of using a play for its anniversary fund-raiser.

"I'm sure Abby's House will be involved in the new work in some

way," Julie Komenos, development coordinator, said.

Komenos is also sure "Abby" will be seen again. "It's a great piece of theater, and it is an important work related to Worcester's history."

Most people interviewed leaving the auditorium said, without hesitation, that they would attend a repeat performance of "Abby."

"It's so amazing that it takes place in Worcester," said Wendy Harding of Worcester, summing up the reactions of many in the audience.

Joan Daughney, who lives in the Tatnuck area, empathized with the hardships experienced by the Fosters in the play.

"They were dedicated and courageous. If someone threw tomatoes and eggs at me, I'm not sure I'd ever go back or get up and speak to a group again," she said.

Keith Dixson of Oakham would see "Abby" again. "It was very interesting. I learned a lot of history by just listening," he said.

---

12 Nazis sentenced to death

The Nuremberg trials at which surviving Nazi leaders were prosecuted for "crimes against humanity" began in November 1945 and lasted for nearly a year. Of the 22 Nazis tried by the international tribunal, 12 received death sentences, three life imprisonment, four shorter prison terms, and three were acquitted.

Melissa (Mom) and Bonnie

Holly and McKinsie (4 1/2 mos.)

March is
Women's History Month

Join us for a mournful, merry musical, menopausal celebration

washed-up
middle-aged
women

Worcester's only performance

a montage of real-life stories & songs about women growing older and coming into their own.

Cast: Debra Wise, Kate Charney, Christina Bynoe & Ruth Roper
Directed by: Wes Sanders
Music by: Steven Cummings
Written by: Debra Wise & Elaine Koury

March 15 @ 8:00 p.m. *(ASL Interpreted)*
Hebert Auditorium • Quinsigamond Community College
670 West Boylston Street • Worcester

Tickets in advance: $25 Golden Circle (preferred seating); $15 Adults; $10 Seniors/Students. **Tickets at door:** $20 all seats; no preferred seating available.

To order tickets call: 767-2505.
MasterCard, VISA & Discover accepted.
Checks payable to: YWCA - Play, 1 Salem Square, Worcester, MA 01608

Proceeds to benefit: Abby's House, Quota International of Worcester, Rape Crisis Center of Central Massachusetts, Worcester Women's History Project & YWCA of Central Massachusetts.

CHAPTER 21 *Guardians, Bright Minds and Good Hearts*

By March of that year, the board of directors received the report and recommendations of the long range planning committee, a very affirming publication, but one which underscored a number of areas for growth and improvement. For example, 82% of the respondents believed that Abby's House should be a center for women's information, parenting workshops, support groups, education, and job training resources. I wondered myself how many of the respondents remembered the days of "Worcester Connection" that had been Abby's educational arm for nine years, but closed because funding sources seemed resistant to supporting programs of consciousness raising. If it hadn't been for a few faithful feminists and communities of religious women, we would never even have lasted one year. Had the Connection's time come again? Was the community realizing the necessity of addressing the root causes of poverty, domestic violence, substance abuse and low self-esteem through formal education sessions? And were we being urged to do our own job training? Perhaps we had not done enough to promote our Abigail Program, geared to do this very kind of skill building with our residents. Interestingly, a smaller percentage of those responding, 73%, believed Abby's House should concentrate mainly on safe, affordable housing development. We were certainly well aware that safe housing was the fundamental need that had to be met before we could address other personal growth areas. Without stability, rootedness, and structure in place, the educational programs would bear little fruit. So many of the women who came through the shelter were at some level of crisis or transition; until all their immediate needs could be met, women, especially those with children, were in no position to focus on longer term educational options. All of these proved to be warning signs of overextending ourselves and risking the possible diminishing of our focus, which would adversely affect the quality of programs. It was no surprise that as a committee we recommended taking into consideration our mission, its internal capabilities, and the external environment that:

> "Abby's primary future direction should be to maintain the high quality level of its existing programs. In terms of growth, the primary focus should be on the development of safe, affordable housing."

Since there were educational programs that might be available elsewhere in the community, we offered the following:

> "That, as a secondary recommendation, Abby's staff, both core and volunteer, develop a targeted plan to network with other programs and community resources to ensure that women are aware of, and able to participate in the areas of job training, parenting and other women's issues."

While the board of directors was busy reading and mulling over the contents of the long range planning committee's report, the local newspapers were once again flooded with Abby's House publicity, which confirmed exactly what the report stated—educating and networking. First, "Abby," the original play performed at the 20th anniversary, was back by popular demand. In Jane Dutton's words which appeared in Dianne Williamson's March 18th column in the *Telegram and Gazette*:

> "They [Abby and Stephen] were so much in love and so different, which is what makes the play so much fun. She [Abby] was practical and didn't have much of a sense of humor; he [Stephen] was romantic and tender. Once I hit on Stephen, I thought, 'This is just great.' So I wrote the play for the two of them. I didn't want this to be a history lesson. I wanted it to be entertaining, but educational at the same time."

WORCESTER'S INDEPENDENT VOICE SINCE 1976

APRIL 2-8, 1997

worcester maga...

FREE

What they're making at non-profits ... and elsewhere

Payday

| Michael Madden on Meegan Garrity | A decade of Joy of Music | Safri Duo thumps tubs |

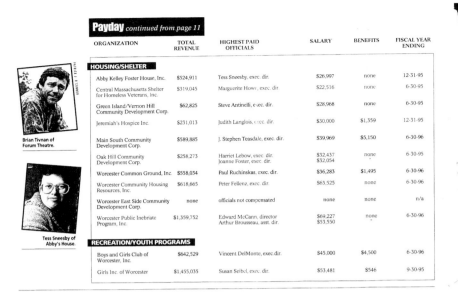

Payday continued from page 11

ORGANIZATION	TOTAL REVENUE	HIGHEST PAID OFFICIALS	SALARY	BENEFITS	FISCAL YEAR ENDING
HOUSING/SHELTER					
Abby Kelley Foster House, Inc.	$524,911	Tess Sneesby, exec. dir.	$26,997	none	12-31-95
Central Massachusetts Shelter for Homeless Veterans, Inc.	$319,045	Marguerite Howe, exec. dir.	$22,516	none	6-30-95
Green Island/Vernon Hill Community Development Corp.	$62,825	Steve Antinelli, exec. dir.	$28,968	none	6-30-95
Jeremiah's Hospice Inc.	$231,013	Judith Langlois, exec. dir.	$30,000	$1,359	12-31-95
Main South Community Development Corp.	$589,885	J. Stephen Teasdale, exec. dir.	$39,969	$5,150	6-30-96
Oak Hill Community Development Corp.	$258,273	Harriet Lebow, exec. dir. Joanne Foster, exec. dir.	$32,437 $32,054	none	6-30-95
Worcester Common Ground, Inc.	$558,034	Paul Ruchinskas, exec. dir.	$36,283	$1,495	6-30-96
Worcester Community Housing Resources, Inc.	$618,665	Peter Fellenz, exec. dir.	$63,525	none	6-30-96
Worcester East Side Community Development Corp.	none	officials not compensated	none	none	n/a
Worcester Public Inebriate Program, Inc.	$1,359,752	Edward McCann, director Arthur Brousseau, asst. dir.	$69,227 $53,550	none	6-30-96
RECREATION/YOUTH PROGRAMS					
Boys and Girls Club of Worcester, Inc.	$642,529	Vincent DelMonte, exec. dir.	$45,000	$4,500	6-30-96
Girls Inc. of Worcester	$1,455,035	Susan Seibel, exec. dir.	$53,481	$546	9-30-95

Brian Tivnan of Forum Theatre.

Tess Sneesby of Abby's House.

Smile, Tess, and say "cheese"

Great Gardeners!

Marion Twining

Hilda and her fiddleheads

Karen Stevens

Ellen Grimm joins the staff

And then, as we were clipping out all this publicity about the return of Abby Kelley Foster in play form, Julie Komenos, now our development coordinator, was busy networking with other women's groups who had been gathering to bring The Underground Railway Theater of Arlington to Worcester's Quinsigamond Community College for Women's History Month. The theater group brought to Hebert Auditorium a staged montage of true stories about women maturing called, "Washed-Up Middle Aged Women." The merry musical had, of course, a very serious purpose: to raise funds for organizations like Abby's House that did direct service with abused women.

The first week of April was play time again. For the second year in a row, "Abby," starring Susan Nest and Victor Kruczynski, played to sold-out audiences and financially benefitted Abby's House. The response was far better than Jane Dutton, playwright, had anticipated and, when asked if "Abby" would become an annual April event, she said with some hesitation, "Oh, I don't know. I'm working on a new play." Julie was less hesitant in her response to the same question, "I'm sure "Abby" will be seen again. It's a great piece of theater, and it is an important work related to Worcester's history."

I believe part of our commitment to the spirit and the life of Abby Kelley Foster is to continue to let every citizen of this city learn about this remarkable woman, surely the city's most famous abolitionist. If I had the wherewithall, I'd fund this production to travel about the city, to perform in every school; I'd underwrite the performers and the director's salaries, so that they could give their talents full-time to the art of theater. We can't afford to have Abby's life disappear. She must be here to stay! Ordinarily, this dream would require a "sugar daddy." I like to envision myself as the Dutton-Nest-Kruczynski "sugar sister."

The very week that "Abby" played to packed audiences at Hebert Auditorium, *Worcester Magazine* featured once again, "Payday: What They're Making at Non-Profits." Ellen O'Connor, author of the article, answered her own question simply and truthfully: "Why did we focus on non-profits more than on for-profit companies? Because we could. Most for-profits are not required to make their salaries public." Of course, there we were again at the bottom of the salary scale listing. There was our executive director, Tess, on page 12 looking the readers in the eye

as if to say, "Ok, everyone. Now you know exactly how much I earn, and it's embarrassing to have the whole world see this in black and white. To add insult to injury, my photo is just horrible. My driver's license photo is more flattering." Feelings aside, such an "exposé" always reaps rewards for Abby's House. Full houses, such as Jane Dutton's plays which attract increased donations, new supporters and volunteers, don't happen in a vacuum. In the future, when an event is billed as a benefit for Abby's House, everyone will know where the largest percentage of those proceeds will go. The same article emphasized that most of our donations come from those sources just mentioned and small grants carefully researched and written by our new grantwriter, Ellen Grimm, who joined our staff part-time in March. Abby's commitment to the mission is what impressed the reader. So, Tess Sneesby, smile once again and say: "Cheese, please!"

Spring transformed our backyard garden into paradise overnight. It was that time of year again for flowers and for Hilda's annual "time-off" to go in search of fiddleheads, a delicacy within the Acadian community. Fiddleheads have a very short growing season and must be harvested and prepared at just the right moment. If the truth be known, I think I'm the only staffer who enjoys sharing Hilda's crop. I'm not Acadian, but trace my love of those fiddleheads to an eighth grade experience provided by my beloved junior high school teacher, Clara Barton Turner (grand-niece of Clara herself), who introduced me to that courageous woman, "Evangeline," Longfellow's famous historical poem. She had to have eaten fiddleheads! In the fall of 1997, I visited Acadia for the first time and imagined what it was like for my heroine to have been so cruelly banished from the land that was home. I must admit that I did look around in search of fiddleheads, but found none. Like so many native crops, they, like the original inhabitants, had disappeared. Well, we weren't going to let that happen to the plants and flowers at Abby's. Thanks to many women and groups, like Emma Flores, Wachusett Regional High School students: Karen Stevens, Marion Twining, Maggie Wain, Laura Callahan, Dynamy, the women of the Tatnuck Garden Club and grantwriter Ellen Grimm, also a part-time gardener, our gardens and landscaping are just beautiful to behold. As coordinator of gardening, Ellen continues to guarantee garden longevity by requesting perenni-

Sue Bastardo and her daughter, Jena, bring vegetables

At Tower Hill

Hampton Beach for a day

Our 77 Chatham Street hero

Jena, Julia, Alex, and Cait

Fun and Food inside

Gwen

Kim and Jocelyn

Kate and Kendra

als from anyone willing to drop off seeds or cuttings at our back door. What a wondrous place, this Abby's House, that combines long range planning for services with long term planting plans. It could only happen here that bread and roses would be as important for the spirit as lavender, phlox and thyme. Readers of our newsletter support this concept, as well. Every week when crops appear in our land, Acme, a produce company, brings us fresh produce and Mike and Sue Bastardo of Holden have arrived faithfully for years with their garden produce. As Tess reminded us in her writings:

> "For all of us who are a part of Abby's, there needs to be room within our community's cycle for changes, for surprises, for possibilities and for growth and healing. Abby's provides many important and needed services. But, above all, we are guardians of the cycle, being careful to maintain it with loving care." As May Sarton says:

> *'Help us to be the always hopeful*
> *Guardians of the spirit*
> *Who know that without darkness*
> *Nothing comes to birth*
> *As without light*
> *Nothing flowers.'*

During the summer the Day Center guests traveled to Tower Hill and to Hampton Beach, which gave several women their first opportunity to see the ocean. There were other "firsts" that summer, some expected, others not. The Day Center was forced to close for several days due to water damage caused by a fire in one of the 77 Chatham Street units. The cause was a lighted candle left unattended by the occupants. This was certainly unfortunate for the guests of the center as well as for the woman and her family in that apartment. But, within a short time, the center re-opened, meals were being prepared by happy-to-be-back volunteers, and the conversation among the women was loud, long-lasting and interrupted with bursts of hearty laughter. The "first" setback was forgotten by dessert time. But the staff will long remember the fire and will be thankful forever for the sprinkler system and the on-site security person who responded to the hard-wire fire alarm, evacuating all the residents safely. Our 21st anniversary date gave us the opportunity to express that gratitude.

Another 1997 "first" was the arrival of four high school students for summer internships. We welcomed Emily Athy, Kim Fletcher, Kendra Kartheiser and Kate Melkonian, all of whom proved to be an enormous help especially in the office and in the thrift store. I can't overlook the presence of Jenna Fletcher, Alexandra Kartheiser, Julia Fletcher, Rose and Fernando Rodriquez, the younger generation who were always willing to do odd jobs for us. For a few weeks we had the pleasure of a fifth student, Jocelyn Black. We learned so much from these young women, each of whom brought her own special personality and talent to enrich the staff. And that was another "first." Consciously or unconsciously, bringing younger women into our community to be participants in our work had been a move that boosted our spirits, relieved us of some responsibility and taught us new ways of dealing with old problems. It was evident by early fall that "old" dogs *can* be taught new tricks. I felt privileged to work with these young women. In fact, their presence made me feel younger and more energetic. Bright minds, good hearts best describe them and they will, again, make a difference someplace, sometime.

Joining those young women in their efforts at Abby's was another group of young women and men from all over New England and New York state. They called themselves Young Neighbors in Action and they spent a week with us. Under the capable and watchful eye of Hilda, they painted the new fence that had been installed around the 77 Chatham Street property. Dynamy students were also part of this effort. It proved to be a difficult assignment, but they finally accomplished it with lots of moans and groans and pizza. The poet Robert Frost reminded us that good fences make good neighbors, and that proved to be true for Abby's. Painting the fence initiated a new relationship with Spring Valley Nursing Home, our neighbor next door. Gwen, from 19 Crown Street, began volunteering there as a friendly visitor. All of us toured the facility and met staff and residents, many of whom had no families. They were particularly grateful and appreciative of our visits. Gwen had started another tradition that continues to grow and endure.

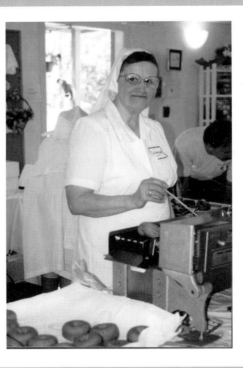

A6 TELEGRAM & GAZETTE   SATURDAY, OCTOBER 18, 1997

ENTERT

'Hugger' impresses in its debut

By Richard Duckett
Telegram & Gazette Reviewer

WORCESTER — "Hugger Mugger" embraced its audience with plenty of cleverness and marvelous acting as Jane Dutton's play about reunited sisters made an impressive debut last night at Quinsigamond Community College.

Dutton, a Worcester playwright who has mainly focused on works depicting local historical figures (for example, "Abby," which chronicled the life of 19th century activist Abby Kelley Foster), shows that she has the versatility and confidence to delve into fresh areas. True, the dramatic-comedy sisterly subject matter doesn't arrive without some echoes, but Dutton (who also directs) and the cast combine to make this production uniquely and enjoyably their own.

The sisters are brought together again after the sudden death of their mother, and in the process have to confront some home truths and secrets that they've kept from each other. The eldest of the trio, Barbara (Linda Oroszko), is the seemingly happily married Mom-type, who has had a difficult time accepting that her middle sister, Roslaind (Kathleen McGrath Jordan) is gay. It doesn't make matters easier for Barbara that Roslaind has brought along her "friend," Carol (Gwen Mason). The youngest sister, Lucy (Susan Nest), is mildly retarded, but has the disconcerting habit of always speaking, and knowing, the

CHRISTINE PETERSON
The cast of "Hugger Mugger" gets close. They are: Susan Nest (top, smiling) and, clockwise, Gwen Mason, Linda Oroszko and Kathleen McGrath Jordan.

Theater review

HUGGER MUGGER; written and directed by Jane Dutton. A Theatre Unlimited production. Performances 8 p.m. tonight and Oct. 24 and 25; 2 p.m. tomorrow. At Hebert Auditorium, Quinsigamond Community College, 670 West Boylston St., Worcester. Tickets: $10; $9 for those attending with a sister.
With Linda Oroszko, Susan Nest, Kathleen McGrath Jordan, Gwen Mason.

truth.

The play has been carefully thought out, and within 10 m Dutton and the cast not only l situation set up and the char superbly defined, but they al several good laughs under the The audience of 340 (last opening was a benefit for House) was immediately wor

and rightly so.

Dutton shows a particular propensity for well-crafted and witty one-liners that cap a situation perfectly. The play also successfully balances its efforts to be both a drama and a comedy. The second act, however, developed a tendency to be bottom heavy and in need of some trimming near the conclusion. And while the proceedings have an engaging naturalness, one wonders whether "Hugger Mugger" (the term means secrets) might be in need of an even more shocking skeleton or two in its closet in order to have a dramatic impact that resonates for a long time in the memory.

Still, the play is a joy to watch in

Standing, Polly, Fran, Eva, Margaret,
Elaine Kneeling: Anna Marie and Annette

CHAPTER 22

Reminders of Our Mission

Summer months, usually slow, served up a series of fundraisers: Bhadon's Gift Gallery, Classic Toy Shoppe, Price Chopper, Sam's Club and our own annual tag sale helped considerably in putting final financial touches on the capital campaign, leaving leftovers for shelter and supportive housing expenses. As I often write in my thank you notes, "Every bit makes a difference here." And, by the way, the new location of the tag sale was greeted with loud, long cheers of approval. We had relocated to the spacoius backyard of 77 Chatham Street from the smaller space behind the shelter. The tent had saved our many volunteers from sunstroke. Sister Gertrude's homemade doughnuts were the hit of the day—the pièce de résistance, so to speak, of the many culinary delights served up by the food committee. It was at the tag sale that announcements of the upcoming exhibit at City Hall were distributed:

BEYOND SURVIVAL: RECLAIMING OUR LIVES
Art and Photographs depicting the
issues of violence against women and children

City Hall - Week Without Violence
October 19-25, 1997

Although this event was a collaborative effort involving the Clothesline Project, Inc., YWCA, Girls, Inc., Art X!!, the Rape Crisis Center and the Committee on the Status of Women, Abby's House provided the leadership under the creative direction of Day Center coordinator, Ellen Laverdure. Selecting City Hall as the site of the exhibit was a conscious decision: the impact of the artwork would be strengthened by its presence as a backdrop to "business as usual" in the community. Adding her talent to the project was Donna Talman, a professional photographer and therapist. Ellen designed a tee shirt to help raise money for the exhibit, the first of its kind, which portrayed each woman's dignity as she moved beyond victim status to strong survivor and reclaimer of her life. Abby's had truly provided the Worcester community with two opportunities to reflect on powerful and thought-provoking issues: A Women's Equality Day in August raised up the memory of many former guests who died violently. This exhibit in which women who survived and created lives of worth beyond their abuse surely reminded the community of our mission. From the joys of getting bargains at our tag sale, the excitement of receiving the results of fundraising, the heights of experiencing well-deserved strokes of success, we are always called back to the reality of why we exist.

We were fortunate in the fall to have Jane Dutton's new play, "Hugger Mugger," performed on opening night at Quinsigamond Community College's Hebert Auditorium for the benefit of Abby's House. Once again, the theater was filled with Dutton devotees, a following that swelled considerably after her stunning production, "Abby." Featured as the stars were Susan Nest, Kathy McGrath Jordan, Gwen Mason and Linda Oroszko. It was, as I'd grown to expect from Jane's works, an immediate hit. The title, "Hugger Mugger," means "secrets." Believe me, it's no secret how much we owe these women, especially Jane and Susan, for their dedicated service to Abby's.

And, speaking of dedication and commitment, a November "reunion lunch" brought together a few of Abby's early pioneer women—those who blazed the trails and endured their share of trials and tribulations. The occasion, November 11, 1997, marked the launching of these memoirs and it had to take place around that dining room table where so many hours had been spent in the mid-1970s. What better place to eat and reminisce?

My quilts

Kris Komenos helps us out!

Some random notes collected during the three-night **Phish** stand at the Worcester Centrum Centre:

Abby's House, the Regional Environmental Council and the Worcester County Food Bank were invited to bring information about themselves to the concerts. Each of the organizations benefited from funds raised through the sale of raffle tickets for backstage passes and Phish merchandise. The band has set up the Water Wheel Foundation to "give back to the communities it comes to," said Mike Hayes, who keeps the operation going along with Henry Schwab. Phish started the Water Wheel to help fund charitable works in its home state of Vermont. This is the first time the organization has gone on the road to work with local groups.

Saturday's show ran longer than three hours and featured a senses-reeling 45-minute jam in the second set. When the band did Led Zeppelin's "Moby Dick" during the encore, some of the young pups around us had no idea what it was. That's when I felt old.

A debate between a Phish fan and a Deadhead was overheard Sunday at the Food Court in the Worcester Common Outlets. The guy in the Dead T-shirt with his family was a little miffed that Phish is always being compared to his favorite band, and felt the new group was riding the coattails of a legend. The considerably younger Phish fan was emphatic in claiming that Phish and the Dead were representative of two completely different worlds. "It's like comparing steak to cheese steak," the Phish fan proclaimed.

We didn't stick around to figure out which band was which.

Elaine, Santa and families

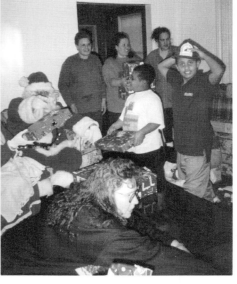

Those able to attend were: Ellen "Polly" Kierstead, Fran O'Connell, Eva Engel, Margaret Baillie, Elaine Lamoureux, Anna Marie Kane, SSJ and I. Margaret won the "I came from the farthest point—Norway, Maine" award, and Elaine copped the award of courage, hobbling in on her crutches, the result of "The one who hit me was on a cell phone" automobile accident. In the photo here, Anna Marie and I are the ones on our knees symbolically reliving the gratitude we felt when the house at 21-23 Crown Street was finally secured in May of 1976. Over coffee and sweets we recalled many memories of former guests, and they all gave suggestions on what format might be used for this book. I think it was at this meeting that I mentioned a preference for a "scrapbook" style, since all of the early history was kept in scrapbooks which took the place of file cabinets in those days. That particular model (the scrapbook) always appealed to me and seemed a very appropriate memory storage box for a woman's organization. Our foremothers preserved their precious memories in the same way. They also pieced together family and community history in quilts, another art form dear to my heart. Although I am far from an accomplished quilter, I have achieved a certain proficiency in creating quilts and wall hangings with the log cabin design, one of the oldest patterns used by women to tell their stories. As I put these thoughts down on paper, it became very obvious I had already decided what the best format would be. At the reunion I did my darndest to absorb other suggestions, but I confess, as far as I was concerned, it was too late for changing the format. Since that November get-together, I have spent months of solitude in the history room reading, researching, and recording. I always kept in mind that this would be a formal historic account of our 25 years. However, as the weeks passed, that resolve gave way to what seemed more natural and spontaneous for me as designated keeper of memories: a memoir of my own experiences at Abby's House would produce the kind of written quilt that would jog others' memories. I hoped it would reveal untold "secrets," bring a smile or even cause an outrageous burst of laughter, possibly a flood of tears, a furrowed brow, and, above all, an appreciation of women's courage and caring. Finally, I wanted it to show that so much goodness exists in this community. Just expressing this has relieved me of the guilt I felt for putting aside the idea of doing a scholarly history. I guess confession is good for the soul after all.

The events that took place in that final month of 1997, reflected the variety of "spirits" that come floating through Abby's House on a regular basis. Early in the month, Waterwheel Foundation's Henry Schwab and Mike Hayes, who manage the comings and goings of "Phish" (a rock group), provided us with an opportunity to be part of their fundraiser for local Worcester charities. The result would be a goodly share for Abby's of the funds raised through the sale of raffle tickets for backstage passes and "Phish" merchandise. It took Kendra Kartheiser, Kim Fletcher, Kris Komenos and Ben Chates to make those three "Phish" performances successful for us.

Spirits of generosity and kindness moved Barbara Herman to hold her Third Annual Wisewomen Gala and stirred the hearts of Worcester Academy sophomores to adopt us for the holiday season. Courtesy of UMass Medical Center, Santa Claus came to our families via an ambulance, with lights and horns blaring. It caused more of a stir than a sleigh with reindeer attached would have! The more noise, the better for this generation of gift recipients. Lastly, items on our holiday needs list published each year by *Worcester Magazine*, began appearing everywhere, brought into Abby's by those generous "spirits" we recognize as our supporters and donors. By the time the Crown Hill Neighborhood Association carolers arrived at our door, announcing in song the tidings of the season, we were in the best of spirits. It had been another full year and in an attempt to describe the feelings we had on that December 31st, I chose W.E.B. DuBois' poem, "Prayer for a New Year":

"We pray tonight, O God, for confidence in ourselves, our powers and our purposes in this beginning of a New Year. Ward us from lack of faith and hesitancy and inspire in us not only the determination to do a year's work well, but the unfaltering belief that what we wish to do, we will do. Such Faith is born of Works. Every deed accomplished finishes not only itself, but is fallow ground for future deeds. Abundantly endow us with this deed-born Faith."

Celebrating
Worcester's 150th

Joyce Harter's welcomed presence

P. 2   DATEBOOK   AUGUST 24, 1997

TUESDAY

Worcester observes **Women's Equality Day** with special commemoration of former shelter guests, poetry readings and interpretive dance at 6 p.m. at the gravesite of Abby Kelley Foster in Hope Cemetery, 119 Webster St., Worcester.

Tess and Elaine

With Lamoureux's help, parents find trust again

Continued From Page One

nary," says Jeannette Atkinson, a spokeswoman for the group.

"Her group members know that they can rely on her, week after week and year after year. Slowly, leaders help their groups become families with a sense of hope. When leaders such as Elaine are trustworthy, members gradually learn to trust and are able to become the parents," she says.

The majority of the members in her group are women, and some are single parents. Members come from throughout Central Massachusetts. Confidentiality is prized, so the location of meetings and the full names of members are not disclosed.

"The group meetings are a very, very safe place for parents to share their problems," says Lamoureux.

Parents' group honors years of help

By Mary Anne Magiera
Telegram & Gazette Staff

WORCESTER — Elaine Lamoureux thrives on watching other people solve problems.

Every Tuesday night, she listens and watches as 10 parents wrestle with the stress and emotional issues of bringing up children. She's been at it so long — more than a decade — and she's so good at it, that Parents Anonymous of Massachusetts is singling her out for recognition.

Lamoureux facilitates one of two Worcester chapters of the national self-help group, which was founded in California in 1970. She is being honored as part of the observance of Child Abuse Prevention Month in April. She will be recognized in June

> ❝I am continually inspired by the parents. It takes a lot of courage to pick up the phone, call someone and tell them you need help. ❞
>
> ELAINE LAMOUREUX

at the group's annual meeting, which is going to be held in Worcester.

Parents Anonymous offers weekly support meetings for small groups of parents who help one another control their anger and stop abusive behavior toward their children. Each group is led by a trained facilitator who works with a parent leader. There are more than 65 Parents Anonymous groups in Massachusetts.

"I am continually inspired by the

parents. It takes a lot of courage to pick up the phone, call someone and tell them you need help. Their determination to do a good job at bringing up their kids, day after day, is inspiring," Lamoureux says.

The hardest part of being a facilitator, according to Lamoureux, is "allowing the parents to come to their own conclusions."

PARENTS HELPING PARENTS

The group is structured so that parents help one another; Lamoureux describes her role as providing support and information about services.

"Elaine's commitment to her Parents Anonymous group is extraordi-

Turn to WITH/Page A5

TELEGRAM & GAZETTE   MONDAY, MAY 11, 1998   **A5**

House that Lamoureux received a flyer from Parents Anonymous asking for a one-year commitment as a volunteer facilitator.

"I thought I would do the year and be done with it, but I got hooked by

home — drugs, alcohol, violence — are frightening to them," she says.

Lamoureux says she's not ready to retire from her facilitator's job, but she's also not promising she'll last another decade.

Miriam Torres,
Tammy Zelaya and Annette

HAPTER 23 *Fallow Ground for Future Deeds*

Little did any of us realize how much we would need that confidence and faith in the early days of 1998. We received word the first week of January that one of Abby's young Holy Cross staffers had died unexpectedly on December 31, while on vacation with her family in England. Michele Webster died three weeks before her 21st birthday, leaving her parents, Carol and Walter, devastated by the loss of their only child. As a sociology major concentrating on women's studies at the college, Michele had written her final paper on her experience working at Abby's. In that paper she expressed her desire to dedicate her life to improving conditions for women, especially poor women. Carolyn Howe, her professor, forwarded to Abby's the final exam paper which clearly revealed an understanding of the effects of poverty on women well beyond Michele's young years:

"At about 7 p.m. the silence was broken as 'Terry' arrived with her two upbeat sons, the youngest of whom was quickly titled the man of the hour in honor of his birthday. Terry's foremost concern is the well-being of her children, a sentiment shared by many poor women struggling to make ends meet. Seeing the joy in this woman's eyes as she watched her children play, was a heartbreaking moment. While she is doing her best to provide for the children, the government and Clinton administration are drafting plans to make her job even

harder—when we recognize the struggles of all of these women as our own, change in our society will become possible—statistics concerning welfare, homelessness and poverty will never again be seen as mere numbers. Now, names and faces are attached—[it strikes me] that no one is secure."

Michele Webster understood the importance of connection between people and felt that, as a woman, she had made that connection with the women and children of Abby's House. And today, several years after her premature death, Michele's connection remains real at Abby's, carried on by her best friend, Debbie Gobron and her beloved mother, Carol, who was finally able to take her daughter's place as a night staffer. The spirit of DuBois' "faith born of Works" came to rest on these two women—devoted mother and best friend! So, dear Michele, it's true—you are with us still and "every deed accomplished finishes not only itself, but is fallow ground for future deeds." All of us at Abby's House were reminded by Michele's death not only of the brevity of life, but also of the unbelievable commitment made to Abby's women and children by the young women of Holy Cross College. Imagine, 25 years of staffing our night shelter during fall and spring semesters, three nights a week, never missing a beat, befriending and listening and learning things their books will never teach them. Female profiles in courage, one and all!

Close on the heals of sadness and sorrow came reasons for rejoicing. Joyce Harter joined our staff as administrative assistant, providing the organization with her expertise and her kind, respectful and caring heart. Our services were expanding and the time had come for someone as skilled as Joyce to reorganize those files that had long since replaced the old scrapbooks. It still amazes me to think of how much had accumulated in 22 years. Then came news that Abby's would be participating in the 150th anniversary of the official incorporation of the City of Worcester. I, along with hundreds of other women and men, had been selected to represent all who had preceded us as citizens and to honor the positive contributions each of us had bestowed on the city. February 28th dawned clear and crisp and crowds soon descended on City Hall for the formal celebration. It was a day filled with excitement and, as a native of Worcester,

I felt a strong sense of pride in being a daughter of the city's family. One hundred and fifty years earlier in 1848, Abby Kelley Foster had initiated Worcester's first antislavery fair held in the city's largest auditorium, Brinley Hall. Much to her surprise, it was a huge success. As a result of Worcester's enthusiasm for the cause, one thousand dollars was raised for the treasury of the American Anti-Slavery Society. As I stood on the steps of City Hall that day, I concluded that, in spite of our aches, pains and complaints about Worcester, the citizenry would always respond favorably with support and in large numbers to either a good cause or a splendid celebration. As a city we need only a rallying call for community spirit and, of course, the enticement of good food and drink to create that unified front. February 28th was one of those memorable occasions in our city's history. Twenty-two years of caring attention to the needs of homeless and battered women and their children is an ongoing example of this kind of support citizens have contributed to the archives of Worcester's amazing achievements. All of these thoughts occupied my mind, standing on those hard steps in dress shoes I seldom wear, listening now to state and federal politicians praise Worcester. Only a sense of decorum inherited from my Irish parents prevented me from crying out to them:

> "Look at us up here, standing five deep across the width of these steps. Ask us who we are and whom *we* represent today. For me, it's the women and children of Abby's House who need a lot more from *you*. When we gather on these same steps for the 200th, I won't be here and I hope no one will be here to take my place because *you* made safe, decent, affordable housing a city priority and everyone now has a home."

By the time I had refocused my attention on the outdoor podium, the speaking had stopped, mercifully, and the crowd began cheering and the afternoon activities were underway. When I looked around at those standing to the right and left of me, most of whom I knew were personally involved in some concrete work with poor people, I wondered if they had read my mind. I was dead certain they had and, no doubt, had added other demands to the city's "must have as soon as possible" list.

By the way, don't think it didn't occur to me, as I meandered around the Common, that Abby Kelley Foster was probably "steaming mad" that I had been too cowardly and polite not to have used that staircase as a pulpit and let those politicians hear exactly what was on my mind. Sorry, Abby. If I ever have another chance—let's say at the 175th, I promise to do better.

The celebration of the 150th just kept going, with another woman in our community having been chosen as a 1998 Woman of Distinction—our own Elaine Lamoureux. This is an honor given each year by the Montachusett Girl Scout Council to a woman nominated by the organization in which she works. As a staff we were thrilled that Elaine, the heartbeat of Abby's House, had been selected and, finally, properly recognized for her years of dedication to our guests. Elaine's nomination read as follows:

> "Elaine Lamoureux was one of the founding members of the Abby's House team 22 years ago. Today, she is the guest advocate for the women coming into the shelter and for Abby's House permanent housing at 19 Crown and 77 Chatham Streets. Her personal touch and love for what she does is reflected in her attitude towards women and the connection she makes with those who seek shelter at Abby's. Elaine helps women seek and find safe, affordable housing, stability in their lives and to experience hope and success.
>
> In addition, Elaine leads a group of women in Parents' Anonymous and proceeds to support those parents in their struggles to do the best job they can, sometimes under the worst conditions. Elaine is an inspiration to the people who work with her every day, and is truly a Woman of Distinction."

Ordinarily, there would be nothing more to add to this tribute, so well expressed and so accurate in its portrayal of Elaine, but, for me, after 22 years of friendship, of sharing many different adventures, most of them told in the previous pages of this memoir, the nomination words were just the tip of the iceberg. This is an amazing human being who thinks positively 24 hours a day, whose heart embraces the whole world and who is a "sister" to every woman. Instinctively, Elaine knows what each woman needs most at any given time. Her specialty is empowerment and she serves it up with a smile and a sense of confidence that inspires the most discouraged woman to develop, almost overnight, a strong, "can-do" attitude. Elaine can also set limits and if rules that would endanger staff or guests are violated, the violator is dismissed from the shelter. But typical of Elaine, she'll always drive that woman or those women to another destination, help them with their belongings and, inevitably, former guests and advocate part on friendly terms. In all my years here, I've never known anyone with such skill in human relations. I know all of us are gifted and talented, but Elaine, in her chosen work as advocate, stands out and above us all. Elaine is linked in my mind with Abby. She's a person who inspires the kind of statement made by Lucy Stone on the occasion of Abby's death. "She had no peer and she leaves no successor," Lucy said of Abby. I say the same about Elaine.

Michele Webster

1977–1997

Abby's friends from Holy Cross

Jeanne Adler at her

new position

Ellen MacDonough invites

all into the Day Center

Ginny Lindsay and

France Guillette serve

dinner at noon while

Jeanne and Joyce look on

ELEGRAM & GAZ

WEDNESDAY, JULY 22, 1998 • WORCESTER, MASSACHUSETTS

Jill E. Plunkett and Kristen L. Ryan, students from Brentwood, N.Y., paint a fence around Abby's House.

T&G Staff/BETTY JENEWIN PHOTO

HELPING HANDS

Student volunteers bring relief to the city's needy

By Bronislaus B. Kush
TELEGRAM & GAZETTE STAFF

WORCESTER — Sarah Higgins is quite the basketball player, and this fall has a pretty good chance of becoming a member of the varsity girls' team at Xavier High School in her hometown of Appleton, Wis.

The slot, however, is not guaranteed, so, every minute of court time over the summer helps.

Students Sarah A. Higgins and Mark L. Lee remove

T&G Staff/BETTY JENEWIN
Katie A. Ewald of the Academy of St. Joseph in Brentwood, N.Y., paints a fence at Abby's House.

Students lend a hand

VOLUNTEERS/From **PAGE ONE**

But rather than practicing her fade-away shot, the 16-year-old is in Worcester this week, along with 10 fellow Xavier students, helping the folks of Jeremiah's Inn.

In all, 82 kids from around the ... volunteering their time ... Abby's House, the Ed-... Day Care center, The ... olate, Dismas House, ... se, The Mustard Seed, ... YWCA, St. Agnes ... ville House.

... second year that volun-... e to Worcester to help ... needy through the ... bors in Action pro-

... d the work does have ... aid Higgins, taking a ... sembling a bookshelf

... one of 16 communi-... h school students are ... with tutorial, recre-... ral maintenance pro-... the country, 1,350 stu-... cipating.

... is sponsored and di-... Center for Ministry ... a nonprofit agency ... h 100 Roman Catholic ... e United States and

... a lot of programs

where kids do volunteer community service," said Laurie A. Delgatto, a CMD spokeswoman. "But, with Young Neighbors in Action, the students get together after a long day and discuss what their particular work has meant. It's a way of living the Gospel."

GREAT HELP

Beth A. Tobin, a local organizer who is involved with the youth ministry at St. Mary's Church in Southbridge, said the program helps students learn to understand why the particular needs have come about.

She said it also gives teen-agers an opportunity to learn about local cultural and ethnic groups.

Andres Vera, assistant executive director at Jeremiah's, said the work performed by the students will greatly benefit any handicapped people staying at the inn.

The students are at work making two rooms at the Webster Square building handicapped accessible.

"It's really great to have them here helping us out," Vera said.

Sarah Simon, a campus minister who's accompanying the group from Appleton, said the experience also helps the students to learn about each other and how to work together. Simon said the students are staying at the Oakhurst Retreat and Conference Center in Whitinsville.

T&G Staff/BETTY JENEWIN
Katie A. Ewald of the Academy of St. Joseph in Brentwood, N.Y., paints a fence at Abby's House.

Let the bidding begin

WORCESTER – Mike Komenos of Worcester examines the tusks of a granite walrus he bought for $250 yesterday during an auction sponsored by Abby's House at Christ the King parish hall, 1052 Pleasant St. Annette Rafferty, Abby's House founder, is helping Komenos. 'bout 200 people attended the auction, which raised about $10,000 for the homeless and battered women and children.

STEVE LANAVA

Wally the Walrus!

ABBY'S HOUSE

22nd Anniversary Celebration

featuring

ABBY'S ANNIVERSARY AUCTION

June 3, 1998 • 6 to 9 p.m.

Christ the King
1052 Pleasant Street
Worcester, MA 01602

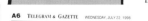

A6 TELEGRAM & GAZETTE WEDNESDAY, JULY 22, 1998

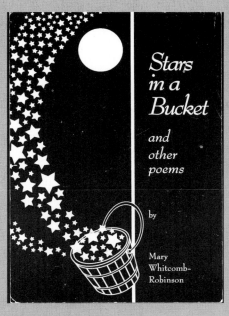

Stars in a Bucket

and other poems

by

Mary Whitcomb-Robinson

Mary Robinson and her wonderful poetry

Betty and Annette at Seneca Falls 1998

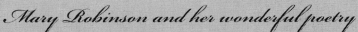

'Equality' participants tip their hats to Abzug

By Kathleen A. Shaw
TELEGRAM & GAZETTE STAFF

WORCESTER — More than 50 women and a few men gathered at the grave of Abby Kelley Foster early last night to renew their com-

D-Worcester, who read an essay titled "Gloria Steinem on Bella Abzug," wore a black, wide-brimmed creation with a striped hat band. Annette Rafferty, a founder of the Abby's House women's shelter, —— re a straw creation. Some wore hats and others wore small hats. ew wore no hat.

he hats were in honor of Bella S.

Turn to W

WORCESTER,

A2

Local women gather at Foster's grave site

WOMEN/from PAGE ONE

Abzug, a feminist and former congresswoman from New York, who died in March. Those attending were reminded of the time she said, "Stop apologizing and just do what needs to be done." Abzug also sponsored the legislation that created Women's Equality Day.

Foster, an early feminist and campaigner for women's rights, and Abzug, a late 20th century leader of the modern women's movement, were honored together for their commitment to this issue. The seventh annual Women's Equality Day celebration was organized by the

people of Abby's House, a place for homeless women and their children, that was named in Foster's honor.

SIGNING A DECLARATION

At the end of the program, those attending lined up to sign the 1998 Declaration of Sentiments drafted last month in Rochester, N.Y., by delegates to a National Organization for Women conference to celebrate the 150th year of the women's rights movement.

The movement began in 1848 at Seneca Falls, N.Y., as a local endeavor, and led to a national meeting in 1850 at Brinley ——

A14

The Worcester Women's History Project is planning a major event in the year 2000 to commemorate that session.

The "sentiments," in part, call for a world in which women can determine their own destiny, where all people have social and economic justice and where "nonviolence is the established order." They asked for a world where "women and girls are heard, valued and respected."

Foster's grave in Hope Cemetery was decorated fo—— with died hus-

Betty and Elise, Abby's very creative women

WEDNESDAY, AUGUST 19, 1998

WORCESTER DIARY

The Seventh Annual Commemoration of Women's Equality Day will be held at 6 p.m. Aug. 26 at the grave site of abolitionist and women's rights advocate, Abby Kelley Foster.

In addition to the annual remembrance of Abby's guests, staffers and supporters, there will be a special tribute to the late Bella Abzug, who sponsored the legislation for the observation of Equality Day. A tribute to the late Michelle Webster, a Holy Cross staffer who died in December also will be held.

The public is invited and to wear Bella or Abby-like hats.

The celebration, sponsored by Abby's House, continues observation of the First Women's Rights Convention of Seneca Falls, N.Y., 150 years ago and is a prelude to the observation of the First National Women's Right Convention held in Worcester in 1850. Worcester Women's History Project is planning a weekend-long celebration

and re-enactment to be held in October 2000.

Carmen, Lucy, Julia

CHAPTER 24 *Departures, Arrivals and Sidetrips*

The winter refused to leave us and in late April 1998, flowers remained in seclusion under the earth, afraid to appear for fear of dying prematurely. Our gardeners who had expected to be totally involved in planting by this time, were frustrated by the continued cold and rain. Inside, hearts were heavy, too, because Ellen Laverdure had resigned as Day Center coordinator and the process of hiring her replacement took over six weeks. We were looking for someone who, miraculously, would be a combination of the talents and the personality of all previous coordinators. Finally, Jeanne Adler of Charlton, a former shelter staffer and volunteer coordinator at Sturbridge Village, familiar with Abby's philosophy and the organization's mission, was selected. She surely carries on the tradition of compassion, optimism, good humor and commitment to the mission so central to the heart of the Day Center. Jeanne was warmly welcomed by volunteers, staff and guests. She had been the finalist—the one who once again opened the Day Center door. As Adrienne Rich reminded us in her poetry, "The door itself makes no promises. It is only a door." The promise rests in the efforts we all make to befriend, to listen, to encourage, to inspire and to know what it is we can and cannot accomplish in the course of a day. Such is the courage required to walk through the Day Center door, and it felt reassuring to me that our new coordinator would be there.

At long last the rain stopped, the bright sun reappeared, warming us and resurrecting the gardens while injecting a resurgence of energy into every area of Abby's activities. It was that time again, the time to celebrate another anniversary—the 22nd. This year a silent auction and raffle marked the occasion at Christ the King Church Hall on June 3rd. Everyone was invited. A variety of most unusual items had been donated: 20 tables of precious artwork, glassware, linens, gift certificates, crystal clocks and jewelry boxes were among the treasures up for bid. And to help with the bidding was hostess Toni Ballard (who, by the way, had to compete for the mike with Julie Komenos and Patti Conzo). Those two were born, not to shop, but to talk! The trio of Toni, Julie and Patti provided unexpected and hilarious entertainment. It made the fight for the mike worthwhile and profitable for us. Every item was auctioned off, even Wally the Walrus, won by Julie's husband, Mike. When his name was called as the highest bidder, I saw Julie grimace at the prospect of housing Wally, about whom she had already expressed unkind thoughts. But Mike had fallen hopelessly in love with this exquisite sculpture and it would be a useless task trying to relegate it to the garage. Today Wally resides in the Komenos' living room. Need I say more?

Students began arriving at Abby's from all over the United States to give that fence at 77 Chatham Street another coat of paint. What a job they did. Those Young Neighbors in Action were even better than last year's crew. In the office area, we were fortunate to have the services of Burke Dunphy, a junior at Notre Dame Academy. It was another summer in which we were reminded of how confident and competent young people are. We needed that reminder since we see how much self-esteem is lacking in younger shelter guests who often make poor decisions regarding relationships. This year was also a year to stand back and admire the stamina of older women, like Mary Whitcomb Robinson of Auburn who, at the young age of 85, published her first book of poetry, *Stars in a Bucket*, and designated Abby's House as one of the organizations to receive proceeds from the sale of this delightful anthology. Mary arrived with books to be sold out of Abby's office. I wondered why she had waited so long to finally publish but found my answer in her introduction of the book:

"Perhaps one could say 'If not now, when?' The clock is certainly ticking louder and louder each day.... It took years of living and learning and much writing to finally write what I could, at last, term poetry."

Mary is living proof that older is bolder and I hoped she'd follow her daughter Gail's advice to begin a second volume immediately.

Thank you, one and all, Burke, Bancroft students, Northboro Cadette Scouts, Ladies of Harley, who again raised money for camp scholarships and provided camp supplies and, thank you, Mary Whitcomb Robinson, for reminding us in your poetry that age is ageless:

"What is age?
A generation catcher; a feast
of generations spread before one
North, South, West and East."

The "feast of generations" stayed with me the remainder of the summer months and was certainly in my mind when, in July, at Seneca Falls where the 150th First Woman's Rights Convention was celebrated, Elaine and I unexpectedly came face to face with Betty Friedan in the Women's Hall of Fame. She was one of my idols, and I felt honored to have her stand next to me while Elaine took our picture. I'm sure there aren't that many years separating us, but I surely was the awestruck teenager and she, the venerable mother of feminist thought. What a feast of generations! The ladies of Seneca Falls were fluttering around Betty who was asking what came next on the schedule. Suddenly, after learning about the busy day ahead, she sat down and said in a rather loud voice, "I can't do any of that until I've had a pedicure. My feet need attention." The fluttering ladies were obviously dismayed. Where in the world was there a pedicure available in Seneca Falls or vicinity? After much ado, practical-minded Elaine spoke up, "Check the yellow pages. There should be information there." It was as though some cutting edge, scholarly paper on women's rights and feminist thought had been delivered. The ladies-in-waiting flew from the room to find a telephone book and, hopefully, a pedi-

curist. Elaine saved the morning and had provided the Friedan attendants with a solution. The two of us headed out of the Hall of Fame happy to have been of service and thrilled to have had our own moment with the always young, never old Betty Friedan. At 9:30 in the morning, we had tasted a real live feast of generations.

When we returned to Worcester, Elaine and I shared our experience of Seneca Falls with anyone who would listen. Especially interested were Betty Hoskins and Elise Kreiger who had stories of their own stemming from a conference they had attended in Rochester. I had no idea how much those two creative women absorbed from our experience until I read the script they had carefully prepared for our annual Women's Equality Day. It was a wonderful blending of the generations, another pattern on life's loom as the contributions of Abby Kelley Foster, Bella Abzug (who had died in January) and Michele Webster (dead at 20 years) were beautifully detailed in word and song. A Congresswoman, an effective orator and thinker, and a young student—all with visions of creating a better world for women—came together that evening at Abby's grave to be remembered along with guests and supporters:

"Our lives make a difference. We do what needs to be done. The effect of voting is not assured; the double standard flourishes; women work within the home and outside, too, but we always have poor women. Women retiring into poverty. We are the successors of Abby, Bella and Michele. They did what needed to be done. And so we recommit ourselves to the work we do together."

As those who participated in that celebration gathered afterwards in the Day Center to enjoy supper and one another's company, that recurring theme kept surfacing—what is age? A generation catcher—a feast of generations. August 26th was the best of feasts; it will be impossible to duplicate such a deeply moving ceremony, made beautiful by Betty, Elise, violinist Sheila Reid, musicians Lucy DeJesus and Julia Vigliotti, the family of Michele Webster and all those women who wore colorful hats in memory of Bella Abzug.

Tag Sales 1998–2000

The crowd arrives

Charlene Z.

Maryellen Lamoureux (center)

Leah Hazard and
Hawley Eckstrom

Linda McClendon and
Toni Heard

Lise Plante

Molly Donahue

Lauri Fletcher and
Sue McNamara

Mollie Rosenbaum and
Marvalie Gorden

Marielle and Danielle Anas

Jenn Harter and
Julia Fletcher

Predictably, in the fall we were caught up in the whirlwind of organizing another successful tag sale. Once again, doughnuts were the main attraction in the food department and whatever treasures the hundreds of buyers found netted another $12,000 for Abby's. This event, for the first time, involved over 200 volunteers who gave up a morning, an afternoon, or the whole day to socialize and sell their wares. We expanded the number of tables and added a second tent, thanks to the help of Worcester's business community.

And, watch out, Broadway. Jane Dutton's "Hugger Mugger" took the stage for another round and the opening night was, once again, for the benefit of Abby's House. Theater companies in Cleveland and Washington, D.C. had already expressed interest in staging this touching theatrical production. Even though Jane thought this was just another nice little play, we at Abby's had news for her. Broadway, Off Broadway and Off Off Broadway will soon be knocking on her door. And when the call comes, Jane, opening night will always be reserved for Abby's, right? After the successful second-time run of "Hugger Mugger," I learned that Susan Nest, our own Abby Kelley Foster, had been called on by Charlotte Wharton, the artist appointed to execute a portrait of Abby for the much anticipated hanging in Mechanics Hall, to pose for the painting since the only existing photographs of Abby show her only from the shoulders up! Wharton pointed out in an article that appeared in *Worcester Magazine* that, "How the body stands is three-fourths of the portrait."

In her research, Charlotte Wharton had discovered that Abby was taller than most women, very pretty with ice-blue eyes, chestnut hair and a fresh complexion. Her hands were slender, her posture erect and Abby had remained thin and trim into old age. Who better to be a living stand-in than Susan, who so closely resembles the subject and who knew her spirit perhaps better than any of us? Once again, just the thought of Abby gracing the walls of Mechanics Hall, along with Clara Barton, Dorothea Dix and her beloved friend, Lucy Stone, filled my mind with visions. I imagined what could happen in October of 1999, the month and year determined for this historic event. There would be thunderous applause; drums and trumpets hailing all four; media from everywhere; flashing cameras; women,

like myself, shedding tears of joy; men, like Albert Southwick expressing sincere joy that this moment had finally arrived. Now, the world had truly grown better. But it was only the fall of 1998. Could I possibly exercise the kind of patience it would take to get to the fall of 1999? Even if my dreams of that night weren't realized, one thing was going to happen: those connected intimately with Abby and the organization which carries her name, would cheer. No more being too polite, Abby! Since I might not make the 175th City Anniversary, this is my chance to give the last hurrah.

I never have to dig too deeply into my stored memories to recall people's generosity, particularly during the holidays. It's right there on the surface. Articles that appeared this year in local papers seemed to highlight the giving nature of our community. Interviews with donors revealed the roots of their generosity as well as their reasons for supporting certain non-profit agencies. This approach was welcomed by those of us on the receiving end who are grateful year-round and, in our case, are dependent in great measure on donations and donated services. It was refreshing to read how donors to our organization view us and to better understand their commitment to our mission. Of course, there are always the phone interviews with journalists curious to learn how Abby's fared at Thanksgiving time. In 22 years, we've never had to say anything other than what Julie Komenos told George Griffin of the *Telegram and Gazette* whose article appeared in the November 26, 1998 edition:

> "Thanksgiving is a good season not only for the spirit of giving it brings out in people, but for the opportunity it offers us to meet the people who have provided support for Abby's House. It's also the time of year when people respond to the needs of women and children."

The year came to a close quickly, but not without that "feast of generations" making a final appearance at Abby's House. Our friend Victoria Podbilski and her daughter Margaret Cardwell donated their forty year old Colorado blue spruce behind their 16 Perry Avenue home to the city of Worcester (now officially 150 years old) for its annual Christmas tree and donated money to Abby's House in thanksgiving for the life of that noble tree.

Susan Nest delivers the "Bloody Feet" speech

Crusader in black and white

Artist seeks her subject in the past

By Clare Karis

"Why have *I* been given this?"

That was artist Charlotte Wharton's first reaction when she learned she would be executing a portrait of Abigail Kelley Foster, whose likeness, along with those of three other notable women — Clara Barton, Dorothea Dix and Lucy Stone — will be gracing the walls of Mechanics Hall before 1999 is rung out, a year before the 150th anniversary of the first National Women's Rights Convention in 2000.

The project "Honoring Women in Mechanics Hall" emerged as an initiative of the Worcester Women's History Project. The objective is to honor and recognize women's societal contributions through portraits of mid-19th-century women with connections to Worcester.

Art

At present, all 19 portraits hanging in the balconies of the Great Hall are of men, from Stephen Salisbury II and President James Garfield to Elbridge Boyden, a carpenter and self-taught architect who designed the Hall and whose company was awarded the contract for its construction. Boyden had the dubious distinction of being the first person whose portrait was exhibited before his death. He was 87 at the time his likeness was hung, and some have speculated that they simply couldn't wait any longer.

Wharton's initial mixed reaction to the challenging assignment gave way very soon to fervor. Looking back, she feels that some sort of special karma sent the assignment her way.

"This is a Worcester project, and somehow I feel it was put out there for me to do. And because Abby Kelley lived in Worcester, we have access to the research materials. I was following the project in the newspaper for years, even cut out the first article I saw and wrote to the reporter and said it would be a shame if a Worcester woman didn't do this portrait. It's turned out to be one of the most fun, exciting projects I've ever done."

Why, one might ask, is so much research necessary to paint a portrait? Because all the portraits of males at Mechanics Hall are full-length ones, with most or

the press and clergy decreed that women should be silent and submissive. Labeled a Jezebel, a harlot, an infidel, at every meeting she ducked and dodged a barrage of rocks, tomatoes and rotten eggs hurled her way. But it would take more than a tomato or two splattered across her Quaker gray for Kelley to drop her efforts for the cause.

She carried on the good fight wherever and whenever she could find a venue: at Boston's Faneuil Hall, at Christmas fairs, at Fourth of July picnics. She kept audiences on the edge of their seats, telling stories of children taken from their mothers and pressed into slavery, of women flogged and forced to be concubines. She tugged at people's heartstrings, and just as important, loosened their purse strings; she herself set an example of self-sacrifice by never taking a penny in pay, even mortgaging her home when the financial forecast was bleakest.

In one speech, she appealed, "My soldiers must have money. If it can be raised in no other way, it shall be by mortgaging the little farm that I in part own. I have pledged myself to raise $10,000 to carry on this work. I will give a hundred dollars and if necessary a thousand, and if that will not do, two thousand. ..."

And she did not stop with the antislavery campaign. The fact that she took the floor at conventions that until now had been exclusively male and addressed mixed audiences made her a heroine with women, her passion and commitment coaxing

all of the body depicted. It was decided that the new portraits should be done in the same style in order to blend in with the existing ones. And therein lies the rub; the only existing photographs of Abby Kelley show her from the shoulders up.

"How the body stands is three-fourths of the portrait," Wharton points out. So it was essential that the artist find written descriptions of Kelley in order to nail down her physical demeanor. Wharton discovered Kelley was taller than most women of the time, at 5 feet 4 or 5; she was considered very pretty with her ice-blue eyes, chestnut hair and fresh complexion. She had delicate hands. Her posture was very erect; thin as a young woman, she remained trim into old age. Her voice was soft but could ring with commanding passion at speaking engagements.

Above: The earliest known portrait of Abby Kelley, a lithograph drawn from a daguerreotype.

Artist Charlotte Wharton with preliminary sketches of Kelley.

Kelley was a Quaker and Wharton researched her on the Internet in that connection. She discovered that in the Quaker faith, boys and girls are equal. The congregation doesn't speak or sing songs, but girls are encouraged to speak at the pulpit. "They are brought up to have a voice, so it was not unheard of for Abby to do public speaking. A woman's voice was very important to the Quakers, so her husband encouraged her to go out on the road."

It was in 1835 or thereabouts, while a teacher at the Friends school in Lynn, Mass., that Kelley was swept away by the abolitionist fire when she read William Lloyd Garrison's *Liberator*. She began to crusade for the abolition of slavery and fo... women's suffrage, and actually went on the road wi... troupe to deliver speeches to groups of both... which were referred to at the time as "prom...

Kelley began her crusade in 1838, a deca... women's rights convention. She did her speak...

hundreds of Abby Kelleyites out of the kitchen ... Scores joined her on the platform; Lucy Sto... ny and many others were trained b... campaign for women's right...

Though Kelley wa... "a simple Q... ple...

TELEGRAM & GAZETTE MONDAY, DECEMBER 29, 1997 B1

Mechanics Hall gallery walls may go coed

LOCAL

TELEGRAM & GAZETTE ■ WORCESTER, MASS.

generosity shows many big hearts

Susan M. Foley

Ellen Shepard

For two Worcester businesswomen, Ellen M. Shepherd and Susan M. Foley, the opportunity to give to others can't be overlooked.

Foley and her husband, Jay, are the owners of Foley Inc., an industrial engine distributor here.

Susan Foley said she contributes food to the Mustard Seed, accompanied by nieces and nephews. It's important for youngsters, she said, to see neighborhoods that are different from their own and to see children their own age who are in need.

Shepherd and her husband, Robert, give their largest donations to Abby's House because of the agency's ability to provide a place where women can reaffirm themselves.

General manager of the couple's business, Shepherd Engineering Inc., Ellen Shepherd said the feeling she gets from making contributions is similar to a warm, internal smile.

Holiday reaps fresh farm food

By Richard Nangle
TELEGRAM & GAZETTE STAFF

WORCESTER — Yesterday was a long day for the Holidays with Heart volunteers who drove to Western Massachusetts farm towns, like Hadley and Deerfield, to pick up 19.5 tons of fresh produce.

Then, a human chain of more than 100 people moved bag after bag of food from the trucks to a number of locations, including The Mustard Seed, Abby's House, AIDS Project Worcester and finishing up at the AME Zion Church at 21 Belmont St.

Jack Reardon got up at 4:30 in the morning to make the drive. He is with the Strike Force at Teamsters Local 170.

"There are a lot of unfortunate people in this city, and you just want to make a difference during a really nasty time of year. The holidays are particularly tough on people who

Turn to **FOOD**/Page B3

SUNDAY TELEGRAM NOVEMBER 22, 1998 **B3**

One-day army harvests farm-fresh holiday food

FOOD/From **PAGE B1**

don't have anything," Reardon said.

"We're able to make a small difference by getting some fresh produce, things they normally wouldn't be able to get at a food bank or at a pantry," he said.

There were onions, carrots, broccoli, parsnips, apples, butternut squash, cabbages, and more. Program Coordinator Jennifer Callahan of Sutton, who ran unsuccessfully for the 2nd Worcester District state Senate seat this year, said more than 200 people participated yesterday.

GIVING OF THEMSELVES

She said the food is bought with every penny contributed to the organization, and all of the effort is the work of volunteers.

The Rev. Nathaniel K. Perry, of the AME Zion Church, said, "I'm so impressed with the group of people that Jennifer gets, the army to bring the food, basically because they are giving of themselves. They will never see the faces or the hands that receive these goods. It shows that they have a lot of heart."

Callahan said she explained to the volunteers that this has not been the best of farming years. For example, "this year we had no native carrots, the crop was so low," she said.

Vanessa Williamson, a trustee for the Teamsters local, said there is no doubt that the people who will receive this food desperately need it. She went on a dropoff run to a shelter in Spencer, where there were already 500 bags of food ready to be picked up by needy families.

"They had gotten calls for 127 more, and they had no more food until we showed up," Williamson said.

On Dec. 19, Holidays with Heart will be at it again. And when the volunteers finish up again at the AME Zion Church, they will be treated to a Southern barbecue, said volunteer Willie Andrews of Worcester.

Anyone who wants to donate their time or money to Holidays With Heart should write to 112 Uxbridge Road, Sutton, MA 01590.

A Feast of Generations!

Happy Thanksgiving

TELEGRAM & GAZETTE

THURSDAY, NOVEMBER 26, 1998 WORCESTER, MASSACHUSETTS

Flock of donations lands on Turkey Day

By George B. Griffin
TELEGRAM & GAZETTE STAFF

WORCESTER — For Judith A. Langlois, Thanksgiving doubles as a holiday and a time to get in a little extra exercise.

The exercise — hauling frozen turkeys and sacks of fresh vegetables and stacking boxes of canned goods — is an added, though sometimes fatiguing, benefit of the generosity of those who donate food and other items to Jeremiah's Inn during the holiday season.

Langlois, executive director for Jeremiah's Inn, pitches in to carry and store the food people bring to feed the needy, and finds the work both exhausting and rewarding.

"Turkeys," she said, "are heavy."

When the gifts of food arrive at the Webster Square shelter and treatment center for homeless men, whoever is around pitches in to help put them away.

"Our donations this year are going pretty good," Langlois said. "We've been fortunate. The turkey migration is occurring and that's good, but the biggest thing we tend to run out of is the stuff to go with the turkey."

Staff and volunteers at Jeremiah's Inn began distributing Thanksgiving food baskets last week. Langlois said local contributions have been steady and the public has been very generous.

Many other area organizations that help the needy also reported an outpouring of holiday generosity from people wanting to contribute food and other items.

Maurice Boisvert, executive director of YOU Inc. on Plantation Street, said people have been very responsive to the needs of the less fortunate.

Turn to **CHARITIES**/Page A6

FROM PAGE ONE

Charities report good year

CHARITIES/From **PAGE ONE**

"The community has been really great," he said. "It is a time of the year when people really experience a sense of community. And the thing with giving is that oftentimes it's the giver that gets the most out of it. It's enriching to us when we give to others."

Jean G. McMurray, executive director of the Worcester County Food Bank in Shrewsbury, said the donations this year have been exceptional.

"I can tell you we are doing very well," McMurray said earlier this week. "But I didn't really have a sense of that until Saturday, because on Friday we didn't have as many turkeys on hand as we did at this time last year."

> "I can tell you we are doing very well. But I didn't really have a sense of that until Saturday, because on Friday we didn't have as many turkeys on hand as we did at this time last year."
>
> JEAN G. McMURRAY
> EXECUTIVE DIRECTOR, WORCESTER COUNTY FOOD BANK

The shortage was of great concern to her because the food bank is one of the main distribution centers for donations to benefit local social service agencies.

She worried, she said, that the food bank would not be able to keep its commitment to provide more than 9,000 turkeys to area organizations for holiday food baskets and Thanksgiving meals. But on Saturday, donations started pouring in — and by Monday, the food bank had received almost all the donated turkeys and other food items it would need for the distribution.

'WONDERFUL WEEK'

"Once again, the community has come out and shown support, and that's what makes this possible," McMurray said. "I think we're going to have a wonderful week."

Gordon P. Hargrove, executive director of Friendly House, said his agency has been handing out food baskets since Saturday.

The Friendly House goal this year was to provi... to 2,000 famil...

"It looks li... that by 200 ... grove said.

Each day s... as 600 famili...

front of Friendly House for the food baskets.

"It gets so busy at times that we have to have people directing traffic," Hargrove said. "The community support is so great. People come in with one turkey to donate. There was a lady in my office almost in tears who had come in with donations and so forth. It's really upsetting to know that with the economy and things going so well, that unfortunately there are some who are not doing as well."

Julie M. Komenos, volunteer development coordinator for Abby's House, a shelter for women and children, said the community has always been generous.

GOOD TIME

Thanksgiving, she said, is a good season not only for the spirit of giving it brings out in people, but for the opportunity it offers to meet people who have provided support for Abby's House.

"This is the time of year when people respond to the needs of women and children," Komenos said.

Anne Gillespie, case management supervisor at HOAP, the Homeless Outreach and Advocacy Project, ...

dren.

She said that even more basic than a Thanksgiving turkey is the need of the homeless for items to help them get through the cold winter months.

"We always need gloves and knit hats and socks," Gillespie said. "Those are the kinds of things we need so desperately throughout the winter."

Ronald E. Charette, executive director of the South Worcester Neighborhood Center, said community support this year has been "phenomenal."

Donors have ranged from people who drop off a bag or two of vegetables, to corporations.

'THE BEST YEAR'

"Folks really understand there are truly working poor in the community," Charette said. "In the 24 years I've been here, this is the best year I've seen in terms of community support."

Elmer Eubanks, executive director of Centro Las Americas, said Centro has been doing very well this year collecting donations for the needy.

"We've collected $5,000, and we've worked with Goya Foods, who do...

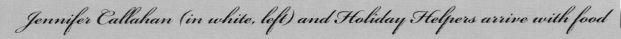

Jennifer Callahan (in white, left) and Holiday Helpers arrive with food

TUESDAY, NOVEMBER 10, 1998 TELEGRAM & GAZETTE ■ WORCESTER, MASS.

Family gives 50-foot spruce to city for the holiday season

By Bronislaus B. Kush
TELEGRAM & GAZETTE STAFF

City's holiday tree.

WORCESTER — About 40 years ago, Alexander Podbilski planted a Colorado blue spruce behind the family three-decker at 16 Perry Ave.

He'd been told that if he talked to the young tree, it would grow to a tremendous height. Taking the advice to heart, Podbilski made it a point to share some type of pleasantry with it.

Nobody is sure what he said to the fledgling tree, but it flourished and quickly became entwined with the life of Podbilski, his wife, Victoria, and his two daughters.

Podbilski died a couple of years ago, just about the time family members began to become concerned about the safety of the tree, which was nearly as high as the roof of the Vernon Hill house.

"The tree is special to the family, but we began to worry about it falling over," said Margaret M. Cardwell, one of Podbilski's daughters. "It was a matter of time before we would have had to cut it down."

This morning, the full-bodied tree, which Podbilski so carefully nurtured, will be felled. But there will be no regrets from his family, because it will be anchored behind City Hall as Worcester's 1998 Christmas tree.

"We're just happy to share it with the city," said Cardwell, who still lives in the family three-decker at Perry Avenue and Suffield Street.

The tree was one of about a dozen in Worcester and surrounding communities that city officials considered, according to Deputy Parks, Recreation and Cemetery Commissioner Robert C. Antonelli.

A Palmer tree service will cut the 50-foot spruce this morning and truck it across busy Kelley Square to Worcester Common, where it will be decorated. A lighting ceremony is scheduled for late afternoon Nov. 27, the day after Thanksgiving.

The Podbilski tree was actually the city's second choice.

A tree on Healy Road was selected but later nixed when arborists discovered they would have to pare it down drastically because of structural problems.

Cardwell had offered the tree to the city last year, but officials opted for a Canadian spruce at the Housatonic Avenue home of former Mayor Thomas J. Early.

Cardwell said the tree at Perry ...enue has meant a lot to her fami...

So much so that her mother donated $300 to a local food bank ... $300 to United Way in lieu of th... moval costs.

"We asked the tree-removal ... vice how much it would have co... cut it down," Cardwell explai... "They figured at least $800, so ... mother wanted to make some ki... donation in thanks."

She said Victoria Podbilski plans to make contributions [illegible] relief efforts.

Sadly, in February of the following year, Victoria died, joining her husband, Alexander, who had not only planted the tree but talked to it, having been told that if he did, the young tree would grow to a tremendous height.

As Alexander's private conversations with the tree apparently performed magic, so had Victoria's and Margaret's gift to Abby's House, coming just in time to provide Christmas dinner with all the trimmings for one of our young families. The 1998 city tree with all its sparkling lights dazzled on-lookers, while at 77 Chatham Street a family gathered to celebrate a feast spread before them, unaware of what had been a modern Gift of the Magi—the Gift of the Podbilski's blue Colorado spruce. One more pattern on the loom of life had been formed reminding us that all living things respond to gentle whispers, to coaxing, encouraging, affirming words. Had one of us been doing just that to the original Abby's House building and its guests that produced two more houses and hundreds more women and children? Abby Kelley Foster, is it possible you're still here?

November 2000
Art Auction

139

Paul R. Cernauskas, left, and Juanita E. Madison stand outside the door to the PIP shelter in yesterday morning's frigid temperatures.

City shelters are filling up

SHELTER/From PAGE B1

who are under influence of alcohol or drugs are admitted if they need a place to sleep. The staff is concerned about the welfare of these street people, but DiCenzo said they are being called on more often to help other people in the neighborhood at a time when people in the community want the shelter to be relocated.

MENTAL HEALTH CLIENTS

DiCenzo said a number of their regular guests are also mental health clients, so seriously impaired they cannot easily fend for themselves.

"There are people who live in this neighborhood who work and have apartments, but once they pay the rent they have nothing left for food." About 25 to 30 neighbors are coming by to eat at the PIP "and we are giving them warm coats," she said.

DiCenzo said the idea that some people want the PIP out of the present location is "frightening" to a number of neighbors, particularly the elderly, who need the help that the PIP gives them, she said.

With onset of the cold wave, with temperatures dipping below zero in recent nights, the shelter at 701 Main St. was filled up by 9 p.m., she said. The PIP turns no one away. They took out all the blankets and mattresses they could find and let people sleep wherever they could find space. DiCenzo said more than 100 people came to the shelter Friday night to escape the cold tempera-

tures.

A nurse supervisor at the University of Massachusetts Hospital said yesterday they have yet to see people coming into the emergency room with cold-related injuries, but believed they will begin seeing people affected as the cold snap continues.

GO TO SHELTERS

The street people know to go to the PIP shelter if they need to get in from the cold, DiCenzo said. "The people who come here also look out for each other. If someone is not in here by a certain time, people will go out and look for them. They know where their spots are," she said.

"The police are also very good about picking up people they find on the street and bringing them here," she added.

"The PIP shelter is the bottom line," said Julie M. Komenos of Abby's House, a shelter for women and their children. She said all the city's shelters are doing their best, but the PIP has a particularly special place among them because it turns no one away. "They really deserve credit for what they are doing," she said.

Abby's House was also full yesterday, but was turning no one away. "We make referrals," Komenos said. Komenos said she just got a telephone call from a woman with two children and her mother. She had gotten an eviction notice saying she's got to be out of the apartment by today. "She was panicking, espe-

cially because it's supposed to be so bad tomorrow," she said.

Komenos said Abby's House is filling up not because of the cold, but because of the welfare reform law that forced many women off welfare without insuring proper job training. "You can't get much at $5 an hour," she said.

SHELTERS FILLING UP

Other city shelters were also filling up, although people are usually admitted through referrals from social service agencies.

Lois Gibbs, staff person at the Friendly House shelter, said the shelter is full with 11 families, but no one is being turned out into the cold. "We put people up in motels if we have to," she said. Friendly House and other local agencies are given public emergency money for that purpose.

Gibbs said the Friendly House shelter can also use donations, not of clothing, but of household items like linens, dishes and small appliances, for families moving out into new apartments.

At the Central Massachusetts Shelter for Homeless Veterans, referrals are made during the week, but one staff member said they were expecting three new people to be admitted this weekend.

The veterans shelter also does not turn people away at the door, preferring to refer them to the PIP or other places known to take people in on short notice.

Cold wave strikes hardest at homeless

By Kathleen A. Shaw
TELEGRAM & GAZETTE STAFF

WORCESTER — Blankets. Winter coats, boots, hats and gloves.

Liz DiCenzo and the staff of the city's Public Inebriate Program need all of it with the start of the current cold wave. "We need anything that will keep people from getting frostbite," she said. "Our supplies are running low," she said.

Other city shelters were also

DiCenzo said the PIP staff is concerned with keeping its regular clients warmly clothed during the cold spell, but the PIP staff increasingly is being asked to help working poor people who live in the neighborhood who cannot afford meals or warm clothing.

The PIP shelter is one of the area's few "wet" shelters, meaning people

Turn to SHELTER/Page B4

Lidia and Maria Bardequez

TRI-TOWNS

Wallpaper Guild takes on community service projects

Volunteer team hits Abby's House

Bob Smith

By Mary Donovan
RECORD STAFF

NORTHBORO — Abby's House has a totally new look inside and Bob Smith is partly responsible. Smith, of S & R Wallcovering Inc., was part of a volunteer team

that did over every room in the Worcester shelter for women and children — and he did this as part of his professional life.

Smith is a member of the Central Massachusetts Chapter of the National Guild of Paperhangers. The guild's plan is to do one charity project a year. Repapering the rooms in Abby's House was the first such project for the two-year-old Central Massachusetts chapter.

Julie Komonos, development coordinator for Abby's said, "They did the whole shelter. It is so uplifting for the women. We couldn't be more happy."

Abby's House at 23 Crown St. in Worcester provides emergency shelter for women and children. The needs that propel women into this kind of situation are varied, said Komonos. They could be economic, the result of mental illness or because of domestic violence. Abby's maintains 10 beds and three cribs. It is a volunteer organization that has been

in operation for 23 years.

Some of the rooms had not been repapered in 15 years, Komonos said. Members of the guild came to Abby's to talk to her about their offer. When they saw the rooms in the much-used house, they knew they could do a job that would make a big difference.

"They saw what we needed, they were thrilled; I was thrilled," she said.

Making that difference is a part of his work that appeals to Bob Smith. He said there is a huge satisfaction, a great sense of accomplishment when he finishes a job and looks back on a room that was shabby and ugly when he began to work on it.

Smith has been working in the business for 24 years and has had his own business in Northboro for much of that. He started when he was first married, he said. He was offered a job working with a paperhanger. The enticement at the time was a better hourly rate than the work he was doing. Once

he got into the work, however, he found he enjoyed it, he said.

He liked the work so much, as a matter of fact, that when he tried other work, he came right back to paperhanging.

"I thought, there's got to be a better way to earn a living than working with my hands, but I wasn't happy. I just like it," he said.

Larry Johnson of A.J. Robbins Co. Inc. of Worcester is president of the Central Mass chapter. He organized the work at Abby's House. The entire job was done with donations and volunteer work, he said.

Students from Worcester Vocational High School prepared the walls and did the painting with paints donated by Worcester Commercial Paint Company. The guild crew spent a day putting up the paper, which was donated by Imperial Home Decor, wallpaper manufacturers.

Johnson said the chapter has 10 members now and is looking for

more. The chapter would welcome women paperhangers to its membership, he said. According to him, 25 to 30 percent of all professional paperhangers are women.

The guild is a national organization that helps the average paperhanger, Smith said. If members find defects in products and lots, the guild will let the manufacturer know. Quality control is not what it used to be, he said.

In addition to providing the power of a large organization to solving an individual member's problems, the guild offers such resources as educational conventions, seminars and workshops, a product-testing program and a retirement plan. Professionals interested in joining the local chapter of the guild may contact Larry Johnson at A.J. Robbins, he said. The number is 799-7297.

In addition, the guild offers its members an opportunity to join each other in using their skills on a volunteer project. Johnson said the local chapter is currently looking for next year's charity project so its paperhangers can brighten up someone else's life.

Floral Street students reach out to veterans

*Jeanne and Patti, Abby's 1999
Women of Distinction*

CHAPTER 25 *Compañeras, Take Heart*

And bright days will rise
From the fertile dark."

By the third of January 1999, the city was in the grips of a severe cold wave. The shelter was full partly because of the cold, and partly because women were beginning to experience the chilling effects of the so-called welfare reform. The supportive housing residents who were lacking adequate training to keep a decent job, were out in the cold, literally. Those lucky enough to have a worthwhile job, meaning one with more than minimum wage and benefits, were struggling to pay their rent and buy food. The economy for anyone in the shelter or housing units was a far cry from what marketing departments were busy spinning. A predicted warm spell at week's end might ease the frostbite, but nothing short of a miracle would warm things up for these women.

It was at week's end, as a matter of fact, that the first miraculous warming occurred. Lidia de la Cruz, who served on our board of directors while working in case management for Community Healthlink, joined our core staff as service coordinator for the women in the supportive housing units. She was our miracle! I knew the warmth of her personality would help combat the cold and that her excellent advocacy skills would steer the women into warmer economic waters. Jan Phillips, the poet, had Lidia in mind, I'm sure, when writing these words:

"Take heart, compañeras!
Though roots be torn
They will grow again in new ground.

Like every other core staffer, Lidia had already discovered that the sentence in her job description, "includes, but is not limited to" is there for a reason. Replacing fear and hopelessness with inner strength and resolve was a tall order for a tiny woman. Lidia jumped right in, true to the origins of Abby's House, and took the lead. The women jumped in after her. That was our second miracle. Nothing changes overnight. The economy is still out of sync with our women's lives, but when someone can give you the will to move ahead, to find a way out, then a miracle has happened. Cold be gone. Lidia is here.

Spring came early, bringing with it some unexpected events and one special occasion that was no surprise: the inclusion of Patti Conzo, past board president, and Jeanne Rosenblatt, full-time volunteer, into the circle of Women of Distinction, sponsored by Montachusett Girl Scouts. Patti and Jeanne joined past recipients, Julie Komenos and Elaine Lamoureux.

Surprises came when Doherty High School sophomore Randi Ford, an Abby's after-school volunteer, was named United Way's Community Hero. Randi asked that the $1,000 check she received from BankBoston be given to Abby's, the charity of her choice. Within the same week, a visit from members of the Massachusetts Chapter of the National Guild of Paperhangers, resulted in a project of painting and papering all the first floor shelter rooms. Larry Johnson, president of the Guild, organized each step. First, the students from Worcester Vocational High School prepared the walls (no easy task when you're removing paper with horsehair plaster underneath). Then they painted the woodwork—lots of it! On the morning of April 10th, the guild members arrived, nine men and one woman. Just one look and they knew they could make a difference. They did just that. By late afternoon the task was done. Volunteer Guild member Bob Smith expressed the group's sentiment: "What a sense of accomplishment." They had even put up matching borders which pulled the colors of the rugs, chairs, couches and curtains together. The house was beautiful and as I roamed into each room, I could imagine it saying, "Come in, sit down and admire me." I did just that, thinking how fortunate Abby's was again

On the greens
for Abby's
1999

June 2000
Kettlebrook

The Kringel Team

The Anger team

this year to have new groups and so many young people involved in our mission. They had made life a little more bearable and a lot more beautiful for all of us.

With the exception of anticipating Abby's House first venture into the world of golf, the summer passed quickly with behind-the-scenes efforts to execute the usual annual events. I must say that the Holden Hills Golf Tournament was a gala affair, unlike any tournament I'd ever seen on television. There were no tense moments, only rounds of laughter as balls sailed into the woods and helpers ducked to avoid getting beaned. There was no Tiger Woods or Dottie Pepper in the crowd, only wannabees, or so it seemed, having fun in the sun. Every golfer, female and male, had only one thing in mind—raising money for Abby's. That was prize enough. Announcements made at lunch on the patio indicated that there would be a second annual tournament. And there was—on June 13, 2000 at Kettle Brook in Paxton. Our fundraising committee, along with Tony Vigliotti and friends, have created another annual win-win event. By the year 2010, we will have tried every golf course in town!

As in everyone's life, patterns begin to form. Certain occasions become sacred and, like a stream bubbling along day after day, a sameness sets into the daily routine. We keep swimming alongside that stream with sure strokes, hardly aware that much of what we do is part of that sameness. They provide a sense of security, of familiarity, of continuity. Such sameness and satisfaction is found in the annual tag sale, in the commemoration of Women's Equality Day and Abby's annual strawberry festival, held on or close to June 7th, our anniversary date. The history of this organization is unique in one major respect. Those who come as guests and those who transition into our supportive housing make the difference. Because of them, every day is different, every night at the shelter is a challenge. In other words, although the organizational structure is in place, what keeps us on our toes and flexible are the women and children of Abby's. In the midst of sameness, they bring shades and hues of color, varying degrees of needs and personal resources, a range of personalities and issues, all of which make this a most exciting and, at the same time, a most demanding place to work.

That does not mean we are not all forced to deal with unexpected, often unwanted, interruptions. In late fall 1999, as our beautiful gardens went underground hiding from the approaching winter, we were sadly interrupted by death. We lost Liz Culhane, a member of Abby's community of women. Those with whom she quietly socialized on a daily basis at the Day Center were inconsolable. They had lost a dear friend—one who had been loved by all, without exception. She had brought peace and calm into their circle. During the month of November, a pall of sadness hung over the Center. I don't remember any other woman's death having had such an impact. For a time, it seemed as though the sorrow, like a dense fog, had settled in forever. But as the days passed and Thanksgiving approached, spirits lightened up as we planned the dinner and began talking about the annual Harley Holiday Party for the children. Just when hearts were free of past pain, death once again unsettled our lives. On December 3rd, we lost a very special friend in the tragic Worcester Cold Storage fire. Timothy Jackson was part of the Harley-Davidson family and had done innumerable "runs for Abby's Kids Camp Scholarship." Our tears flowed on Saturday, December 4th, when Tim's friends arrived with Santa, presents and food for the children. They came because they knew Tim would have wanted them to be at Abby's. The children couldn't be disappointed. Eventually, we learned that the fire had been caused by an overturned candle. A homeless couple was later identified and charged with having left the scene of the fire without reporting the incident. As shelter providers, we were overwhelmed by the loss of the six courageous firefighters and doubly saddened by the circumstances surrounding the fire. Everything about the fire was tragic. Was there anything about that night that could ease our mourning? I found it in the December newsletter:

> "In one fiercely courageous act,
> those firefighters proclaimed
> the inherent value of all persons...
> In sacrificing their lives for
> those they knew only as 'homeless people,'
> these men, in an electrifying instant,
> gave meaning and importance to everyone,
> regardless of his/her station in life."

Women's Equality Day, 1999

Annette introduces Shirley Wright, guest speaker

Liz Culhane

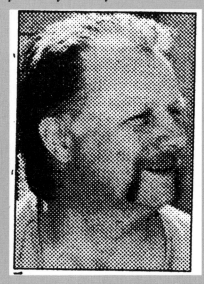

Tim Jackson - a friend to Abby's children and community hero

Harley Holiday Party 1999

Rep. Harriette Chandler brings greetings from Boston

Mary Dean announces the good news

May they all, firefighters and Liz, be in a safe place where there are no more tears, only peace.

Much to the surprise of the gloom and doom prophets, Y2K came without a hitch. The world didn't end, but fortunately for us, the grief and pain endured last month, last year were gone. Blue skies were smiling on us and it was time to plan a party. I thought the celebration of my seventieth birthday would be the perfect occasion to have fun, to laugh again, to bring friends together. Besides, what else can you do in February? Arrangements fell into place quickly, and on February 6th we lived it up at the Tatnuck Bookseller. Larry and Gloria Abramoff, as hosts of the occasion, outdid themselves extending hospitality and good food to over 300 guests. Music by the Highlights, Janet and Louis Borelli, filled the air. Jane Dutton's talk "Friends of Annette" and Representative Harriette Chandler's presentation of a proclamation from the Massachusetts House were well received by everyone. The true birthday surprise came when our board president, Mary Dean, announced the renaming of the Abby's Woman's Survival Fund to the Annette Rafferty Survive to Thrive Fund. And I thought I knew exactly what would happen at MY birthday party! Never too late for surprises, never too old to be shown you don't know everything. Seed money for the fund was initially a generous donation from the Evangelical Congregational Church of Westboro. Karen Nunley was the one responsible for urging the Mission Committee to seriously consider Abby's as the recipient. Additional monies came from bequests made by Betty Dadmun Kettell and Jean Dewey. Party guests added over $7,000. As it states in the fund:

> "Many women at Abby's do not have enough money for a security deposit to obtain decent housing. Others cannot afford simple necessities such as a phone that would keep them connected and safe. Still others do not have access to educational or cultural or spiritual opportunities. This fund is meant to be an effective part of a woman's support network, not a stop-gap measure. It is meant to help a woman on her journey from mere subsistence to a thriving existence."

Because of this fund, women and their children have a better chance in life. Betty, Jean and so many friends are really the ones responsible for the thriving that will come in the days ahead.

June 7, 2000, marked the beginning of our 24th year. It was a year like every other featuring the sameness and the surprises that make up our daily Abby's House life. On one hand, a steady stream of women and children came through the shelter still unable to say that they are better off now than they were four, ten, fifteen or twenty years ago! The plus side of that situation is the support these women receive at Abby's. There are very few who leave us without the tools to "grow again in new ground." Some were fortunate enough to transition to 19 Crown Street and several new families moved into 77 Chatham Street. The down side is, of course, not enough safe, decent, affordable housing and too few decent jobs available for these women. Twenty-four years of sheltering and going beyond shelter has failed to solve this problem, now a national disaster. We've certainly made a big difference in individual lives and have left a legacy of how to solve the problem. We continue to educate our newsletter recipients of the seriousness of homelessness, pointing out effective ways of addressing the crisis by writing or phoning state and federal legislators. It's at this level that policies can be changed; it's in each person's power to decide to live more simply so that others can simply live. I remember well our staff meeting discussions about our role in the ongoing dilemma and thinking, "Can we continue to jump in headfirst? Where do we jump?" If Abby's risks another building, and we all know more housing is needed, will any woman have the money for rent? That's how dismal the economic picture remains. Our meetings inevitably resulted in a rousing call of reassurance. Take heart, compañeras! Was there ever a time we didn't see the glass half full? Was there ever a time we weren't faithful to forging ahead? A phone call in late November refocused my energy. A student hurrying to complete an assignment (due that afternoon) asked me if I ever envisioned a time when Abby's House would cease to exist. I answered:

> "Yes, we always envision an end to the need for Abby's House. But, looking at the signs of the times, it seems

that vision is far off. I think we're closer than ever to being a nation of rich and poor. There's no middle class left. We'll stay the course as long as it takes. Abby's will continue to be a solution for as many as possible."

A final question about whether we had social analysis sessions about the problem and discussions about social justice and the part religion played in our work elicited the following response:

"Our social analysis is done on the front line. We're the ones looking the homeless and the battered right in the eye, hearing their horror stories, responding as best we can, while trying to make sense of it all. Their religion? That's not our concern. Most everyone who comes to Abby's is clinging to hope for a better day. The volunteers and the staff are the people trying to help them take heart. That's our job and it's not easy. In some respects we're like a hospital trauma team. Our religion? I've just described it."

I ended the conversation with an invitation to do a training session, to read a brief summary of Abby Kelley Foster's life and to think about doing some personal social analysis on the politics of anti-slavery and institutional homelessness. Abby would have loved that challenge! She had to be proud of us all, when, at our first staff meeting of 2001, we framed our next project and agreed to unveil those future plans at the Volunteer Appreciation Dinner, Monday, January 8. This is what we said at that dinner:

"Abby's House is serously considering a request made by the Sisters of Mercy of Worcester. The following statement, taken from a letter written to us by their President, Suzanne Elliott, describes the request, which may become the unexpected, very exciting project for our 25th year.

'After discussion and prayerful consideration, it was the recommendation of the Assembly to the Leadership Team that we proceed to turn over the mission of St. Joseph's Home at 52 High Street to another housing provider. We desire to enter into formal discussion with you in order to fulfill our Assembly mandate.'

And so, we are anxiously standing by, hoping that this request has a positive ending."

Will we jump in again, headfirst? Of course. And I can hardly wait!

Abby's kids on Camperships

John Bowler

Barbara Dusoe

Maybelle Ward

Ron Dusoe

Epilogue

wouldn't have it any other way. We've become more than shelter providers. We're landladies, supportive service women, public relations workers, fundraisers, correspondents, writers, organizers, competent volunteers in so many areas of service. But above all, we remain dreamers, creators and believers in the power of women to overcome the odds of living on the edge, even over the edge! Like Abby Kelley Foster, our inspiration, we continue to raise our voices and to give witness by our commitment to the mission. Sometime, next year, the year after or ten years from now, those bright days *will* rise from the fertile dark. Meanwhile, the lights are still on at Abby's House.

*I*t's morning and shelter guests are busy getting the kids ready for school. Breakfast is over and Hilda has put the sheets in the washer as Mercedes and Edith, the only women without children, help out with the vacuuming. A taxi is blasting the loudest horn in Worcester outside the front door. Finally, Naomi and the children dash out en route to school. It takes a while to arrange for city transportation, so in the meantime, Red Cab is on the job.

Downstairs, the office staff is answering the back door. It's Maybelle from 19 Crown Street who just wants to say hello before she begins her busy day at PIP and the Lighthouse Mission. Phones are ringing and before 9 a.m. more requests for shelter are being transferred to Elaine's office. By 11 a.m., two application requests for 77 Chatham Street residents are in Lidia's hands. Barbara is preparing a mailing. Over at 19 Crown Street, Frank is occupied with painting Room #5 readying it for occupancy. Ron has finished repairing a broken fixture and John is carefully moving furniture. The Day Center has opened at 77 Chatham, and the women are awaiting Sandi who will cut and curl and do nails. A poster leaning against the piano announces a budget planning session that evening for residents of the building. Another poster reminds anyone curious enough that Karen will be doing artwork on Wednesday. Come prepared to paint!

It's the same and yet so different. We're bigger and things are more complex. In retrospect, life in 1976 was much simpler. But when I consider what we have become in these 25 years, I

Pat Austin

Barbara and
Gary Englander

Helen and Bill
McLaughlin

The Gagnons

Ginny Allen

Liz Iandoli-Raab
and her family

Jim and Margaret
Diggins

Barbara Lucci

Voices of Volunteers and Supporters

"It's hard to say how or why. I think at some point in one's life you have to start giving back a portion of what's been given to you. I guess I'm a little late in starting, but anyway, I'm here! Another point that appealed to me was the fact that Abby's is funded by private donations….and doesn't get bogged down by unnecessary red tape."

Pat Austin

"I've known Elaine (Lamoureux) for many years, and when I was involved with Worcester Connection, I learned about Abby's House. For some time I kept telling Elaine I ought to come to staff. Finally, in 1986, I began….and I'm still here."

Anne Laliberte

"I became involved in Abby's House shortly after it opened in 1976. Margaret Baillie asked me to attend a meeting with her at Abby's House. It was then that I realized the need for a shelter for women and knew that I wanted to become involved. I cleaned along with 4 or 5 other women for 8 years, and I also staffed overnight (and still do) starting the first or second month of Abby's existence. Sometimes I wonder if I am too old to staff and then a guest asks me, 'Are you coming back tomorrow night?' or 'When will you be back?' and that is when I know that age doesn't make a difference. Here I have met wonderful women….volunteers who steadfastly give of their time and guests who literally have nothing. So, Abby's has made me a better person."

Eva Engel

"I became involved, probably about 1977, through the persistence of Eva Engel. I first heard of Abby's through a notice in my church bulletin. My deepest and most constant impression of Abby's House is that of the full-time, round-the-clock, round-the-year always generous and cheerful dedication of the wonderful women who are the staff."

Carol Burns

"When my children were grown, I felt the need to go on nurturing somewhere in my life. I read about Abby's and called to see if there was something I could do. I wanted to work with people, hands on. I have never regretted the move to do overnight staffing. I've never spent a night without feeling glad I came….I've learned so much from the women. They have such strength."

Marie Maclaren

"An ad in the paper told of the different needs of the house. It had been several years since I had been involved in volunteer work, but felt I lacked the necessary skills to offer Abby's house. But, I mustered the courage and took the plunge. I called and started in Abby's Day Program in 1987. Surprisingly, I loved the women and eventually started staffing at night as well. Here at Abby's House, women are treated with the dignity they deserve."

Ellen Shepherd

"I really can't remember the year….I was at UMass one day for an appointment, and one of the nurses was wearing a House Pin. I asked about it and learned a bit about Abby's Mission. Then I attended a training session, which led me to volunteer every other week in the Thrift Store. Abby's is a bright spot in the city and in my heart. The staff and volunteers are quite remarkable….there's a oneness of purpose here….I always leave there walking a little taller, with a glad feeling in my heart that I am part of such a network of women who give so much to those women whose lives have been a daily struggle."

Helen McLaughlin

"I first came to know Abby's in the early '80s through the Worcester Connection….it has been inspiring me ever since. What wise women can accomplish! Although I have been only tangentially involved at Abby's, I believe it is unique among organizations in the personal, respectful, open, loving attitude which permeates every aspect of Abby's programs … it restores a sense of self-esteem and personal courage."

Ginny Allen

"I became involved with Abby's House through acquaintance with Annette Rafferty. I learned about her effort to shelter women and victims of domestic abuse sometime before the opening of Abby's House. In the early days (after the shelter opened) Abby's was without a washer and dryer. So, I washed and ironed (!) sheets and pillowcases each week until I left for a sabbatical. By the time I returned, there was an on-site laundry. Prior to the opening of the shelter, the Worcester City Council was asked to vote to accept a small gift or bequest, for which no purpose had been specified. My fellow councillor Barbara Sinnott had the smarts to suggest quickly that funds ($1,000.00) be designated to support Annette's project….I wish I had thought of that! (But Barbara voted it in, along with all the councillors!) To me, Abby's is an exciting and important example of what one determined woman can start and other women can build. The ambition and imagination of those responsible for this growing enterprise are stunning."

Barbara Kohin

"After retiring in 1988 after working in the corporate world for 48 years, I looked for an organization with which to get involved as a volunteer. I read that Abby's was looking for volunteers. So I called and made an appointment with Tess (Sneesby, Ex. Director), and I was on my way! I have worked in most every one of the programs since arriving at Abby's. It's impossible to zero in on any one experience that stands out except to say that working at the annual Tag Sale is "GREAT.""

Gloria Todd

"I became involved while a student attending Assumption College and while working part time at Mercy Centre for Developmental Disabilities. At the time, I was working with Sr. Eileen Marshall (since deceased and a former shelter staffer herself). She has a special place in my heart for what she taught me! One afternoon in the auditorium the two of us were talking about my classes. Knowing that I was interested in social work, Sr. Eileen said: 'I know what you would be good at.' When I asked what, she replied with a big smile…'Abby's House.' Sr. Eileen never got into details, saying only that it was a home for women and children in need of services. Because she was my boss and I respected her work, I asked how I could get involved. The following week, I started my overnight volunteering. It was such a good beginning for me; it opened my eyes to lives I had only heard about or read about in the paper. It gave me an opportunity to give what I know I had inside….love, compassion, understanding and guidance. I was especially good with the dear little children who would come in with their mothers, just as afraid as their Moms were. I remember Alice, Sharon, Julie, and, of course, Barbara. One night I had to ask her to leave because she had come in drunk and proceeded to be extremely abusive verbally to me and to the other guests. I was nervous, but led her to the door, listening all the while to swears and curses. The next morning I reported to Elaine (Lamoureux) what had happened. Elaine knew exactly who she was and said with a smile that Barbara was known for her "feisty" behavior, but supported me in my decision. Asking someone to leave Abby's is quite rare, but Barbara had earned the dismissal! A few years later, I remember reading about her in the local papers. Barbara had spent the night at P.I.P. and was found the next day beaten to death in a nearby dumpster."

Liz Iandoli-Raab

"I got involved early on because I had an interest in the needs of women and children that were not being met by the system. I did a lot of staffing, patching and painting in those first years and became involved in the women's center, Worcester Connection, and the first Tag Sale. In fact, my claim to fame is starting the Tag Sale in the cellar of the #21 side of the house! I continue to come every year to the greatest Tag Sale of them all."

Irene Mizula

"I got involved through our friend, Annette Rafferty, who worked hard to establish Abby's House. Our support and involvement had been financial and spiritual. We know that we are helping women everywhere, but especially those who are at Abby's House....for them there WILL be a future."

Jim and Margaret Diggins

"About 1998, a co-worker of mine at the time suggested I look into doing volunteer work at Abby's House. So, once a month I did an overnight in the shelter and followed that experience with a year spent in the Day Program. My volunteer work at Abby's was very meaningful in my life. I learned so much from the women that stayed there, and this education was helpful to me in the work I do today and in my own personal life."

Barbara Lucci

"I have been a shelter volunteer for about 3 years. Many years ago I spent some time at Abby's House myself due to an abusive situation. I never forgot the peace and safety I felt and the concern and help I received from the staff. My main focus has been as an overnight staffer...my main goal to listen, empathize and help a woman validate what she is trying to do. I always feel that I receive much more that I give, and I am extremely impressed with the courage and strength of our guests. These past two years I have served as a Board Member of the organization, and I was thrilled to have given back to Abby's House my own strengths and abilities."

Sally Roy

"I got involved with Abby's House through an invitation to a fund-raiser (during the Capital Campaign for 77 Chatham Street). It was then I knew I wanted to give time, so I have staffed at the shelter for the past three years. Abby's is my only outlet for the 'pure possibilities that women are.' Every time I go there, I get to contribute to the guests, but equally important, they allow me to see how blessed I am. Being here is a privilege and very full of emotion and opportunity."

Betsy Abeles Kravitz

"After retiring, I looked for volunteer work, and being a neighbor of Abby's, I just walked down the street. It was June 1990. Starting part-time in the Thrift Shop, I then asked to be more involved and began staffing the shelter. I can't remember how that evolved into helping in the Food Pantry, the Day Program, the mailings, covering the phone, going on the Board of Directors, and in general working where needed. I am honored to be included in staff planning. There are many, many examples of courage and strength among the guests. However, particular staff members stand out—the guest advocate is a genius. She has endless compassion and wisdom. And, as for myself, after years as a rather inactive feminist, this 'job' has defined what real feminism is. The staff is untiring in efforts to help women and families. Their mission is so clear, and their advocacy is fearless. It is a great pleasure to be a part of Abby's mission."

Jeanne Rosenblatt

"About 18 years ago while answering service calls (Com Gas Co.), I stopped at the traffic light at Piedmont and Pleasant Streets. A woman with two small children knocked at my truck window. All of them were weeping. I opened the door and told them to get in. The kids had red welts on their bodies. The temperature was well below freezing. The father had kicked them out of the house. I took the family to the Waldo Street Police Station, went inside with them, explained the situation to the desk sergeant and asked that he get them shelter. That incident made me think that a place like Abby's House is what this family needed. My wife, daughter and I have given support to Abby's ever since."

Chester and Ada Gagnon

"In all the areas of volunteering I've done at Abby's House from the shelter to the tag sale, I have always felt I've helped other women. I'm always reminded of my blessings, as well."

Barbara Englander

Steering Committee and Board of Directors 1976 - 2001

Pat Albrecht
Jean Anger
Mirjam Auger
Margaret Baillie
Annette Bleau
Carol Burns
Ann Carlson
Lucky Clarke
Patti Conzo
Jacqueline Cote
Patricia Daly
Tracy Dankwah
Mary Dean
Lucelia DeJesus
Lidia Dela Cruz
Leona Donahue
Eileen Dooley
Angela Dorenkamp
Karen Dorhamer-Fadden
Beverly Dumas
Theresa Eckstrom
Eva Engel
Maddy Entel
Fran Fajana
Patti Falcone
Evelyn Fowler
Rachel Girard
Marie Gleason
Jane Grady
Veronica Griffin
Mary Haberstroh
Leah Hazard
Holly Heggie
Martha Hosey
Suzanne Howatt

Pauline Kalagher
Anna Marie Kane
Nancy Kane
Julie Komenos
Maureen Kroyak
Mary Labunski
Claudia Lacerte
Elaine Lamoureux
Carolyn Leary
Vida Maczyk
Peggy Marengo
Theresa McBride
Helen McCarron
Mary Ann McGrain
Ginny Mischitelli
Carmen Negron
Nancy Nobert
Karen Nunley
Frances O'Connell
Joyce Perron
Beverly Plucinski
Vickie Powers
Michelle Prunier
Annette Rafferty
Jeanne Rosenblatt
Sally Roy
Pam Ruah
Mary Salkaus
Edna Sexton
Eileen Sheedy Curry
Sharon Smith Viles
Gloria Todd
Mary Pat True
Fran Wall
Charlene Zimkiewicz

Volunteer Names 1976-2000

Abbie Gagnon
Abby Becker
Abby Driscoll
Abby Klotz
Abby Markle
Abby Ruettgers
Abby Schalz
Adrienne Featherstone
Adrienne Lamoureux, P.F.M.
Agnes Broderick, S.P.
(deceased)
Aimee O'Rourke
Aina Lanigan, P.B.V.M.
(deceased)
Alexandra Kartheiser
Alice Audie-Figueroa
Alice Bourdeau
Alice Guertin
Alice Laferriere, S.A.S.V.
(deceased)
Alice Petty, R.S.M.
(deceased)
Alice Ploysungwan
Alice Stearns
Alicia Porter
Aline Paradise
Alison Bagg
Alison O'Neil

Allisa Doyle
Allison Crane
Allyson Spadora
Alyssa Dorsey
Amanda Guarino
Amanda Matlak
Amanda Newton
Amanda Oyler
Amanda Tobey
Amy Baker
Amy Brogna
Amy Desrosiers
Amy Grove
Amy Koch
Amy Morehouse
Amy Phillips
Amy Richardson
Amy Starvaski
Anabella Vasconcelos
Andrea Fincke
Andrea Lance
Angela Dorenkamp
Angela Reyes
Angela Stolfi
Angie Hotchkins
Anita Wallent
Ann Bowman
Ann Carlson

Ann Curtis
Ann Dean
Ann Gibbons-Smith
Ann Hajkuk
Ann Harrington
Ann Hedge
Ann Holden
Ann Hynes
Anne Marie Wildenhain, S.S.J.
Ann McLaughlin
Ann Murphy
Ann O'Connor
Ann Pax
Ann Saunders
Ann Sheehan
Ann Stamm
Ann Sweet
Anna Marie Kane, S.S.J.
Anne Doucette
Anne Baressi
Anne Carroll, S.S.J.
Anne Driscoll
Anne Humes
Anne Hunt
Anne Laliberte
Anne Lipp
Anne Lund
Anne Matuskowitz
Anne McSweeney
Anne Oehling
Anne Rogers Jones
Anne Schneider
Anne Vozzella
Anne Wickwire
Annmarie Carr
Annmarie Drumgoole
Annemarie Flynn
Ann-Marie Blaber
Anne Marie Chrosniak
Anne Marie Grattan
Anne Marie Kaune
Anne Marie Wielund
Annette Bleau

Annette Quatrano
Annette Rafferty
Annie O'Connor
Annie Wolfe
Aracely Carabellos
Arlette Grubbs
Ashley Dineen
Ashley Hall
Audrey Kracke
Audrey Robinson
Ave Leonard
Avis Fleischer
B.J. Cavicchi
Barbara Dusoe
Barbara Englander
Barbara Fuchs
Barbara Guillette (deceased)
Barbara Kohin
Barbara Lucci
Barbara O'Neil
Barbara Parys
Barbara St. Laurent
Barbara Trifilio
Barbie Dolan
Becca Ford
Becky Fauth
Ben Chates
Berna Iris
Bernadette Antaki
Bernadette Furtado
Bernadette Thompson
Bernice Gellagher (deceased)
Berry Martona
Berta Boegel
Beth Berstene
Beth Blodgett
Beth George
Beth Murphy
Beth Petro-Roy
Beth Schaefer
Beth Sullivan
Betsy Davidson
Betsy Kravitz

Betsy Nolan
Betty Ann Janek
Betty Cahill
Betty Cole
Betty DeWolfe
Betty Dowd
Betty Guimond S.S.A.
Betty Hoskins
Betty Jenewin
Betty Jones
Betty Judd
Betty Martone
Betty Tamburro
Bev Davis
Bev Dumas
Bev Plucinski
Beverly Iott
Beverly Johnson
Bill Fletcher
Bill McLaughlin
Bob Brown
Bonnie Duckworth
Bonnie Kraus
Bonnie Krupi
Bonnie Millett
Brenda Kartheiser
Brenda Nagle
Brenda Spinney
Brenda Starkus
Brenna Cusen
Bridget Daly
Brigitta Karlson
Brigid Franklin
Brooke Dusoe
Bruce Hurter
Bruce Plummer
Burke Dunphy
Cait Maynard
Caitlin Farrell
Camille Brillon
Cara Winters
Carla Cicerchia
Carla Inangelo

Carmel Sandock
Carmella Hutchings
Carmen Negron
Carol Alderson
Carol Blair
Carol Burns
Carol Carpenter-Levine
(deceased)
Carol Cross Johnson
Carol DiSalvatore
Carol Donovan
Carol Gilbert
Carol Harrington
Carol Lareau, S.S.J.
Carol Mercurio
Carol Precobb
Carol Proietti, S.S.A.
Carol Ramig
Carol Rizzo
Carol Smith
Carol Socia
Carol Walsh
Carol Webster
Caroline Mockler
Carolyn Fratto
Carolyn Hall
Carolyn Howe
Carolyn Morrisette
Carolyn Freeman
Carolyn Kendall
Carolyn Kogut
Carolyn Leary
Carolyn Sheldon
Carrie Martin
Carrie Pucko
Casie McNamee
Cassandra Clark
Cate Melkonian
Cathy Zajac, S.S.J.
Cathy Deliandes
Cathy Meagher
Cece Wood
Cecilia Curd

Cecilia Denning
Cecilia Novelle
Celeste Lussier
Celia Medina
Celine Toomey
Charlene Zimkiewicz
Charlotte Boutellette
Charlotte Fitzgerald
Charlotte Hanks
Charlotte Higgins
Cheri Grant
Cheryl Almeida
Chloe Leary
Chris Ciabetti
Chris Degon
Chris Ford
Chris Healy
Chris Kowalchek
Chris Larry
Chris Leach
Chrissy Kinsman
Chrissy McCabe
Christina Barillaro
Christina Jackson
Christina Ranelli
Christine Barber
Christine Boutiller
Christine Buell
Christine Dailey
Christine Erickson
Christine Forgione
Christine Jackson
Christine Kowalchek
Christine Levesque, S.S.A.
Christine Lombard
Christine Lovecchio
Christine Marie, S.S.A.
Christine Nealy
Christine Pipchick
Christine Quigley
Christine St. Germain
Christine Stone
Christine Trinceri

Cindy Crus
Cindy Dube
Cindy Nero
Cindy Zmijewski
Chuck Harter
Claire Dugan, S.S.J.
Claudia Hamlet-Lacerte
Claudia Kulhanek
Claudia Russo
Claudia Simonian
Clint Beuscher
Cofe Uber
Coletta Aberdale
Colette Daigle
Colleen Blake
Colleen Carrigan
Colleen Crowley
Colleen Keyes
Colleen Smith
Connie Hill
Connie Kelly
Connie Maynard
Courtney Langell
Crystal Upshaw
Cynthia Delotto
Dana Palermo
Danielle Anas
Danielle Risotti
Dara Ely
Darlene Bustin
Darlene Kamel
Dawn Reddy
Deanna Polli
Deb Greene
Deb Hutchinson
Deb Johnson
Deb Whittredge
Debbie Arey
Debbie Brunnet
Debbie Burlingame
Debbie Coughlin
Debbie Gobron
Debbie Gendron

Debbie Hovey-Mangine
Debbie Kirk
Debbie Valenza
Debbie Wernholm
Debbie Whitman
Debi Erickson
Deborah Chaulk
Debra Cotter
Deidre Gillin
Dell Marrone
Denise Benoit
Denise Graney
Denise Lavallee
Denise Rao
Denise Simon
Denise Thomas
Diana Dioppa
Diane Brown
Diane Desorcy
Diane Downie
Diane Feeney
Diane Pokorny
Diane Tasse
Dierdre Gillin
Dolores Buckley
Don Lamoureux
Donna Bisceglia
Donna Doyle
Donna Finlay-Cavaretta
Donna Kesseli
Donna Rollins
Donna Valentini
Donna Wentzell
Dorilda Flynn
Doris Weishaus
Dorothy Cellucci
Dorothy Joseph
Dorothy O'Brien
Dorothy Scesny P.B.V.M.
Dorothy Tise
Dorrie Hutchins
Dot LaFratta
Douglas Hotchkin

Edie Galindo
Edie Joyce
Edna Ouelette
Edna Sexton
Eileen Crowley
Eileen Daley
Eileen Dooley
Eileen Dunn
Eileen Durkin
Eileen Joseph S.S.J.
Eileen Keavy
Eileen Kenneally
Eileen Marshall,
  R.S.M.(deceased)
Eileen Meehan
Eileen O'Neil, S.S.J.
Eileen Phelan
Eileen Ryan, S.S.J.
Eileen Sheedy
Elaine Caron, S.S.A.
Elaine Lamoureux
Elaine Peck
Elaine Potvin, S.S.A.
Elaine Razzana (deceased)
Elaine Robinson
Eleanor Gaucher
Elice Chiapulis
Elimore Sanchez
Elisa Zawadzkas
Elise Kreiger
Elizabeth Do
Elizabeth Dowd
Elizabeth Drake
Elizabeth Kay
Elizabeth O'Donnell
Elizabeth Shiland
Elizabeth Wolff
Ellen Grimm
Ellen Guerin, R.S.M.
Ellen Gugel
Ellen Laverdure
Ellen Liberty
Ellen MacDonough

Ellen Neville
Ellen Sexton
Ellen Shepherd
Eloise O'Neil
Elsa Ekblaw
Emily Athy
Emily Collins
Emily Dempsey
Emily Hogenboom
Emily Moore
Emmanuela Bucci
Erica Hill
Erika Gutierrez
Erika Paige
Erika Sullivan
Erin Hickey
Erin Lane
Erin McAleer
Erin McLaughlin
Erin Turbitt
Estelle Jussaume
Ethel Donaldson
Eva Engel
Evelyn Brault
Evelyn Fowler
Eveyln McKenna, S.N.D.
Everett Lacerte
Faith Buscone
Faith McGillicueey
Faith Golden
Fern Gagnon
Florence Dion
Fran Duckworth
Fran Keller
Fran Wall
France Guillette
Frances Claire
Frances Kelley
Frances O'Connell
Francesca Fajana
Frank Cassidy
Frank Kartheiser
Gail Bourdon, S.S.J.

Gail Harmon
Gail Holland
Gail McQuown
Gail Stubbs
Gail Zimmermann
Gemma Kallagher
Genevieve Georges
Georgette Arsenault
Georgette Martinez
Georgia Brown
Georgia Poulopoulos
Geri DiNardo
Gerry Ashworth
Gertrude Emonds, P.F.M.
Gina Martins
Ginger Brooker
Ginny Lindsay
Ginny Mischitelli
Giovanna Spets
Gisele Duplessis
Gloria Todd
Gloria Whorton
Grace Blaber
Grace Casello
Gretchen Ekeidt
Halimat Warziri
Hannah Longo
Harriet Willins
Hawley Eckstrom
Heather Binder
Heather Cline
Heather Downey
Heather Drury
Heather Lynch
Heather McArdle
Heather Raferty
Heather Thompson
Heather Tomkinson
Hedy Santo
Heidi Golicz
Heidi O'Donnell
Heidi Swanik
Helen Dussault

Helen Gagnon
Helen Gannon
Helen P. McLaughlin
Helen May
Helen McCarron
Helen Smith (deceased)
Helene Dussault
Helga Hofman
Henry Sweet
Hilary Clark
Hilda Chasse, P.F.M.
Holly Brown-Saldana
(deceased)
Holly Heggie
Holly Sullivan
Ida Primus
Ingrid Esser
Irena Wallace
Irene Allaire
Irene Dupont, S.S.A.
Irene Mizula, S.S.J.
Irene Moran, M.V.P.
Irene Pineiro
Irene Rawding
Irma Gendreau, P.F.M.
Isa Bayon
Isabelle Bowler
Ivanette Osborn
Jackie Laflash
Jackie Pratt
Jackie Roe
Jacqueline Cote, S.S.A.
Jacqueline Swan
Jamie Thomas
Jamie Welch
Jan Bergeron
Jan Dell'Olio
Jan Marie Drury-Dugan
Jan Silveri
Jane ClarkJane D'Agata
Jane Goland
Jane Grady
Jane Knight

Jane Oliver, P.F.M.
Janelle Berg
Janet Borelli
Janet Cronin (deceased)
Janet DeJesus
Janet Flaherty
Janet Judge
Janet Provost, S.S.J.
Janet Rier
Janet Romanoff
Janice Connelly
Janice Garrety
Janice Nadeau
Janice Starziski
Janice Yee
Janine Christiansen
Janine Walsh
Janine Woods
Jayne Rohrbacker
Jean Andes
Jean Anger
Jean Dahler
Jean Donado
Jean Dumais
Jean Johnson
Jean Lafond, S.A.S.V.
Jean Landry
Jean McPherson
Jean Risotti
Jeanne Adler
Jeanne DelSignore
Jeanne Martineau
Jeanne Mattson
Jeanne Nordquist
Jeanne O'Shea, S.S.J.
Jeanne Rosenblatt
Jeanne Stepan
Jeannette Corneau
Jeannine Broadnax
Jeannie Seidler
Jeff Dean
Jen Ganem
Jen Lamson

Jen O'Neil
Jen O'Toole
Jen Papa
Jen Prescott
Jen Schmolz
Jenna Amato
Jenna Fletcher
Jennifer Del Gizzi
Jennifer Harter
Jennifer Travis
Jenny Garber
Jess Zimmerman
Jessica Eagle
Jessica Goodall
Jessica Logan
Jessica Massey
Jessica Slowick
Jessica Vellaccio
Jessie McMahon
Jill Anger
Jill Douglas
Jill Naigle
Jill Stockman
Jillian D'Urso
Jim Ludy
Jim Lukes
Jo Dascanio
Jo Dorman
JoAnn Amico
Jo Ann Fitzgerald
Jo-Anne Bachorowski
Joan Brennan
Joan Bull
Joan Cassidy
Joan Dumais, S.S.J.
Joan Gold
Joan Herlihy
Joan Liggons
Joan McGinn
Joan Polwrek
Joan Roche
Joan Rogers
Joann Infante

Joanna Chowaniec
Joanna Rosenblatt
Joanna Smith
Joanne Cantwell (deceased)
Joanne Demers (deceased)
Joanne Furmonavicius
Joanne Harvey
Joanne Kalat
Joanne Lambert
Joanne Martin
Joanne Owens
Joanne Russo
Joe Abramoff
Johanna Rosenblatt
John Anas
John Bowler
Joy Carroll
Joyce Gorgeglione
Joyce Harter
Joyce Packard
Joyce Perron
Joyce Tolson
Juanita Beuscher
Juanita Miranda
Juanita Robichaud, P.F.M.
Judy Colognesi
Judi Bulman
Judi Milott
Judie Cofsky
Judie Love
Judith Connelly, P.V.B.M.
Judith Kane
Judy Darzal
Judy Dukas
Judy Evangelidis
Judy Gauthier
Judy Lazarz-Weathers
Judy Webster
Julia Crowley
Julia Fletcher
Julia Sheehan R.S.M.
(deceased)
Julia Vigliotti

Julianne Early
Julie Anderson
Julie Casey
Julie Dorval
Julie Fidler
Julie Gomeau
Julie Komenos
Julie LaFerriere
Julie MacDonald
Julie Ranieu
Julie Zimmerman
June Fletcher
June Sanchez
Justina Daley S.N.D.
Justine Andrews
Justine Wellstood
Kara Harris
Kara Kitteredge
Karen Arsenault
Karen Belsito
Karen Blongastamer
Karen Brown
Karen Burns
Karen Dorhamer-Fadden
Karen Grass
Karen Hilliard
Karen Kappes
Karen Keefe
Karen Kleinkopf
Karen McFadden
Karen Mileski
Karen Mills
Karen Nell Smith
Karen Nunley
Karen O'Sullivan
Karen Scharfenberg
Karen Schussler
Karen Schroeder
Karen Staropoli
Karen Stevens
Karen Talarico
Karen Taylor
Karen Walsh

Kari Wren (deceased)
Karin Hobman
Karina Alder
Karla Ruzicka
Karyn Brown
Kate Crowley
Kate Donnelly
Kate Melkonian
Kate Montweiler
Kate Warren
Kate Winters Corcoran
Katherine Lucas
Katherine Lyrintzis
Katherine Schmidt
Kathianne Hilton
Kathleen Carr
Kathleen Desy
Kathleen Joyce
Kathleen Keating, S.S.J.
Kathleen Luthman
Kathleen Manseau
Kathleen O'Keefe
Kathleen O'Leary
Kathleen O'Sullivan
Kathleen Scavone
Kathleen Sullivan
Kathy Bates
Kathy Cain
Kathy Carr
Kathy Coleman
Kathy Correia
Kathy Fox
Kathy Gallagher, S.S.J.
Kathy Hughes
Kathy Kardokas
Kathy LaCasse
Kathy McSweeney
Kathy Meade
Kathy Meagher
Kathy Murdock
Kathy O'Connor
Kathy O'Keefe
Kathy O'Rourke

Kathy Trainor
Kathy Waterhouse
Kathy Wedemeyer
Katie Blaisdell
Katie Cahill
Katie Caruana
Katie Harrison
Katie Johnson
Kay Kroyak
Kay Shepard
Keira Harris
Kelly Belli
Kelly Callahan
Kelley Chipman
Kelly Kinsella
Kelly Meno
Kelly Pereira
Kelly Sweeney
Kelly Turner-Cooke
Kendra Kartheiser
Kerri Bullock
Kerri Blumenaur
Kerry O'Brien
Kerry Palmer
Kerry Sullivan
Keti Sekuj
Kiki McMahan
Kim Fletcher
Kim Perkins
Kimberly Hicks
Kimberly Kepler-Gennert
Kimberly O'Malley
Kimberly Tharp
Klio Sekuj
Konnie Lukes
Kris Hersey
Kris Komenos
Kristen Homan
Kristen McCue
Kristen Norris
Kristen Squeloce
Kristin Cavalier
Kristin Conley

Kristin Griffiths
Kristin Hiensch
Kristin Paquette
Kristin Wahner
Kristina Hines
Kristina Smith
Kristyn Duvre
Lacey Cochrane
Lara Allen
Larissa Lucas
Larry Laverdure
Laura Blimmel
Laura Ciaramicoli
Laura Cutone
Laura Failla
Laura Lia
Laura MacDonald
Laura Molinari
Laura Peeke
Laura Sales
Laura Sullivan
Lauren Chite
Lauren Fiske
Lauren Friend
Lauren Malloy
Lauren O'Connor
Lauren Schnare
Lauri Fletcher
Lauri Johnson
Laurie Cutts
Laurie Moran
Laurie O'Neil
Leah Hazard
Leia Zitola
Leigh Lesko
Leona Donahue R.S.M.
Lesley Birmingham
Leslie Crockett
Leslie Ruzzo
Libby John
Lidia DelaCruz
Lidy Overbeeke
Lilani Muth

Lily Ann Divino
Lin Morris
Lina Gerber
Linda Gustafson
Linda Clement
Linda Kosik
Linda McClendon
Linda Mulcahy
Linda Norton
Linda Rurka
Linda Wakefield
Linda Wilk, S.S.J.
Lindsay Sampson
Linnea Stead
Lis Corrigan
Lisa Bafaro
Lisa Batista
Lisa Clement
Lisa Connelly Cook
Lisa Courtney
Lisa DiLeo
Lisa Doan
Lisa Domal
Lisa Germer
Lisa Goncalves
Lisa Grabish
Lisa Guay
Lisa Kiernan
Lisa Koffinki
Lisa Maio
Lisa Paollotti
Lisa Pichor
Lisa Root
Lisa Simon
Lisa Wilson
Lise Plante
Liz Baptiste, S.S.J.
(deceased)
Liz Brennan
Liz Buell
Liz Cafferty
Liz Cavanaugh
Liz Constabile

Liz Iandoli-Rabb
Liz Morancy
Liz O'Connor
Lois Edinberg
Lois Hirschberg
Loree Griffin Burns
Loretta Giacomelli
(deceased)
Loretta Ivich
Lori d'Entrement
Lorraine Crawford-Mapp
Lorraine Fletcher
Lorraine Gaston
Lorraine Henry S.S.J.
(deceased)
Lorraine Morse
Lorraine Parent
Lorraine Tegan
Lou Ann Branche
Louis Borelli
Louise McCarthy
Louise Miracle
Lucie Bouchard, P.F.M.
Lucilia DeJesus
Lucille Reno
Lucille Virzi
Lucky Clarke (deceased)
Luisa Santana
Lydia Dafonte
Lydia Nichols
Lynn Boutote
Lynn Connor
Lynn Glauber
Lynn Gostyla
Lynn Liberatore
Lynn Murphy
Lynn Vaccarelli
Maddy Entel
Madonna Sgro
Mag Carra, S.S.J.
Maggie Wain
Mandy Wentworth
Marcia Reni

Marcy Lepore
Margaret Adams
Margaret Baillie
Margaret Boden
Margaret Carney
Margaret Clark
Margaret Curran, S.S.J.
(deceased)
Margaret Olivieri
Margaret Post
Margaret Sullivan
Marge Borg
Marge Flood
Marge Pasceri
Margie Streeter
Maria Hendrickson
Maria Jimenez
Maria Louise Louden, S.S.J.
Maria McQuaid
Maria Negron
Maria Pedone-Whalen
Marian Gianetta
Marianne Bardsley
Marianne Murrah
Marie Berthiaume
Marie Bissonette, R.S.M.
Marie-Claire Daou
Marie Dugas, S.S.A.
Marie Edward, R.S.M.
Marie Faulkner
Marie Gleason
Marie McClaren
Marie Melanson
Marie Therese Martin, C.S.J.
Marie Thrain
Marielle Anas
Marilyn Boucher
Marilyn Crandell
Marilyn Dron
Marilyn Hildick
Marilyn Kramarz
Marilyn Martin
Marina Moriarty

Marion Twining
Marj Murtagh
Marjorie Ropp
Marlene Rosenfield
Marty Pierce
Marty Rogers
Marvalie Gorden
Mary Ann Daly
Mary Ann McGrain
Mary Ann Smith
Mary Bath
Mary Bettley
Mary Beth Arnold
Mary Beth Belmler
Mary Beth Benison
Mary Beth Kerns-Barrett
Mary Beth Mullen
Mary Blaum
Mary Boucher
Mary Cain
Mary Christopher, S.S.J.
Mary Cocorocchio
Mary Colasuonno
Mary Conway
Mary Cove
Mary Dean
Mary Donnelly
Mary Donovan
Mary Doyle
Mary Duffy, S.S.J.
Mary Ferguson, S.S.J.
Mary Flynn
Mary Gildoy
Mary Green
Mary Guillemette
Mary Haberstroh
Mary Hennessey C.P.
Mary Hennigan
Mary Hill
Mary Hinkley
Mary Holm
Mary Hooper
Mary Jaeger

Mary Jane Proulx
Mary Jo Jackson
Mary Joyce
Mary Juges
Mary Kate Birge, S.S.J.
Mary Kay Cummings
Mary Kay Yanik
Mary Kelley
Mary Kenney
Mary Keough
Mary Lawless
Mary Liz Horan
Mary Lou Campion
Mary Lou Warren
Mary Margaret Kerns
Mary Marron
Mary Matthew Lubunski
Mary Maxwell
Mary McCarthy
Mary McDonnell
Mary Murray
Mary O'Brien
Mary O'Mara
Mary Pat Carr
Mary Pat True
Mary Perno
Mary Peter, S.P.
Mary Plummer
Mary Powers
Mary Quinn, S.S.J.
Mary Read
Mary Salkaus
Mary Sheekey
Mary Sidebottom, S.S.J.
Mary St. Onge
Mary Small
Mary Spahr
Mary Troy
Mary Vachon
Maryann Hall
Maryanne Guertin, S.S.J.
Maryellen Lamoureux
Matt Sullivan

Maura Albert
Maura Forde
Maura Shea
Maureen Bannon
Maureen Carmody
Maureen Chandley
Maureen Egan
Maureen Holahan
Maureen Kroyak (deceased)
Maureen Martin, S.S.J.
Maureen Murphy
Maureen O'Rourke
Maureen Rymeski
Meg Doe
Meg Helmas
Meg O'Connor
Meg Schaefer
Megan Cepetelli
Megan Gaffney
Megan Wright
Meghan MacDonald
Meghan Woodard
Melanie Sullivan
Melissa Bean
Melissa Dworanczyk
Mellen Morrill
Mellesa Bateman
Meredith Bennett
Meredith Bruns
Meredith Michaud
Meredyth Weisman Ward
Meru Lukose
Michele Webster (deceased)
Michelle Ballard
Michelle Bergeron
Michelle Casavant
Michelle Chambers
Michelle Cournoyer
Michelle Charbonneau
Michelle Duguette
Michelle Forgette
Michelle Hurtubise
Michelle Jacques, S.S.A.

Michelle Lefebvre
Michelle Lucier
Michelle Steminele
Michelle Swagler
Michelle Tangredi
Millie Silverberg
Millie Zweir
Mike Komenos
Mijiam Auger
M.J. Regis
Mollie Rosenbaum
Mollie Wittstein
Molly Buchanan
Molly Del Howe
Molly Donahue
Molly Gallup
Mona Metro-Gagnon
Monica Frattaroli
Monica Thornton
Monnie Rockwell
Myra Fortugno
Nadine Beaudet
Nami Ebisawa
Nancy Duhamel
Nancy Bilodeau
Nancy Burns
Nancy Cocchiarella
Nancy Dunn
Nancy Flynn
Nancy Hastings
Nancy Hemenway
Nancy Kane
Nancy Kelly
Nancy Marusak
Nancy McBride
Nancy McGinley
Nancy McKallagat
Nancy Morton
Nancy Nobert
Nancy Senior
Nancy Sestak
Nancy Sheridan, S.A.S.V.
Nancy Symanski

Nancy Welch
Natalie Ackert
Natalie Kostick
Natasha Kerry
Natasha Palucci
Nicholle Lavallee
Nicole Bell
Nicole Damiano
Nicole DiStefano
Nicole Gravel
Nicole Howard
Nicole Martin
Nicole O'Shea
Nicole Thonit
Nicole Williams
Noreen Bisceglia
Noreen Moran
Norma Decoteau
Norma Jean Pratt
Norma Kelleher
Otis Wickwire
Pam Astrella
Pam Brender
Pam Fleming
Pam Hero
Pam Leavens
Pam Miller
Pam Mitchell
Pam Moore
Pam Romano
Pam Ruah
Pam Sawyer
Pam Silvia
Pamela Bronder
Pamela Goodale
Pamela Mamacos
Pat Albrecht
Pat Archibald
Pat Austin
Pat Barkus
Pat Carey
Pat Crupi
Pat Daly

Pat Degon
Pat Dell-Ross
Pat Duggan
Pat Gunderman
Pat Heald
Pat Juneau
Pat Lawler
Pat Lozeau
Pat May
Pat Nedoroscik
Pat Pennucci
Pat Ritchie
Pat Silver
Pat Thomas
Pat Utzschneider
Patricia Ahearn
Patricia Kelly
Patti Conzo
Patti Falcone
Patti Kelly
Patti Soule
Patty McDonald, S.S.J.
Paula Bousquet
Paula Bradley
Paula Kelleher, S.S.J.
Paula Kiley
Paula Miller
Paula Prentice
Paula Sasso
Paula Sleeper Szkoda
Paulette Harper
Paulette Lacoste
Pauline Dauteuil
Pauline Kalagher
Pauline Turner
Peg Benson
Peg Blondin
Peg Brown
Peg Lonstein
Peg Mongeau
Peg O'Leary
Peg Shea
Peggy Eident

Peggy Flagg
Peggy Marengo
Penny Gaumond
Phyllis McGovern
Polly Kierstead
Rachel Clark
Rachel Girard
Rainee Wapner
Ralph Gaston
Ramona Preston
Randy Dunn
Raquel Ruano
Raymonde Forgette
Rebecca O'Brien
Rebecca Smith
Rebecca Wharton
Regina King
Rena LeBlanc
Rena Mae Gagnon, P.F.M.
Renee Desrosiers
Renee LeBlanc
Renee Malowitz
Renee Martin
Renee Vita
Reyna Jovel
Rita LaMontagne
Rita Lunney (deceased)
Rita Pelletier
Rita St. Denis
Rita Santelli
Roberta Mulcahy, S.S.J.
Robin Cutler
Robin El-Hachem
Robin Klar
Robyn Crandell
Robyn Sardelitti
Ron Dusoe
Ron Fletcher, Sr.
Ron Fletcher, Jr.
Rosalie Gagnon
Rosamond Rockwell
Roseanne Ganley
Russ Gagnon

Ruth Corker
Ruth Dow
Ruth Gauch
Ruth Sanders
Sally Brown
Sally Roy
Sandra Buxton
Sandra Landau
Sara McSweeney
Sara Middleswort
Sara Mullaney
Sara Stockman
Sarah Binke
Sarah Connors
Sarah Dalton
Sarah Currykosky
Sarah Evers
Sarah Fairbanks
Sarah Reynolds
Sarah Risotti
Sean Canary
Shamin Hasan
Shannon Handley
Shannon Walther
Sharon Champoux
Sharon Donahue
Sharon Hunt
Sharon Karg
Sharon Lariviere
Sharon Lawson
Sharon Smith Viles
Shawn Feddeman
Shawn Wiggins
Sheila Dombal
Sheila Maher
Sheila McManus
Sheila O'Leary
Sheila Zunen
Shelley Habenstreit
Shelly Simko
Sherry Mingola
Shirley Brady
Shirley Hodges

Shirley Irvine
Shirley Pukaite
Shirley Sherman
Solange Flamand, S.A.S.V.
Sonia Molina
Sonja Sundaram
Stephanie Paolini
Stephanie Picardo
Steve Burlingame
Su Jin Cho
Sue Calabrese
Sue Cameron
Sue Coltrara
Sue Demoga
Sue Ewans
Sue Feitleberg
Sue Gallo
Sue Getman
Sue Haffty
Sue Hunniman
Sue Kasanowski
Sue Laporte
Sue McNamara
Sue Rush
Sue Topalian
Sue Vergase
Sue Yvon
Suneeti Kher
Susan Burke
Susan Bradley-Quaranta
Susan Coleman
Susan Dwyer
Susan Giordano
Susan Kay
Susan Moore
Susan Murphy
Susan Shepherd
Susie Kavanaugh
Susie Sullivan
Suzanne Fricke
Suzanne Howatt
Suzanne Singh
Suzanne Westbrook